D1557640

Advance Praise for *What Justice Demands*

"After hundreds of books on the subject, it would seem difficult to produce a fresh approach, but Elan Journo has done just that in this concise and deftly written volume."

— JOSHUA MURAVCHIK, Ph.D., author *Making David Into Goliath*

"This is a contrarian, thought provoking, relentlessly liberal, fact-rich, lucid, morally serious, constructive, and unapologetically pro-Israel book. Though it makes some arguments with which I disagree, it's an admirable work, very much worth reading."

— DOUGLAS J. FEITH, Senior Fellow and Director, Center for National Security Strategies, Hudson Institute; Under Secretary of Defense for Policy (2001–2005); author *War and Decision: Inside the Pentagon at the Dawn of the War on Terrorism*

"This highly original and thought provoking book argues that only by rethinking the moral premises of its Middle East policy and redirecting its support from local dictators and Islamists to freedom-seekers—first and foremost the region's only democracy, Israel, along with freedom-seeking circles in the Arab world and Palestinian society—will the US be able to help broker Palestinian-Israeli peace. An indispensable book for anyone seeking to think outside the box on the resolution of a seemingly intractable conflict."

— EFRAIM KARSH, Ph.D., author, *Palestine Betrayed*

"Elan Journo captures the essence and nature of the Arab-Israeli conflict in the 21st Century as it is seen through American foreign policy. As more and more groups try to marginalize Israel in American society, Journo gives us the necessary realism to understand this complicated corner of the world and why it matters to America."

— ASAF ROMIROWSKY, Ph.D., executive director, Scholars for Peace in the Middle East; co-author, *Religion, Politics, and the Origins of Palestine Refugee Relief*

"*What Justice Demands* is unwaveringly courageous. Elan Journo's audacity will stun those who refuse to judge, agree or disagree, and always believe 'both sides' are to blame in the Middle East."

—JONATHAN HOENIG, Capitalistpig Hedge Fund and Fox News Contributor

"A quarter century since the Oslo Accords, Israeli-Palestinian peace remains elusive. What went wrong? Elan Journo dispenses with well-worn but tired debates and takes a fresh approach: The missing piece, he argues, has been the failure to appreciate individual freedom and liberty. In this deeply detailed yet readable study, Journo surveys the moral standing of both Israel and the Palestinians and the place of freedom and liberty in each society. He then considers American policy. To side with dictatorship or a society penetrated by jihadist forces over the only free society in the region is not only morally wrong, he argues, but it is also the reason why the peace process has so far failed. Journo is right. *What Justice Demands* is the one new book about the Israeli-Palestinian conflict in quite some time that doesn't simply repackage the failed prescriptions of the past and so is worth reading."

—MICHAEL RUBIN, Resident Scholar, American Enterprise Institute

"U.S.-Israel relations may be mutually celebrated, but Journo argues that 'America has sold out the [Middle East's] only free society, Israel…while empowering jihadist forces.' Strong words, but he convincingly exposes repeated presidential mistakes since 1990, then concludes with a rousing call to fix past errors by supporting an Israeli victory over its enemies."

—DANIEL PIPES, president, Middle East Forum

"Elan Journo's new book offers a refreshing, intelligent, well-written and fundamentally right-headed critique of American policy toward the Middle East. By proposing a policy resolutely based on justice, he illuminates the conflict between Israel and its neighbors in original and startling ways—and offers hope for lasting change."

—YORAM HAZONY, author of *The Virtue of Nationalism*

"Elan Journo brings a much-needed perspective to the world's most pressing crisis: a perspective firmly rooted in deeply considered views about morality and justice. And he demonstrates that nobody is more naïve than the so-called realist to think such considerations beneath them. At a time when our foreign policy debate is focused on considerations of power, Journo shows us that nothing is more powerful than justice, and nothing is resolved that is not right."

—TIMOTHY SANDEFUR, Vice President for Litigation and Duncan Chair in Constitutional Government, Goldwater Institute

"Elan Journo shows that American statecraft's attempts to settle the Arab-Israeli conflict by compromises have always been doomed to failure because they neglect the conflict's essential element: justice. Contrary to conventional wisdom he shows that, far from unrealistic, doing the right thing deals with reality's most inescapable features. Regardless of what goods the Palestinian people might deserve, the reality of Palestinian culture and politics precludes them. Regardless of what Israel has to do to maintain its life, that life is intrinsically in accord with justice and with America's interest. Journo makes a persuasive case that, by decisively supporting Israel's cause and hence acting in accordance with justice, the U.S would be doing the right thing not only by itself and Israel but by the Palestinians as well. A book worth reading."

—ANGELO CODEVILLA, Ph.D., professor emeritus of International Relations at Boston University

"Standing apart from today's rampant tribalism and collectivism, *What Justice Demands* engages readers across the ideological-political landscape. By adopting a principled individual-first, pro-freedom outlook, Elan Journo lays out a compelling analysis of a far-reaching conflict and indicates a path toward a just resolution."

—EAMONN BUTLER, Ph.D., Director, the Adam Smith Institute

WHAT JUSTICE
DEMANDS

AMERICA
AND
THE ISRAELI-PALESTINIAN
CONFLICT

ELAN JOURNO

Post Hill
PRESS

A POST HILL PRESS BOOK

What Justice Demands:
America and the Israeli-Palestinian Conflict
© 2018 by the Ayn Rand Institute
All Rights Reserved

ISBN: 978-1-68261-798-4
ISBN (eBook): 978-1-68261-799-1

Cover art by Cody Corcoran
Interior design and composition by Greg Johnson, Textbook Perfect

Post Hill Press
New York • Nashville
posthillpress.com

Printed in the United States of America

CONTENTS

INTRODUCTION

HOW OUR UNJUST APPROACH HURTS US

In June 2014, a jihadist group linked to Al Qaeda conquered large tracts of Syria and Iraq. After this swift rise to power, which took the world by surprise, the group declared itself a formal "caliphate," or Islamist regime. Within the territory it controlled, the Islamic State in Iraq and Syria, or ISIS,[1] enforced Islamic religious law as a totalitarian system, following in the footsteps of the Taliban in Afghanistan, the Iranian regime, and Saudi Arabia.

The eruption of this new jihadist regime had ripple effects far, far beyond the Middle East. The Islamic State rapidly became a magnet for as many as thirty thousand people who flocked to live, fight, and die under its black flag. They came not only from across the Middle East, but also—astonishingly—from Austria, Belgium, Sweden, Norway, Finland, Switzerland, the United Kingdom, Germany, France, Australia, and the United States.[2] And beyond the territory it conquered in Iraq and Syria—equivalent to the size of the United Kingdom[3]—the Islamic State proved itself a formidable jihadist force with global reach. Fighters linked to the Islamic

State carried out massacres and suicide bombings in Paris, Berlin, Nice, San Bernardino, Istanbul, Orlando, Manchester, London.

Amid an embarrassed scramble to "do something" in response to the Islamic State's initial rise, U.S. Secretary of State John Kerry was dispatched to recruit an international coalition to combat the self-styled caliphate. Upon his return home, Kerry told reporters about a crucial lesson he had learned. While seeking coalition partners in the Middle East, he observed that "there wasn't a leader I met within the region who didn't raise with me spontaneously the need to try to get peace between Israel and the Palestinians, because it was a cause of recruitment and of street anger."[4]

By "recruitment," Kerry meant to the jihadist forces of the Islamic State, a particularly galvanizing faction within the wider Islamist movement. The Palestine issue is one prominent theme in the recruitment videos and literature of assorted Islamist factions, and it has been for years.[5] By "street anger," he meant public hostility in the region about the unresolved Israel-Palestinian conflict, which is bound up with hostility toward the United States. Why? For more than a quarter century, Washington has been neck-deep in the Israeli-Palestinian conflict: it has provided both sides with foreign aid—hundreds of millions of dollars every year—and it has assumed the role of a peace broker in countless rounds of diplomatic negotiations.

Kerry is not alone. The fact that the Israeli-Palestinian conflict festers, many people believe, is a major, if not the chief, source of American (and Western) woes emanating from the Middle East. You can hear variations on that theme from Barack Obama; from Ban Ki-moon, the former secretary general of the United Nations; from President Jimmy Carter, a winner of the Nobel Peace prize; from General David Petraeus, former director of the CIA and

U.S. Central Command; from General James Mattis, the secretary of defense under Donald Trump; from leading intellectuals and academics.[6]

Even if you disagree with Kerry's linkage of the jihadist movement and the unresolved Israeli-Palestinian conflict, even if you've given no thought to the Middle East or the Israeli-Palestinian conflict in particular, it's an inescapable fact that turmoil in that part of the world affects us. What's more, it's undeniable that Washington's approach to unraveling the conflict has come to naught—and arguably, it's made matters worse.

What, then, *should* be America's approach toward the conflict? That's the central question of this book.

The answer I offer in the following pages is unique, in two respects.

First, I address active-minded readers who hold widely ranging political-ideological views: whichever tags—left/right or conservative/libertarian/progressive—resonate with you, that's OK. If, like me, none of those tags fits you, that's fine too. Nor does it matter how little you know about the conflict, nor what views (if any) you already have about it. What matters is that you're open to questioning assumptions and forming (or revising) your own conclusions.

Second, the substance of the answer I present in the book is unique. Something crucial is lacking from the public discussion of what America's approach should be. What's missing is a frank moral evaluation of *both* adversaries and of America's role in the conflict. That moral assessment is what this book offers.

Let me sketch out three salient views on what America's approach should be, pointing out how each is inadequate, and then indicate how my perspective differs.

"Find the Middle Ground"

The prevailing approach to resolving the conflict calls for rebooting diplomatic negotiations, commonly known as the Peace Process. These negotiations aim at a middle-ground compromise between the adversaries. Even if you are sympathetic to one side (or the other), so the thinking goes, a balanced compromise that both sides could accept would deliver some semblance of harmony, perhaps even peace. Here's how President Barack Obama put it:

> For decades then, there has been a stalemate: two peoples with legitimate aspirations, each with a painful history that makes compromise elusive. It is easy to point fingers, for Palestinians to point to the displacement brought by Israel's founding, and for Israelis to point to the constant hostility and attacks throughout its history from within its borders, as well as beyond. But if we see this conflict only from one side or the other, then we will be blind to the truth. The only resolution is for the aspirations of both sides to be met through two states, where Israelis and Palestinians each live in peace and security.[7]

This is widely known as the "two-state solution." In a nutshell: the Israelis keep their state, the Palestinians gain one for themselves, and in theory the two states co-exist side-by-side, in peace. The two-state solution has been Washington's policy for the last quarter century. Each administration clung to that basic approach, while tweaking the timeframe, sequencing, terms of the peace process. To reach a compromise, for example, George W. Bush believed the Palestinians had to be nudged to improve their governance, whereas Barack Obama felt that progress could happen only by pressuring Israel.

No tinkering with this basic model, however, has achieved the stated goal of peace. To judge by the body counts, it has only made things worse. And, fundamentally, there's something profoundly disturbing about a purported solution that pushes aside questions of right and wrong.

Recoiling from that pursuit of "balance," there are two other salient views on what America's approach should be. One demands justice for Israel, the other, in its own way, for Palestine.

"Do Right By Israel"

Many Americans, polls show, are remarkably sympathetic to Israel. One study in 2014 found that, compared with data going back to 1978, "sympathy toward Israel has never been higher."[8] For some, there's a generalized benevolence toward the Middle East's only democracy, beleaguered on all sides by hostile forces, that shares some of our political values. Often that conclusion is impressionistic, lacking detailed knowledge, let alone an evaluation, of Palestinian grievances. So, that pro-Israel stand can, and does, wobble.

Far more stable, however, is the fervent backing of one vocal bloc of voters, Evangelical Christians. They're a significant factor in U.S. politics. By an overwhelming margin, they backed George W. Bush's re-election in 2004, and they helped usher Donald Trump into the White House in 2016.[9] Arguably they constitute the backbone of pro-Israel sentiment in America. For example, John Hagee, the pastor of a megachurch in San Antonio, Texas, has made being pro-Israel his signature issue. Hagee celebrates the post-World War II establishment of Israel as a state with a distinctively religious identity. "Every Christian in America," he explains, "has a biblical mandate to stand in absolute solidarity with Israel and demand that our leaders in Washington stop recommending Israel's withdrawal as the solution to every conflict" (meaning: Israeli concessions to the Palestinians).[10] He insists that "the man or the nation that has blessed Israel has been blessed of God, and to the man or the nation that cursed Israel the judgment of God came in spades."[11] God, the ultimate authority on justice, commands us to back Israel, and rewards those who obey.

Only those of a particular faith could find this view compelling, and if you were to examine it closely, leaving the appeals to the supernatural behind, you'd still come away with at least two thorny, unanswered questions: What are we to make of the morally-freighted claims and grievances of Palestinians and the movement that claims to represent them? (Hagee has no patience for the Palestinians and marginalizes them by rewriting the conflict's history.[12]) And, what if we identify Israeli policies that are unjust; how could it then be just to lend it uncritical support?

"Do Right By the Palestinians"

A widespread opposing view holds just that: To do right by the Palestinians, we must begin by recognizing that they have suffered a double injustice: not only from Israeli policy, but also from Washington's "Israel First" policy, especially in its role as broker in the peace talks. Instead of seeking a fair outcome, we hear, America exhibited a blatantly pro-Israel bias, providing Israel with largely unconditional support, while short-changing Palestinians. At minimum we have to take our thumb off the scales, allowing them to tilt away from Israel and back toward the Palestinians, who suffer acute poverty, unemployment, hopelessness.

Step into a college lecture hall, and you'll hear that justice demands even more. From their professors and from campus activists, many students learn that the mighty Israel ill-treats the weak, impoverished Palestinians—and we Americans enable it to punch downward. They learn that Israel has persistently thwarted the legitimate aspirations of the Palestinian cause—and we arm Israel. They learn that by conniving in Israel's maltreatment of the Palestinians, we stoke hostility against us.

Thus the pervasive indictment: America is way too supportive of Israel—and it should not be. Justice demands doing far
more to support the Palestinians, and distancing ourselves from
the "war-crimes"-inflicting "apartheid" regime in Israel, which
deserves (at least) boycotts, divestment, and sanctions to compel
it to mend its ways.

This outlook, so resonant with many people, is built on
powerful moral claims. But, if we take justice seriously, there are
fundamental problems with this outlook. Here's one: Do the facts
warrant the claim that Washington has pursued a blindly pro-Israel
policy? (The facts, as we'll see, tell a different story.) And another:
This outlook declares its concern about the grievances of specific
Palestinian individuals, but then regards the *Palestinian movement*
as their legitimate agent, fighting to redress those wrongs. Is that
assumption about the Palestinian movement warranted? No, I will
argue, that assumption is belied by the movement's actual goals
and nature. There's no genuine wrong that can be righted by the
creation of a dictatorship or an Islamist theocracy—the goals,
respectively, of Fatah and Hamas, the leading Palestinian factions.

Taking Justice Seriously

In sharp contrast to these salient views about what America's
approach should be, this book presents a distinctive viewpoint.
That viewpoint is the result of taking seriously the principle of
justice.

The moral framework I apply in this book is not religious,
but secular; it's concerned not with collectives, but with the lives
of individual, irreplaceable human beings; and it holds certain
values—human life, freedom, progress—as objective: values for
everyone, at all times, in all places. This secular, individualist moral
framework helps us make sense of an intimidatingly complex

conflict. From this vantage point, the book identifies the essential nature of the conflict, presents an argument about what's at stake in it, and indicates a path toward resolving it.

Has American policy toward the Israeli-Palestinian conflict been unjust? Has our policy fomented anti-American hostility, especially among jihadists?

Yes and yes—*but not for the reasons you may have heard.* The actual injustice is that America has sold out the region's only free society, Israel—along with freedom-seeking people across the Middle East and among the Palestinian community—while empowering jihadist forces. And it is *this* injustice that hurts us. The book's theme is that America should be strongly supportive of freedom and freedom-seekers—but hasn't been, much to our detriment.

To convince you of that, I show why it's necessary to rethink the widely accepted moral assumptions about the conflict's moral landscape. Fundamentally, most of us rely on a conception of justice that's wrong. Only when we apply a proper conception of justice, can we evaluate the adversaries objectively. We start by evaluating the moral standing of Israel (Part I) and of the Palestinian movement (Part II); then we look at what America's approach to the conflict has been and what it should be (Part III).

Much of what we need to know about the moral character of the adversaries is to be found by looking at them in the present tense: at who they are, what they seek, how they behave. But we will look at some of the conflict's backstory to put certain important issues in their historical context. For example, we will examine several episodes in the conflict's history to understand the origin and goals of the Palestinian movement and to understand the inner tension over Israel's "Jewish and democratic" character.

Though we'll explore key elements of the conflict's dizzyingly intricate history, this is not a book about that history (many books deal well with that subject). History matters a great deal. By itself, however, it cannot tell us enough to form a moral evaluation of the adversaries. Nor is the book's aim to provide a comprehensive account of every derivative feature of the conflict. Instead, this book's delimited aim is to clarify the conflict's essential nature and moral significance, which entails questioning commonly held views about justice. To do that, we focus on aspects and issues that are causally basic; that are at the root of the conflict; that are telling; that are, in other words, fundamental.

This requires considerable selectivity. For example, rather than trying to address every Palestinian grievance or claim ever raised, we untangle four of the hardest, well-known, and pivotal grievances; where we find cases of genuine wrongs, we'll consider how these might be redressed. (These analyses, by extension, indicate an approach for how to think about and handle other claims.) For readers keen to dig deeper on various points, I recommend flipping to the endnotes where I cite sources and offer leads for you to explore further.

"OK, so what's the solution?"

When people ask this question, all too often it's in a tone of hopelessness. Understandably, many people have written off the Israeli-Palestinian conflict as irresolvable. The Israelis and Palestinians will always be enemies, people think, and many of us doubt that America can ever secure its interests in the region. Perhaps we should just withdraw. These conclusions, however, are unwarranted. It's true that irrational American policy has inflamed the conflict and empowered forces, especially the jihadist movement, that are hostile to us. It's also true that American Mideast policy, which has been devoid of a principled conception of our interests, is an incoherent mess. But this book shows that if we're willing to rethink our moral premises about the conflict and America's approach to it; if we're willing to recognize and act on what justice demands, then the conflict is *solvable*, and we can secure America's (actual) interests in the region. The book's final chapter indicates the first necessary steps toward a truly just solution.

• • •

What I present in this book is my analysis of an enormously complicated subject. There are many more aspects, issues, and sub-issues involved in the Israeli-Palestinian conflict (and America's engagement with it) than we can possibly explore in this book. I've focused the book on what I judge to be the fundamental aspects. And, unsurprisingly, the aspects we do explore are the subject of conflicting interpretations and debate. I have relied upon sources and scholarship that I find credible, and I've reached my own conclusions. Because of the book's delimited focus and because practically every point is enmeshed in various debates, let me flag one observation and make one request of you.

The observation: I expect that along the way you and I will disagree on some things. And that's OK. We may disagree, for instance, about how I interpret some concrete point or event, or perhaps you find a piece of evidence less than convincing, or perhaps you hold a contrary view of some specific issue. Although I've researched the book's subject in depth and reached a considered analysis of the Israeli-Palestinian conflict, it may turn out you're on to something, and you'd change my mind on the particular point at issue. (Looking back at some of my past writings, there are various points that today I'd present differently, and still other points on which my view has changed.)

Here's my request. Give the book's central argument a fair hearing: where you and I disagree on some point, consider how it affects that overall argument. Yes, you might decide that it defeats the argument, but I believe that's unlikely, and my hope is that you'll find the central argument cogent. I invite you to judge for yourself in the following pages.

PART I

WHERE WOULD YOU RATHER LIVE?

CHAPTER 1

THAT "SHITTY LITTLE COUNTRY"

Scarlett Johansson. Hardly the first person who comes to mind when you think of the Israeli-Palestinian conflict, and yet for a protracted news cycle in 2014, the actress found herself unexpectedly embroiled in it. No, unlike other Hollywood figures who engage in so-called personal diplomacy for some political cause (think Jane Fonda in Vietnam, Sean Penn in Iraq, Dennis Rodman in North Korea), Johansson merely signed on to be the first "global brand ambassador" for SodaStream. That company sells machines for making soft drinks at home. The star had filmed a TV spot for SodaStream, and that ad was going to air during the Super Bowl. So what was the problem?

SodaStream is an Israeli company with a manufacturing plant in the occupied West Bank territories. Activists critical of Israeli policy were outraged that Johansson agreed to front for a company that, in their view, should to be ostracized. How, some people wondered, could Johansson condone malignant Israeli policies? The charity Oxfam International had appointed Johansson as a representative for its cause, but, in horror at her deal with SodaStream, it publicly rebuked her (she later resigned from her Oxfam post).[1]

The ScarJo/SodaStream episode brought to the surface a wider phenomenon. The activists pressuring Johansson were aligned with the Boycott, Divestment, Sanctions (BDS) movement, which campaigns for such measures in order to force changes in Israeli policy. BDS is a commonplace on universities and colleges throughout North America and Europe, but less well-known off campus. Every year at colleges nationwide, BDS-linked groups put on "Israel Apartheid Week" with speakers and protests. Sometimes the student activists dress up as Israeli soldiers and stand at mock checkpoints, hassling other students. Sometimes they build a replica of Israel's controversial security wall (installed to prevent Palestinian suicide bombers). The point of all this role-play? To raise awareness of the daily plight of Palestinians living under the Israeli regime.

The use of the term "apartheid" is a deliberate equation of Israeli policy with the state-enforced white supremacism of South Africa (where apartheid formally ended in the 1990s). For years, international boycotts, divestments, and sanctions pressured the South African government to end its horrendous policy; the same methods, we are told, should be applied to make Israel end its putative oppression of Palestinians.[2] Lending prestige to this movement are such voices as President Jimmy Carter and Archbishop Desmond Tutu, both Nobel laureates, and flocks of professors in assorted disciplines. Many professors have shown their solidarity by campaigning to impose boycotts on Israeli scholars and universities.[3]

On this widespread view, Israel should be treated like a pariah, and student activists have taken that to heart. Consider an incident that took place at the University of California, Irvine. Michael

Oren, Israel's ambassador to the United States at the time, was invited to speak to students on campus, under the auspices of the political science department and five student groups across the political spectrum. As the event began, however, a coordinated gang of student hecklers caused such a disruption that Oren was prevented from delivering his talk. Having earned a Ph.D. at Princeton, Oren is an accomplished historian and bona fide scholar of the Middle East, yet at an institution of higher education, the students silenced him. Message received: the ambassador of Israel is undeserving even of a hearing; he, like the regime he represents, is beyond the pale.[4]

Look beyond the tree-lined quads of college campuses, and you will hear many echoes of this indictment of Israel. By a wide margin, the United Nations Human Rights Council has passed more resolutions targeting Israel than it has against any other member state. Ever. More than the rest of the world combined. To put that into perspective, North Korea, Syria, Iran, Libya, China— none of these notorious authoritarian regimes has been subject to as many official rebukes as Israel.[5]

Delve into the reports of this U.N. organ, nominally entrusted to uphold individual rights, and you'll find horrifying charges leveled against Israel. Take one high-profile example, which became known as the Goldstone Report. Following a war between Israel and Hamas-controlled Gaza in 2008–9, the U.N. Human Rights Council launched a fact-finding mission "to investigate all violations of international human rights law and international humanitarian law" that occurred.[6] The mission's report, named after Judge Richard Goldstone, who led the investigations, validated the suspicions and accusations swirling in the media during the war: it found Israel guilty of massive war crimes. The U.N. General Assembly endorsed the Goldstone Report (despite its many obvious shortcomings)[7] by a resounding vote of 114–18 (with forty-four abstentions). Members of the international community had pronounced a verdict. Israel was certified as an outlaw regime.

Five years later, Israel and the Hamas regime in Gaza again went to war. Once again, protesters in London, Paris, New York, and elsewhere took to the streets to decry Israel's military action. Rashid Khalidi, an eminent professor at Columbia University allied with the Palestinian cause,[8] put into words the sentiment of those crowds, of untold fiery editorials, of numberless intellectuals. The reality of the war, he wrote in the *New Yorker*, is that Israel—"a nuclear-armed power with one of the most sophisticated militaries in the world"—is besieging and killing Palestinians in Gaza, whom he (like many others) portrayed as "the inmates of an open-air prison."[9]

Is it any wonder, then, that Scarlett Johansson faced vitriol for associating her public image with what seems like a pariah state inflicting war crimes? When you listen to credible-seeming critics, nongovernmental organizations, and pillars of the political-intellectual establishment, the obvious conclusion is that Israel stands out for a poor—perhaps horrendous—record on human rights. The "apartheid" epithet is not just plausible, but apt. Israel deserves harsh rebukes, economic sanctions, and zealous pressure.

Maybe its villainy warrants one French diplomat's description of Israel as that "shitty little country."[10]

Fact-Checking Our Moral Assumptions

Or, maybe not. We need to back up. Many people hold a dim view of Israel, in large measure because of the visceral impact of witnessing the suffering of Palestinians—hassled at check-points, living in squalor, bombarded in Gaza—and the sharp contrast with Israeli wealth, progress, firepower. When most people observe misery and frustration, weakness and misfortune, poverty and need, they feel pity well up inside them. They feel that the destitute "have nots" almost certainly deserve our moral endorsement, whereas the "haves" must be suspect, probably guilty. The weak victims, it feels obvious, are suffering at the hands of a mighty villain.

That, however, is quite a leap. If we take justice seriously, we need to fact-check the underlying moral assumption here.

Call it the Underdog Premise. Put into words, the premise tells us that we owe not only our sympathy but our moral backing to the weaker, neediest, most suffering side. It is true that *sometimes* the weaker side has right on its side. For instance: during the American Revolution, the colonial forces were far weaker than King George III's vast war machine. Or take a contemporary example that fits the same pattern: Think of the twelve-year-old Nigerian school girl, abducted from her village and enslaved by the jihadists of Boko Haram. She's far weaker than her captors, and unquestionably she's an innocent victim of their predation.

But for every example that fits the pattern, we can find an endless number where there's no relationship between being the weaker adversary and being in the right. An obvious example: The so-called Manson family. This gang's leader was Charles Manson, who shared Hitler's ideas, hated blacks, and sought to incite an apocalyptic race war in the United States. To trigger that war, in 1969 Manson's gang went on a murderous rampage in Los Angeles. Clearly the gang had many fewer members than the L.A. Police Department. In that sense, it is an underdog. Do you side with this gang of racist murderers? Or consider an example with an even more pronounced asymmetry: the jihadists who hijacked airliners and rammed them into the World Trade Center and the Pentagon on September 11, 2001. That day, thousands of Americans were put to death at the hands of just nineteen hijackers. Even if we counted every last jihadist fighter from every faction worldwide, compared to American military power, their cause is an underdog. No sensible person, however, sympathizes with, let alone morally endorses, them.

From the fact that a conflict is hugely lopsided, what follows? Not much. By itself, the material inequality between two adversaries tells us nothing about their moral standing. The American colonists; the racist gang; the Nigerian school girl turned sex-slave; and the September 11 hijackers: by the relevant measures, they're all underdogs. But morally, they are worlds apart. The Underdog Premise is just plain false. It cannot guide our thinking about the justice of a given conflict. When we encounter the sight of human weakness, our emotional reaction may be profound, but that unprocessed feeling cannot reliably lead us to a considered moral appraisal. The Israeli-Palestinian conflict is no exception.

We need to reorient our thinking about that conflict. To take justice seriously, we have to look at who the adversaries are, what goals they seek, what they say, what claims they make, what they do. These are necessary steps to forming a view of their moral character. It means looking at the actual facts about Israel and the Palestinians, judging the actions and character of each adversary by the same standard, and then treating each according to what it deserves. In this chapter and the next, we'll begin evaluating Israel; in chapters three and four, we will turn to look at Palestinian grievances and the Palestinian movement.

It's Your Life. Where Would You Rather Live It?

Is Israel a "shitty little country"? Well, it's certainly little: it's roughly the size of New Jersey. But "shitty"?

Here's a way to form your own evaluation. Suppose you have to move to the Middle East, for the rest of your life; you get to choose which country you end up in. Ask yourself: Where would I rather live?

Leave aside preferences like "by the beach," "in a big city," or "out in the country." Instead, focus on this basic issue: If you want to have control over your life, to make your own decisions and chart your own future, to speak your mind and shape the politics of your own country, if you want a shot at achieving your goals and flourishing, where do you stand the best chance of doing that? Ask yourself: *Where would I stand the best chance of defining my own path, achieving my own goals, and of thriving?*

With that question in mind, let's evaluate the major countries in the neighborhood: Saudi Arabia, Egypt, Jordan, Lebanon, Iran, several of the Gulf States, and Israel.[11] We'll skip over failed and failing states like Yemen, Libya, Iraq, Afghanistan, and Syria, because they're mired in some form of war—civil, sectarian, and inter-state—if not outright anarchy. Even so, there's a lot to weigh. So for now, consider just three broad aspects of daily life that matter to all of us: your intellectual freedom (what you think and your ability to live according to your own judgment); human relationships; and your ability to prosper economically.

Thought Control

Start in Saudi Arabia, purportedly a close ally of the United States. Despite the ostensible "moderating" influence of a new crown prince, the Saudi regime stands out for its exacting imposition of Islamic religious law, or sharia. Consequently the regime exerts thought control, on a massive scale. What you think, what you say, and what you do must reflect obedience to religious authority—not your own judgment. Religion and state are deliberately one, an indivisible unity. Just that fact by itself has sweeping implications for how you can live your life, what kind of relationships you can (and cannot) have, and what ideas and values you must accept and live by. During the month of Ramadan, for example, when Muslims fast during daylight hours, it's forbidden in Saudi Arabia to eat, drink, or smoke in public. To ensure obedience, the Saudi regime has an actual "morality police" that seeks to prevent vice (e.g., by enforcing bans on music, mingling between unmarried men and women, and worship of religions other than the officially approved strain of Islam) and to promote virtue (e.g., by enforcing the five daily prayer times).

What if you want to clear away some of that suffocating fog of religious oppression and think for yourself? Merely the idea of peeling Islam away from state power is incendiary. Just bringing it up, inviting people to contemplate the *possibility* of secular government, will cost you dearly.

Ask Raif Badawi, a writer and blogger. What's holding back Saudi Arabia, he thought, is the saturation of life with religion. "Secularism respects everyone and does not offend anyone.... Secularism...is the practical solution to lift countries (including ours) out of the third world and into the first world," observed Badawi in one blog post. With stinging sarcasm, he ridiculed a Saudi TV preacher, because the cleric called for scientists to be punished for undermining religious law. Badawi also mocked the kingdom's ban on non-Muslim holidays, such as Valentine's Day, and the enforcement of that ban by the "morality police," whose officers would skulk around flower shops and chocolate sellers, warning people away from infidel customs. Badawi hoped to spur discussion of secularism, gender equality, and what he called liberalism in society: "For me, liberalism simply means, live and let live," he wrote.[12] Though the kingdom vigorously censors the press, books, and the internet, it is emblematic of Badawi's bravery that he was an active blogger, and he established an online forum called "Free Saudi Liberals Network."

Initially, Raif Badawi faced charges of "apostasy"—the crime of leaving the religion of Islam—which in Saudi Arabia carries the death penalty. He narrowly avoided that fate. For "insulting Islam through electronic channels," however, he received ten years in jail, a fine of more than two hundred and fifty thousand dollars, and one thousand lashes.[13]

Turns out that inflicting a thousand lashes all at once would almost certainly kill a person; the flesh on your back just cannot take such a flogging, and you might bleed to death. The regime delivered the punishment in phases: once a week, Badawi would be hauled out of jail to a public square in front of a mosque, flogged fifty times, then thrown back in his cell. Coincidentally—and without any deliberate irony—Badawi's first flogging for the crime of "insulting Islam" took place soon after three self-identified jihadists stormed the office of the magazine *Charlie Hebdo* in Paris and massacred the editorial staff—for insulting Islam.[14]

Raif Badawi is hardly the only victim of the Saudi regime's thought control. Ashraf Fayadh, a poet and artist, was branded an apostate. He was found "guilty on five charges that included spreading atheism, threatening the morals of...society and having illicit relations with women." Only because of an international outcry did the regime deign to reduce his sentence to eight years in jail, public penitence in the media, and eight hundred lashes (again, as with Badawi, on an installment plan).[15] Nor is that horrifying sentence an outlier. By one reckoning, lately the Saudi courts have handed down the "highest recorded number of executions in the kingdom since 1995."[16]

If instead you think Iran could be your home in the Middle East, consider that the Islamic Republic of Iran embodies another variant of Islamic totalitarianism. Like the Saudi regime, Iran demands from its citizens total submission to religious law. Both "insult-ing" the government and "blasphemy"—in line with the regional norm—are serious crimes in Iran. To enforce thought control, the Iranian regime frequently rounds up journalists, writers, editors, and cartoonists; it intimidates them and throws them into jail.[17] Soheil Arabi, an Iranian blogger, was arrested for Facebook post-ings that were deemed "insulting" to the Prophet Mohammad. The authorities extracted a confession from him. In court, he expressed remorse and claimed to have been in a poor psychological condition at the time, but none of that mattered. Initially he was sentenced to death; later that was reduced to seven years in jail.[18]

Express your ideas, question government policy, criticize a politician—at your peril. One artist, Atena Farghadani, drew a satirical picture of government ministers as cows and monkeys to protest their policy of restricting birth control; she was handed a sentence of twelve years in jail.[19] Hashem Shaabani, a poet, was accused of criticizing the regime. The executioner's noose wrung the life out of him.[20]

What about moving to the country of Jordan, a magnet for international tourists who come for the breathtaking ancient ruins and stunning desert landscapes? Reputed to be one of the (comparatively) more liberal countries in the Arab world, Jordan is yet another supposedly close ally of the United States. Yet "offend-ing" the king is a serious crime that could cost you three years in jail. You'll also find yourself up on charges if you offend religious beliefs and question the policies of *neighboring* governments. One schoolteacher in Jordan complained on Facebook that, in his view, Islamic governments in the region were doing too little to address the plight of Muslims in the Southeast Asian country of Burma. He was charged with insulting the king and injuring relations with other countries.[21] The point of such punishments is to instill conformity with the regime's orthodoxy in matters of policy and religion. To hell with what you think.

But you may never know what's really going on in your new home country from watching and reading the media in Jordan (or Iran, or Saudi Arabia). The government vigorously manipulates the press through censorship, physical intimidation, law suits, bribery, and favors. The Jordanian secret police have been known to telephone an editor and instruct him how to cover a story—or what events to keep out of the news. Occasionally, journalists are handed a government-approved text and told to put their byline on it. Many journalists believe that their newsrooms are monitored by government informants, and more than ninety-five percent say they practice self-censorship.[22]

What about the tiny monarchies along the Persian Gulf— notably Kuwait, Bahrain, Qatar, and United Arab Emirates—one of them has to be a better option, right? These countries cultivate a reputation for being forward-looking. When you see the spectacular skyscrapers in Qatar and the United Arab Emirates, what comes to mind is the graceful skyline of Manhattan, amped up. But behind the trappings of modernity, these regimes are shockingly medieval. In their ambition to enforce thought control, they are of a piece with Jordan, Iran, Saudi Arabia.

"Insulting" the emir (monarch) of Kuwait, or just questioning the legal system, has landed people in jail, some for up to ten years.[23] When one well-known government critic was arrested and sentenced to prison, those who came to his defense *also* faced prosecution for publicizing his views.[24] In Kuwait, a blogger was given a six-year prison sentence for "insulting" a *neighboring* regime, Saudi Arabia. A criminal court in Dubai heard a case against a man accused of using (what one newspaper described as) "bad language" in statements about the Prophet Mohammad on Facebook.[25]

Try to count up the number of times you, or your friends, have tweeted or posted about how Congress is bungling its responsibilities, how some law is just plain stupid, or how the president has made a wrong decision. The last thing you'd expect is to land up in court. When Ahmad Abdullah Al Wahdi gave voice to his perspective on the leadership of the United Arab Emirates, where he lives, he was dragged into court for insulting the regime. Then he was sentenced to serve ten years in jail.[26] The United Arab Emirates, like other regimes in the Middle East, actively trolls its own citizens online. Three sisters in the United Arab Emirates who posted comments on Twitter about their brother—whom Amnesty International describes as a "prisoner of conscience"—were punished by being subjected to something called enforced "disappearance."[27] This penalty, used by many dictatorships around the world, is different from being arrested. The government simply abducts you and locks you up incommunicado. No charges, no court hearings; you simply vanish. Sometimes, you're let go. Sometimes you're never heard from again.

What about moving to Egypt, another longtime alleged U.S. ally? The most populous country in the region, Egypt is a quasi-secular military dictatorship. It too has a long tradition of thought control, through official government censorship and behind-the-scenes intimidation. In keeping with the regional norm, the state decides what movies you can watch, what books you can read, and what the newspapers can report. It decides what facts, ideas, and thoughts are forbidden. For example, when the Russell Crowe movie *Noah* came out, retelling the biblical story of the flood, a panel of Muslim scholars called for prohibiting its screening, because the film supposedly violates an Islamic dictum against depicting the prophets. The Tom Hanks blockbuster *The Da Vinci Code*? Banned. So was the Hollywood epic *Exodus: Gods and Kings,* based on the biblical story of Moses in Egypt. Why? Because of "historical inaccuracies."[28]

The Egyptian regime methodically cracks down on writers, thinkers, and journalists. The satirist Bassem Youssef, host of the television show *El-Bernameg,* has been dubbed Egypt's Jon Stewart for his acerbic political commentary. Youssef was arrested for "insulting the president" and "insulting Islam." Facing continued harassment, Youssef announced in 2014 that production of *El-Bernameg* was being suspended indefinitely.[29] Youssef left Egypt, but Liliane Daoud, a journalist of British and Lebanese background, was kicked off the air and abruptly deported. She used to host a TV show called *The Full Picture* that was at times critical of government policies. One night, a team of policemen arrived at her house in Cairo, whisked her to the airport, and bundled her onto a flight for Lebanon. Why? Apparently, in the words of one official, she had "crossed red lines."[30]

Authoritarian regimes often induce citizens to spy and inform on one another, fomenting an atmosphere of stifling paranoia and self-censorship. The history of the Communist bloc teaches us that such a climate of fear effectively induces conformity and obedience. Egypt, like Saudi Arabia and Kuwait, enables any citizen to lodge complaints about immoral conduct and blasphemy. Ahmed Naji, an Egyptian author, was sentenced to jail for "violating public modesty" with his novel *Using Life.* The charges were brought by a man who complained to the authorities after reading an excerpt of the book in a magazine (the magazine's editor was fined).[31] The two lessons here: The Egyptian constitution, which ought to protect Naji's intellectual freedom, is a grim joke; and even getting the government's own censorship board to approve your book—as Naji apparently did in this case—provides no shield against the arbitrariness of an authoritarian government.

Censorship is the norm in the Middle East. It may seem like an essentially political instrument—a means of silencing political opponents and dissidents—to hold on to power. Although censorship does serve this purpose, it goes way beyond that. What makes it so insidious is that many of its effects are often unseen. Preventing you from speaking out; from expressing your ideas about life in writing, film, art; from trying to persuade other people of your views—these are just the most obvious manifestations. The fundamental effect, however, is to negate your independent judgment. Never mind what ideas or values *you* choose to embrace and live by. Never mind what *you* think, what *you* judge to be good or true or right; what *you* think society should look like. No, you must bow to state-approved "news," values, and moral standards. The threat of censorship works to make a whole host of thoughts and ideas unthinkable, taboo, unlivable.

Intellectual Freedom

By contrast, what if you moved to Israel? You'd discover that it protects intellectual freedom. In that country, it's up to you what you think, what you say, and what you do. You're free to arrive at whatever views and beliefs you judge to be right, to live by them, and to speak your mind. Your independent judgment is sovereign.

Many countries pay lip-service to these principles, but the real question is whether unpopular and controversial views can be expressed freely. One test is to see if you can publicly denounce the government, its policies, and leaders—without fear of retribution. Think back to Raif Badawi, the Saudi blogger sentenced to flogging and imprisonment for "blasphemy," and the Egyptian satirist Bassem Youssef, whose TV show was shut down, and Atena Farghadani, the Iranian artist jailed for lampooning government ministers. Now consider, not a blog, a comedy show, or a satirical cartoon, but Israel's so-called newspaper of record.

The daily newspaper *Haaretz* is prestigious. It commands the attention of the government, intellectuals, the public. You could call it the Israeli equivalent of *The New York Times*. *Haaretz* is known for its distinguished staff of reporters. In its opinion pages and in the news coverage, *Haaretz* also publishes fire-breathing denunciations of Israel, its policies, and many of its people. For instance, one of its columnists, Akiva Eldar, has written, "It is hard to find differences between white rule in South Africa [under apartheid] and Israeli rule in the [Palestinian] territories."[32] With meager, sometimes dodgy, evidence, *Haaretz* has hyped incendiary news reports intended to portray the Israeli military as a "war crimes" machine.[33] Whatever anyone might think about *Haaretz's* editorial positions, however, the newspaper and its commentators operate freely.

Ari Shavit is one of *Haaretz's* superstar columnists. A few years back, his book *My Promised Land: The Triumph and Tragedy of Israel* took the country by storm. The book weaves together what *The Economist* described as a "spellbinding" historical narrative of Israel's founding. Shavit described the book as "a painful love story"; painful, because although he admires Israel, the book purports to document heinous misconduct during Israel's war of independence and its continued "occupation."[34] Regardless of whether you would agree with the book's argument, key claims in the book can fairly be construed as attacks on Israel's founders and indictments of its moral character through to the present day.

Imagine a counterpart book, written by a citizen of Saudi Arabia, Egypt, Iran, Jordan, or any other Middle Eastern regime, that comparably lambastes the regime under which he or she lives; would any writer dare overcome the pervasive self-censorship to put such thoughts on paper and would any publisher dare print the book? To do so would mean risking each of their lives. Shavit's book, on the other hand, was a blockbuster, adding greatly to his prominence as a public intellectual. Beyond Israel, *My Promised Land* quickly became a *New York Times* bestseller, and it garnered numerous awards. Both *The Economist* and *The New York Times Book Review* named it as one of the best books of the year.[35]

Israel's protection for freedom of thought is robust. That was underscored in a legal case involving the documentary film, *Jenin, Jenin*. The case went all the way up to the Israeli Supreme Court. The court's ruling brings to mind a maxim commonly attributed to the Enlightenment thinker Voltaire: "I do not agree with what you have to say, but I'll defend to the death your right to say it."

Certainly the film, which provoked widespread repugnance, was an edge-case. To understand why, we need to look at the film's subject matter and the circumstances surrounding it. In 2002, a Palestinian suicide bomber walked into the dining hall of the Park Hotel in the city of Netanya during the Passover meal. He blew himself up, killing twenty-eight people and injuring one hundred and thirty. Following that massacre, the Israel Defense Forces launched a retaliatory campaign which included a major battle in the West Bank town of Jenin. Fevered rumors swirled that Israel had committed "war crimes" and massacres—allegations that Israel flatly denied. Mohammad Bakri, a well-known Arab-Israeli actor, wanted to document only the Palestinian side of the story. So after the fighting ended, he found a way into Jenin, along with a small film crew, and talked to the residents.[36]

Bakri's film *Jenin, Jenin* made some of the worst, most inflammatory allegations of Israeli wrongdoing seem plausible, even true. The conclusion: the Israel Defense Forces had slaughtered untold numbers of Palestinians. Except that the documentary was riddled with editorial bias, inconsistencies, misrepresentations, untruths.

The end credits acknowledge Yasser Abed Rabbo, a public-relations official for the Palestinian cause.[37] Families of some Israeli soldiers who fought in the battle were outraged at the charges leveled against their fallen sons. People challenged the claims Bakri makes in the documentary, seeking to refute its basic theme. What's centrally relevant for our purposes, however, is that the film was initially banned, but Israel's Supreme Court overturned that ban.

Israel's Film Censorship Board is a relic dating back to the 1930s, before Israel's independence, when the area was ruled by the British. The Board has the power to withhold permission for screening commercial films (the board related to theatrical plays was abolished some time ago).[38] The Board's film-censorship powers are similar to laws in several American states which remained on the books until the 1960s.[39] Daphne Barak-Erez, a legal scholar who later became a justice on the Supreme Court, has studied the case. The Censorship Board's reasons for banning *Jenin, Jenin* "related to its being 'distorted,' 'offensive to the public's feelings,' and 'inciting.'"[40] During the deliberations, a member of the Board argued: "This is a Palestinian propaganda film made by an Israeli citizen. Just imagine that in England during the [Second World] war they would have shown a Nazi propaganda film."[41]

When Bakri petitioned to overturn the ban, the Supreme Court followed settled precedent entrenching freedom of speech, and struck down the ban. Barak-Erez writes:

> Regarding claims pertaining to the film being false, the justices rejected them unanimously, relying on existing precedents. In the words of Justice Dorner: "The falseness of an expression is also, per se, insufficient cause for removing protection." Similarly, Justice Procaccia categorically stated: "The question of true and false in human creativity, including artistic creativity, cannot usually constitute cause for restricting freedom of expression."[42]

So here we have a film denounced as enemy propaganda and bound to be used as an instrument of vilification and recruitment. Whatever you might think of Bakri's film, it is precisely cases like this that test one's commitment to the principle of free speech. The episode surrounding *Jenin, Jenin* reveals a government unique in the Middle East, one predicated on the rule of law.[43]

Not only filmmakers, not only dissidents like Raif Badawi, not only journalists, not only authors, not only cartoonists, not only poets need intellectual freedom—we all do. In defining your life path and pursuing your ambitions, you need to rely on your own independent judgment. Imagine trying to flourish amid the region-wide smog of government thought control. Only in Israel can you breath in fresh air.

Poisoning Human Relationships

The Middle East's norm of thought control betrays a profound devaluing of individuals. The underlying premise is that you and I are fundamentally incapable of rational judgment, unqualified to figure out our own path, unable to choose the important people in our lives, and, ultimately, unworthy of pursuing our own goals. Instead, we must think and believe and do only what some authority tells us to. Practically, if crucial decisions are taken out of our hands, our life is no longer ours; it belongs to the authority demanding obedience. That means you have no sovereignty. Such contempt for individual autonomy is poisonous to human relationships, a fact manifest on a grand scale in the lives of women and gays.

Gender Apartheid

Women across most of the Middle East suffer under what could be called "gender apartheid."[44] Under the original apartheid regime of South Africa, blacks were subordinated to the white population, methodically oppressed, and practically dehumanized. Apartheid was institutionalized, legally-mandated racial discrimination against blacks. "Gender apartheid" is institutionalized, legally mandated gender discrimination against women. Most women in today's Middle East are subordinated to men; they are legally subjugated; their lives are treated as dispensable.

The Saudi regime thoroughly demeans women. You've probably heard about *some* of the outrageous constraints that Saudi women live under. Notoriously, for years Saudi women were forbidden to drive cars, until a royal decree condescended to grant them permission *near the end of the second decade of the twenty-first century.*[45] Women may not leave home without a male chaperon, known as a guardian. The guardian is usually a male relative—a husband, father, brother, even a son.[46] Pause for a moment to trace out what that would mean in your own life: Do you want to go to the bookshop? Meet friends for lunch on your day off? Only if your guardian permits it. What about getting a job? Or going to university? Getting married? To hell with what you want—your guardian knows best. What kind of a life is that? Here's what a few Saudi women themselves say:

> "My sister went to a bookstore without taking permission from her husband, and when she returned, he beat her up without restraint."
>
> "[My guardian] forbids visits to my female friends or going to shopping malls by myself. It is a complete and total isolation from all the joys in life."
>
> "It's like I'm in handcuffs, and the society, the law, the people [are] against us. That's why most women choose to marry in their early 20s as a way to escape, and guess what? The man she marries is no different from her brother or father."
>
> "[My guardian] won't allow me to work, even though I need the money. He also doesn't provide all my needs. I can't recall the last time he cared about what I needed or wanted. He is married

to four women and completely preoccupied with them, and he doesn't allow me to travel with my mother. I suffer a lot, even in my social life. He controls it completely and doesn't allow me to have friends over or go to them. He forces me to live according to his beliefs and his religion. I can't show my true self. I live in a lie just so that I wouldn't end up getting killed."

"It's suffocating. I'd rather kill myself than live with it. I hold on to the smallest hope I have that someday this will change."[47]

"I got into an accident once in a taxi," reports another Saudi woman, "and the ambulance refused to take me to the hospital until my male guardian arrived. I had lost a lot of blood. If he didn't arrive that minute, I would've been dead by now." A thirty-year-old medical doctor says: "I've had to give up on a number of educational opportunities because he (my guardian) didn't think a doctor needed a cultural exchange program or a symposium he didn't understand. I've been trying to have him let me marry the man I love for the past two years.... I'm in charge of people's lives every day, but I can't have my own life the way I want." Another medical doctor had to ask her teenage son's permission to travel.[48]

Outside the home, roving patrols of the Saudi "morality police" keep women in line. They harass women on the sidewalks, in shopping malls, and elsewhere for improperly wearing their veils—veils that are required *by law*. Women are generally expected to wear sack-like black gowns that obscure their figures. Failure to comply can lead to punishment. When a video clip of a Saudi woman strolling down a street in a mini skirt and crop top made its way online, the police tracked her down and arrested her. Possibly because the video—and the story of her arrest—went viral, eliciting shock and dismay around the world, the Saudi authorities decided to release her without charge.[49]

Even when Saudi law is not directly oppressing women, a woman's testimony in a Saudi court of law carries less weight. And the legal system works to reinforce women's dehumanization. Take the case of a nineteen-year-old Saudi woman. Some years ago, she was abducted and then a gang of seven men raped her. The Saudi regime does recognize rape as a crime. The rapists, however, got off with lenient sentences (between ten months to five years in prison), and then the court inflicted its own outrage: it sentenced *her* to ninety lashes.

Why? For being in the company of an unrelated man.

Dwell on that point: the court *actually* penalized the victim. And by shaming and punishing her, the regime became an accessory to the crime of her rapists, aggravating her psychological wounds.

To her immense credit, the woman and her lawyer objected. They spoke out to the media. In response, the judge extended the rapists' paltry jail time, slightly. But evidently the woman had again stepped out of line. The court decided to *multiply* her sentence from ninety to two hundred lashes—plus six months in jail. Thus her double infamy: not only was she unchaperoned, letting herself be raped, she also had the temerity to stand up for herself and question authority. Her lawyer, who acted as an advocate for his client as every lawyer should, was also punished. His license was revoked.[50] This travesty was not a failure of the Saudi legal system; instead, this is how a survivor of rape was treated when the courts *worked*.

Women in Iran, as in Saudi Arabia, are subjugated. They, too, are required by law to wear a religious headscarf. They, too, are stalked by patrols of Iran's own "morality police." These squads are responsible for combating "vice" (for example, by hunting down and punishing unmarried couples holding hands in public) and promoting "virtue," which of course includes enforcing the minute regulations on the veil (it cannot show too much hair, it must be the right color, size, etc.). For violating the headscarf law, a woman might get a talking to, a fine, or even arrested. In a show of defiance, some Iranian women have dared to post photos of themselves on Instagram and Facebook without wearing a headscarf. The regime promptly cracked down: in one sweep, it arrested eight women, who were accused of undermining the morals of society. To humiliate them and crush their spirit, the regime forced them to apologize publicly. The regime promised to identify other women from their social media photos and punish them too, while the police announced plans to deploy seven thousand undercover officers to enforce the headscarf law.[51]

Women in Egypt live under a regime that exhibits a winking indifference to their suffering, abuse, and exploitation. It allows violations of their rights to go unpunished. For example, Female Genital Mutilation/Cutting, a barbaric practice common throughout the region, is widespread in Egypt. One survey found ninety-three percent of women (aged fifteen to forty-nine) who have at some point been married have been subjected to FGM/C. That survey also found that fifty-four percent of mothers supported the practice, which is nominally illegal but continues through loopholes and illicitly.[52]

And while many women in Egypt attend schools and university, and many enter the workforce, they face widespread threats of sexual harassment and assault. What brought this to the attention of millions of people outside Egypt was the 2011 gang-rape attack on the CBS News journalist Lara Logan. While reporting from Tahrir Square, the epicenter of Egypt's Arab Spring protests, Logan found herself encircled by a large group of men. They dragged her to the ground, ripped off her clothes, and raped her with their hands. If passersby had not rescued her, she might have died; she had to be hospitalized.

That attack on a foreign journalist put a lurid spotlight on the ugly reality that Egyptian women face every day. "Catcalls, fondling, indecent exposure, and other forms of sexual harassment by strangers are an *everyday occurrence for women on the streets of Cairo*, according to human rights groups, social scientists, diplomats, and interviews with Egyptians. Moreover, predatory packs have brutalized women at several public places, including a soccer stadium, in recent years, according to witnesses and local news accounts." [Emphasis added.][53]

The number of Egyptian women who experience some form of sexual assault, according to one study, is eighty-three percent (for foreign women, it is ninety-eight percent). Fifty-three percent of Egyptian men blamed women for "bringing it on" themselves, while sixty-two percent *admitted* to harassing women.[54] Clearly, a significant part of the problem is rooted in a culture that devalues women and condones their exploitation. But this is not only a cultural problem; it is also a legal-political one, because it is a basic responsibility of government to protect a woman from such predation—and punish her attackers. So thought one woman, Noha Ostath, who told the BBC that she was groped in broad daylight, during a Cairo traffic jam. She was walking on the sidewalk, and a van driver grabbed at her.

> His behaviour made her so angry she ran after the van and held on to the side mirror to force the driver to stop so she could take him to a police station.
>
> She was equally shocked by the attitude of other passers-by. Some tried to dissuade her from going to the police—others blamed her for what she was wearing (a baggy sports outfit).
>
> In the end, after a tussle with the man that lasted for more than one hour, the strong-willed Ms. Ostath dragged the man to the police station.
>
> But even there, police officers refused to open an investigation and insisted on the presence of her father despite the fact that she is not a minor—she is twenty-six.[55]

Imagine facing that every day. Imagine living with the dread that you or someone you love may be humiliated, or even raped, while walking down the street—and that the police brush aside any complaint she summons the courage to register. Can you picture yourself leading a thriving life in such a society?

Jordan and Lebanon likewise follow the norm of devaluing women. For example, in each of these countries, the law has allowed a rapist to avoid (or lessen) his punishment in certain situations. Considering the deeply wounding and lasting impact of rape on the survivor, what could possibly justify giving the perpetrator any leniency? In these countries, the rapist can get a lesser punishment if he agrees to marry the woman he violated. For the woman, however, that simply compounds her suffering and prolongs it with a life sentence.[56]

Perhaps the most grotesque form of dehumanizing women is the practice of "honor killings." The basic premise behind "honor killings" is that a woman is the property of her family—like an object—and thus the family is entitled to slaughter her if she's believed to have brought them collective dishonor. Why have fathers, brothers, and uncles tortured[57] and then put to death their own daughters, sisters, nieces, wives? These are some of the "crimes" for which young girls, teenagers, and women have been murdered in the name of redeeming family "honor": Being the survivor of rape. Falling in love with someone the family disapproves of. Holding hands with a man. Being too strong-willed, too independent. Being insufficiently subservient. Being accused of having sex out of wedlock. Refusing to wear various Islamic clothing (such as the veil). Wanting to choose her own husband or boyfriend. Refusing to marry a first cousin. Being "too Western." Leaving an abusive husband.

Ultimately, the facts (if any) behind an accusation or suspicion are beside the point. If the family *feels* "dishonored" by the women's rumored, insinuated, or imagined actions, that's reason enough to butcher them.[58]

The practice of "honor killing" is illegal in many places, and sometimes those laws are enforced. But it's breathtaking how the laws in certain countries—notably Kuwait and Bahrain—end up trivializing this heinous crime.[59] Suppose a man claims to witness his wife (or daughter, or sister) committing an "act of adultery"— an ominously vague term. If he then decides, in the name of protecting family "honor," to slaughter the woman, what kind of punishment do you think the murderer will face?

The *maximum* penalty in Kuwait is three years in jail and a fine of seven hundred and fifty dollars.[60]

Such dehumanization of women is the norm throughout the Middle East. Not so in Israel. Quite the contrary.

Since the founding of Israel, suffrage has been universal, for all citizens, male and female, regardless of color or creed. Israel's fourth prime minister, Golda Meir, was one of the first women to lead a modern, Western country. She preceded Margaret Thatcher, who served as prime minister of Britain, by a decade, and Angela Merkel, the German chancellor, by thirty-six years. Many other women serve in parliament and as cabinet members; women number roughly half of all judges and lawyers in the country.[61] Four women are justices of the Supreme Court; one of these, Miriam Naor, serves as the Court's chief justice.[62] Many are members of the Israel Defense Forces (more than ninety percent of positions are open to them), serving as intelligence officers, naval officers, and combat troops.[63] Whereas women in Saudi Arabia have long been forbidden from driving a car or leaving home unchaperoned, in Israel women pilot fighter jets.

Put yourself in the shoes of a young woman, dreaming of what she will become. If you're in Saudi Arabia, you might dream of maybe one day going to the bookstore, pursuing a career, choosing a husband, without your "guardian's" permission. If you're in Israel, your ambition is virtually boundless. You can dream of becoming a Nobel Prize-winning scientist (like Ada Yonath, co-winner of the 2009 Nobel Prize in Chemistry); a CEO of a major corporation; a tech entrepreneur. Your life is yours. Women in Israel are full and equal members of society.

Dehumanizing Gays

The gender apartheid of Saudi Arabia, Iran, Egypt, and elsewhere in the region poisons human relationships. So does the treatment of gay men, who are dehumanized.

There's a Saudi gay scene, but it's underground; the law prohibits gay sex, with a maximum penalty of death. For many years, the regime treated the fact of HIV/AIDS infections as a closely guarded secret.[64] The zeal to stamp out the faintest, even unintended, hint of gay life is eloquently captured in the story of one private school in the capital city of Riyadh. In 2015, after the U.S. Supreme Court ruled in favor of same-sex marriage, the Saudi authorities apparently became hyper-sensitive to any expression of gay identity, real or imagined. Someone noticed that a rooftop parapet at the Talaee Al-Nour private school was painted in rainbow stripes. From what I can tell, it was entirely coincidental; there was no subtext behind the rainbow colors. Nevertheless, the school was fined about twenty-five thousand dollars for displaying "the emblem of the homosexuals" on its building, one school administrator was jailed, and the parapet was repainted.[65]

Nearby, in the religiously conservative Gulf monarchies— you might call them mini versions of Saudi Arabia—same-sex relationships are frowned upon, and gay sex is a crime. The penalties vary: it could cost you your life in the United Arab Emirates (where even pre-marital sex is a crime); up to seven years in a Kuwaiti or Qatari prison.[66]

The Iranian regime seems intent on exterminating the gay community. Officially, gay men don't exist. Speaking at Columbia University in 2010, Iran's then-president, Mahmoud Ahmedinijad, was asked about the regime's persecution of gays. He flatly denied that there were any gays in Iran.[67] Obviously he's factually wrong, but his words suggest a sinister implication. Is the regime's rounding up and execution of gay men intended eventually to kill them off? Perhaps so. Or perhaps simply instilling that fear in the gay population is sufficient to drive them further underground.

The hostility to gays, however, is hardly confined to theocratic regimes. Egypt's military-backed regime presents itself as a quasi-secular contrast to—and barrier against—the Islamists. But in fact it has labored to prove its religious bona fides. The centerpiece of that campaign has been the ramped-up efforts of the morality-police division. And among its targets are people in the gay community, which in the last decade has slowly become more visible. After the current military regime took control in 2013, it swept up at least two hundred and fifty people in "a campaign of online surveillance and entrapment, arrests and the closing of gay-friendly businesses," driving "gay and transgender people back underground and, in many cases, out of the country."

> [Some] have been arrested in raids on private homes or picked up on the street if their appearances raised suspicions....
>
> Most, however, have been arrested after officers entrapped them on dating apps like Grindr, which now greets its users when they log in with a warning message about a possible police presence on the site.

[One activist said that] the police used the apps to flirt with people, engaging in sexual banter and asking for risqué photos that could be used as evidence in court before asking them out on dates. When the unsuspecting targets of the stings arrive for the dates, they are swiftly arrested....

Perhaps the crackdown's greatest physical manifestation is in the proliferation of police checkpoints in downtown Cairo and the closings of cafes and other businesses that were gathering spots for activists, intellectuals, and gay people during the heady days of political upheaval.[68]

Those arrested are often charged with "habitual debauchery," under a law used for prostitution cases. Their punishment? Jail. Two to twelve years.[69]

Or take a look at Lebanon. It's one of the region's more secular and religiously diverse countries. And yet the regime—like its Egyptian counterpart—avidly persecutes gays. To the extent their existence is admitted, they're denigrated for promoting debauchery. Gay sex, according to an invidiously worded article of the penal code, is punishable by up to one year of jail time. In one sting operation, police raided a movie theater known to be a popular gay hangout. The thirty-six men arrested were subjected to a pseudo-medical anal examination to determine if they had broken the law. Activists have rightly denounced such examinations, calling them tests of shame.[70]

This incident, along with a similar scandal, sparked a public outcry. The Lebanese Medical Association refuted such probes as ineffectual and humiliating, and it called on its members to stop carrying out such examinations. But the public prosecutor—exemplifying the regime's contempt for the lives of its citizens—argued that these degrading examinations must continue.[71]

Imagine living in place where this can happen to you, your friend, your brother, your son.

To be gay in Saudi Arabia, the Gulf States, Iran, Egypt, Lebanon, and elsewhere in the region is to face brutal persecution. Simply because of whom they are attracted to and fall in love with, gays in those countries face arrest, torture, imprisonment, or death. Coming out takes on a whole other meaning. Contemplate what it must feel like to have to conceal so important an aspect of your self in the shadows, in an underground scene, in a sham marriage to keep suspicious at bay.

But things are again markedly different in Israel.

The country's military, the Israel Defense Forces, has for many years welcomed gay soldiers into its ranks. By contrast, over the span of decades, thousands of Americans have been drummed out of the U.S. Armed Forces for being gay. It was only after 2011, when the policy known as "Don't ask, don't tell" was repealed, that it become legal for gay Americans to serve. The acceptance of gays in the Israeli military is one marker of how social attitudes have progressed over the years. More and more, gays have become integral to Israeli culture, the media, the film industry, the music scene, and politics. In 2002, Uzi Even, a former chemistry professor, became the country's first openly gay member of parliament (Knesset).

Unsurprisingly, neither Cairo, nor Tehran, nor Riyadh, nor Amman, nor any leading city in the Gulf monarchies has a Gay Pride Parade.[72] The annual Gay Pride Parade in the Israeli coastal city of Tel Aviv is a massive street party. It attracts tens of thousands, including many participants from around the world; in 2016, there were an estimated two hundred thousand revelers.[73]

So it is fitting that Payam Feili—a writer who is gay—has ended up in Tel Aviv. He is originally from Iran, where his writings were censored. Before he left, his friends "hesitated to contact him," and after one of his books was translated into Hebrew, "government loyalists wrote articles accusing him of immorality and collaborating with the enemy." Initially, he fled to Turkey, but he was repeatedly detained and then blacklisted. Although he has "no special connection to Judaism" nor does he want one, nor with any other religion, Feili concluded that he would have the chance of a better life in Israel. Now he's hoping Israel will grant him asylum.[74]

Prosperity and Progress

We've already glimpsed how women in Saudi Arabia are robbed of the chance to earn an income, pursue a career. Let's take a look at that issue through a wide-angle lens, and consider: Where would you have the best opportunity to develop a career you're passionate about, to do productive work, to enjoy the benefits of a dynamic, advanced economy?

For a few clusters of people in Saudi Arabia, the Gulf states, and elsewhere, especially those linked to the region's tyrants or royal clans, life is a blur of mansions, limos, private schools, and torrents of petrodollars. For most everyone else, not so much. On the whole, in terms of standard of living, scientific progress, and technological advancement, the Middle East brings to mind the Third World. Think: dead-end poverty, ignorance, stagnation.

But Israel is an outlier. Israel has been dubbed the "Start-up Nation." After the United States and China, Israel has the most companies listed on the NASDAQ exchange, more even than Canada, the UK, France, Germany, India, or Korea.[75] Israeli companies in the high-tech and life-sciences sectors have attracted enormous amounts of venture capital funding. According to the IVC Research Center, in 2017 Israeli high-tech companies raised 5.24 billion dollars.[76] In the same year, the value of Israeli high-tech firms that had an initial public offering (IPO) or were acquired or merged totaled 7.44 billion dollars.[77]

Among the buyers of Israeli companies are giants like Apple, Microsoft, Cisco, and Monsanto. Google's third acquisition in Israel was one of the largest deals at the time. In 2013, the company invested close to one billion dollars to buy out the navigation and crowd-sourced traffic app Waze. A lot of foreign acquisitions are of start-ups that develop apps, but many are for software that few of us ever interact with directly, involving cryptography and code that makes the internet faster. Start-ups working in the life-sciences and medical space are blooming, too. Medtronic, a giant in the field of medical devices, acquired an Israeli firm that invented a gizmo that sounds as if it belongs in a sci-fi movie, the PillCam. It's a swallowable capsule with two tiny cameras that capture diagnostic images of your digestive tract, enabling doctors to look for signs of cancer.

When you hear about start-ups in Silicon Valley, in Israel, or elsewhere, that make it big, with massive IPOs of stock, or that get bought for hundreds of millions of dollars or even more, remember that they represent just the tip of an iceberg. For every start-up that soars, there are many that have yet to succeed—and even more that never will. (The failure rate for most new small businesses is shockingly high; many more fail than survive.)

The Israeli start-up ethos, though, long predates the digital age, and it's deep-seated. The story of one classic, decidedly old-school industrial start-up illustrates what entrepreneurs, left free to operate, can achieve.[78]

When Stef Wertheimer was ten, he and his family fled Nazi Germany and settled in Israel. In his mid-twenties, he started a company in the garage behind the family home in 1952. The company, Iscar, produces industrial cutting tools, used by carmakers, for example, to bore holes, cut grooves and create threads in metal parts. Iscar long ago outgrew that old wooden garage. Then it outgrew its first manufacturing plant in Israel. Now Iscar operates robot-powered manufacturing facilities in the Americas, Central and Eastern Europe, and Asia, and computerized warehouses in North America, Europe, and Asia. The Wertheimer family built Iscar into one of the world's leading manufacturers in its class.

One day Warren Buffett, the legendary investor, received a letter from Wertheimer inviting him to consider buying into the company. You can just imagine how many people call, email, and write Buffett, trying to catch his attention. Buffett has nurtured his company, Berkshire Hathaway, to titanic proportions by saying no a lot, and yes only rarely. Iscar Metalworking Companies turned out to be Buffett's first acquisition outside the United States (price tag: four billion dollars for an 80 percent stake). "If your readers know a company that resembles Iscar, even a little, have them call me immediately," Buffett told one Israeli newspaper, "I want to buy. Let them call me collect."[79] Seven years later, in 2013, Berkshire Hathaway scooped up the remaining twenty percent of Iscar for two billion dollars.

The company Stef Wertheimer built up went from the proverbial (and literal) start-up in an old wooden garage to a multinational, multibillion-dollar enterprise.[80]

When considered alongside its neighbors, and even compared to advanced Western nations, Israel's economic, technological, and scientific dynamism is astounding. One significant benchmark is scientific and technical journal articles published in a given year. The World Bank tracks such articles, by country, in the fields of physics, biology, chemistry, mathematics, clinical medicine, biomedical research, engineering and technology, and earth and space sciences. In 2013, for example, Israeli researchers published 11,300 such articles. Which is a lot, for a country so small.

For context, it's helpful to translate that number into a per-capita output, by asking, how many articles were published per million citizens? For Israel, it's roughly 1,402 articles per million citizens, which compares favorably with the United Kingdom (1,518) and the United States (1,305). And Israel's output of scientific and technical articles towers above other major countries in the Middle East, such as Iran (426), Saudi Arabia (255), and Egypt (102). By this metric, Israel far surpasses all its neighbors and belongs in the same league as the world's leaders in science and technology.[81]

And Israeli researchers have earned some of the highest accolades. Eight Israeli scholars have won Nobel Prizes in the sciences or economics (I'm skipping over the highly politicized prizes for peace and literature); Egypt, with a population tenfold bigger, has one. No other neighboring country is even on the list.[82]

This dismal fact is a marker of a profound insularity in the rest of the Middle East. Another revealing measure is the number of books translated into Arabic from other languages. The "number of books translated in the Arab world is one-fifth of the number translated in Greece," according to a report issued by the United Nations. The aggregate "total of translated books from the Al-Ma'moon era"—that is, since the ninth century—"to the present day amounts to 10,000 books—equivalent to what Spain translates in a single year."[83] The report, published in 2003, was subtitled "Building a Knowledge Society." But a "knowledge society," predicated on the idea that science, technology, and innovation fuel progress, has yet to be embraced in the Middle East—with one exception, Israel.

The gap between Israel and the rest of the Middle East also stands out in data on two classic benchmarks of material progress: life expectancy at birth and infant mortality. The good news is that globally, the rate of infant mortality has been falling, though the pace varies by country. The freer nations—where individuals are able to develop and implement superior medical expertise— have seen the mortality rate (per thousand births) decline to single digits. In the last half-century, for example, the U.S. rate dropped from 22.7 to 5.6. Today in Israel, the number is 2.9, close to Germany and France (both 3.2), and slightly ahead of the U.K. (3.7). In Saudi Arabia, where stupefying amounts of wealth slosh around within the royal palaces, the infant mortality rate (11.1) is on par with Libya (11), a failing state verging on anarchy. Iran (13) and Egypt (19.4) are roughly where Israel used to be thirty-two and thirty-nine years ago, respectively.[84]

The second benchmark, life expectancy at birth, also indirectly reflects a country's progress. Whereas data on infant mortality are based mainly on an actual tally of newborns (along with some esti- mates), there is quite a bit of guesswork involved in projecting how long someone can be expected to live. And those calculations of life expectancy assume that current conditions stay roughly constant throughout a person's life, yet the history of the last century is studded with medical advances and economic developments that no one could have truly foreseen. By this measure, though, Israel (82.1 years) ranks alongside Germany (81.1), France (82.7), the U.K. (81.6), and slightly ahead of the United States (78.7). Much farther behind are Saudi Arabia (74.6) and Iran (75.7). For Egypt (71.3) the gap is ten years.[85]

When assessing Israel's economic advances and its scientific and technological ferment, recall that Israel lacked the enormous oil revenues that buoyed neighboring economies like Iran, Saudi Arabia, and the Gulf monarchies. Add to that the disorienting, often grueling conditions of Israeli life since independence in 1948. The country has survived international boycotts and numerous major wars. It endured decades of random terrorist attacks. And yet within a stagnant region of the world, despite a tumultuous political backdrop, people in Israel enjoy a decidedly First World standard of living, the benefits of technological progress, and the freedom to thrive.

Which in the Middle East is unique: it is only in Israel that individuals in their daily life are free to set and pursue their own path and to achieve their own vision of a good life. So, if you had to pick a country in the Middle East in which to live, the answer is clearly Israel.

CHAPTER 2

WHAT EXPLAINS THE OUTLIER?

Given the international chorus of denunciation against Israel—at the U.N., on campuses, in editorials, from the advocates of boycotts, sanctions, and divestment—you may well be surprised by the conclusion of the last chapter: that in the Middle East, Israel is by far the best place to live. Not only is it surprising, but it also calls into question the moral judgment informing the widespread condemnations of Israel. Notice that there's nothing like the same outrage—indeed, we hear conspicuously little criticism—about the public and institutionalized barbarism and oppression elsewhere in the Middle East. That's not at all what it looks like to take moral judgment seriously.

That sharp difference between life in Israel and life elsewhere in the region demands an explanation. What is it about Israel that enables individuals to pursue their own flourishing—and why is such a life but a mirage elsewhere in the Middle East? What makes Israel the region's outlier?

That's the question we explore in this chapter. For the explanation, we need to take a close look at a crucial aspect of the regimes in the Middle East: their political systems. What we see is that they fall into three broad categories: monarchy, dictatorship, and theocracy. These regimes *deliberately, methodically* work to subjugate their people. With one exception, Israel. Its political system and institutions—like those of the world's freest, most advanced societies—aim at a fundamentally different end.

Let's start by looking at the major kinds of regime in the Middle East, each a variation on the theme of tyranny.

Monarchy

Saudi Arabia, Jordan, and the Gulf states are full-on monarchies. They differ markedly from Europe's few remaining monarchies. For example, there's still a monarch in the United Kingdom, where I grew up, but Queen Elizabeth II is merely a figurehead. The royal family are a kind of living, breathing tourist attraction. Politically, the British monarchy is an inconsequential vestige of the country's cruel, barbaric, medieval past. It lingers on at the periphery of what is essentially a free, modern, scientifically advanced society. Not so with the monarchies of the Middle East. While these regimes invest in the trappings of modernity and technology, seeking to present a forward-looking, welcoming face to the outside world, at the core their political systems are cruel, barbaric, medieval.

Long ago, the monarchs of Europe asserted a divine right to absolute power, a God-given claim to dispose of your life. The ruler expected—and exacted—your obedience. So it is today in the Middle East's monarchies.

The king of Saudi Arabia *actually runs the country*. Assorted princes serve in ministerial roles and as ambassadors. When the Saudi king dies, another is plucked from the teeming ranks of the royal family. Ditto for the Gulf States of Oman, Kuwait, Bahrain, and the United Arab Emirates, where actual power rests with the monarch (or, emir), who usually comes to power by inheriting the position or the decisions of a patriarchal council.[1]

The Jordanian royal family, claiming a direct blood line to the prophet Mohammad, has clung to power for close to a hundred years. The king is the head of state, the chief executive, and commander of the military: he holds supreme power. The Jordanian parliament answers to him, and he can suspend it at whim. Political parties were illegal for many years, then re-legalized, until the king suspended parliament for two years, and, in a throwback to the ways of Europe's absolute monarchs, he governed by decree.[2]

There's no legal way for the people of Jordan, Saudi Arabia, or the Gulf states to change their government.

Rule of Religious Law Even in Monarchies

We've seen in the last chapter just how central religion is to life in Jordan, the Gulf states, and the Saudi regime. Islam is not merely one religion that Saudis can choose to live by; to be a Saudi citizen, you have to be a Muslim. Islam is the official state religion, it is funded lavishly, and it is the source of the law.

Note the many ways the Saudi regime works to enforce its preferred strain of Islam: the pervasive censorship; the patrols of the morality police; the prohibition on buying or consuming alcohol; the persecution of gays; the gender apartheid. If you question, let alone deviate from, the state orthodoxy, you risk your life.

The flogging of a "blasphemer" like Raif Badawi is just one form of religious medievalism under the country's sharia legal system. For "adultery"—an endlessly elastic term—a woman can be sentenced to death by stoning. For theft, the criminal's arm will be amputated. For some kinds of robbery, the punishment is "cross amputation": cutting off the thief's right hand and left foot. For "apostasy," beheading.

Sharia is likewise essential to the legal-political systems of the Gulf states. Dubai, one of the seven United Arab Emirates, goes out of its way to present a hyper-modern face to the outside world. And yet its laws—like those in Saudi Arabia—punish a great many so-called morality offenses. These include holding hands in public, drinking alcohol in public without a license, or sharing a hotel room with someone of the opposite sex that you're not married to. Women who "report being raped can be imprisoned for adultery if they do not have four male witnesses to support their story."[3] The underlying medievalism is never far from the surface. For example, the monarchy of Qatar has laws prohibiting sorcery, black magic, and incantations. So does Saudi Arabia.

By comparison, Jordan is sometimes seen as religiously "moderate." What does that actually look like?

Even there, religion and state are fundamentally entwined. The profound role of Islam in that monarchy was evident in the persecution of one Jordanian writer. Nahed Hattar, a secular Christian, was well known as writer and political activist. To understand his actions and his ultimate fate, keep in mind that for the last few years, Jordan has been menaced by the rise of the Islamic State in next-door Iraq and Syria. Hattar felt it was crucial to push back against such religious savagery. He decided to satirize the barbarians of the Islamic State by posting a cartoon drawing on Facebook. *The Washington Post* reports that the image depicts:

> ...a bearded man, lying in bed under sheets, smoking contentedly beside two women in paradise and jabbing his finger toward God, who asks, "Do you need anything?" The man replies, "Yes, Lord, bring me wine, cashews and an immortal servant to come clean the floor."[4]

The reaction? There was an "across-the-board" backlash as Jordanians took to Facebook and Twitter to harass him, calling for his killing and lynching. Few listened to Hattar when he hastened to explain the cartoon's meaning. The point was to skewer the warped beliefs of the jihadists of Islamic State. The cartoon was intended, he said, to mock "how they imagine God and heaven, and does not insult God in any way."[5] Going a step further, Hattar removed the image from Facebook, apologized for posting it, and proceeded to shut down his Facebook account altogether. Never mind the apology, one of Al Qaeda's ideologues tweeted, he's still an infidel.[6] The obvious implication: he should be killed for his blasphemy.

Even more alarming than the public's reaction, however, was the response of the government. *It came after Hattar.* He was arrested and held for two weeks, then released on bail pending his trial. It was clear the government was ready to throw the book at him. Almost certainly, he faced a jail sentence. What prevented the government from handing out such a sentence, however, were the bullets of a religious vigilante who shot Hattar to death on the steps of the courthouse.[7]

What's so revealing in this tragic story is that it was the ostensibly religiously "moderate" Jordanian government that arrested Hattar, charged him, and sought to punish him—for posting a cartoon that rebukes the jihadists of the Islamic State.

Arbitrary Power

The legal system and the courts in these monarchical regimes serve the rulers. They are politicized and therefore arbitrary. It's the rule of men, not the rule of law.

The Jordanian constitution theoretically protects the rights of its citizens, but in reality—and with impunity—the regime (like the region's other monarchies) methodically flouts the rights of its citizens. Quite apart from the regular police force, Jordan has a notorious secret police modeled on the Soviet Union's dreaded KGB. The Jordanian secret police deliberately works to subjugate. It engages in pervasive surveillance, with the help of a vast network of informants, and it carries out arbitrary arrests.[8] The secret-police facilities have been called "fingernail factories," because one common way of making you confess—regardless of whether you're guilty or innocent—is to rip out your fingernails.

Being arrested in the Gulf states, even arbitrarily, is something of a step up from being "disappeared," because at least your family can find out where you are. But if you fail to confess to whatever crime you're accused of, the Bahrain authorities, for example, may go after your family and pressure them as a way of extracting your confession.[9] Typically, though, the security forces are more direct. People detained in the United Arab Emirates have reported being subjected to "mock executions, in which prison guards blindfolded a detainee and dangled a noose in front of him, joked he would be executed, and then had him sign a confession"; they also complained of being "whipped, sleep deprived, electroshocked by taser gun, drugged, given laxatives then deprived of the use of a bathroom, and forced to stand under an air conditioner after having water poured on them."[10]

When people in Western countries make the case for "enhanced interrogation" tactics or, to be blunt, torture, the argument usually relies on a ticking time-bomb scenario, an emergency with many lives on the line. The argument is that extraordinary national-security circumstances require such severe measures. But the torture inflicted in the UAE, Kuwait, Bahrain and across the region is a routine matter. Even if you're never subjected to it, simply knowing that you might be tortured instills fear and submissiveness.

The courts of law in the Gulf states are politicized. Although in theory the judiciary is independent, in practice judges must heed the wishes of the king and his court. Family and tribal connections can get you out of trouble, if you know someone with pull.[11] If you're daring enough to complain about the police barging into your home without a warrant, or wrongfully arresting you, or brutalizing you in custody, expect to lose.[12] On the other hand, if the monarch feels like it—or if a particular case has aroused critical coverage in the international media—his highness may overturn the court's ruling. Sometimes authorities may turn a blind eye to people breaking certain laws (including "morality offenses")—until, arbitrarily, these laws are enforced. The irrationality of such legal systems leads people not only to view the law with contempt, because of its systemic injustices, but more important, to live in fear, because of the law's unpredictability.

These monarchs, like so many other tyrants throughout history, rely on fear and brutality to dominate their victim populations.

Dictatorship

Dictatorship is the second broad kind of political system common in the Middle East. Let's consider three regimes—Egypt, Lebanon, and Turkey—that represent variations on this model. And while each in some sense is at least quasi-secular, their through line is a politics of domination again saturated with religion.

Egypt

Egypt's monarchy was overthrown in the 1950s. What replaced it was a succession of quasi-secular dictators. From 1981 until the so-called Arab Spring that began in 2011, Hosni Mubarak ran the quintessential police state. An "Emergency Law" suspended the constitution (such as it was) for some three decades, and it empowered the regime to do whatever it pleased. Arbitrary arrests were common. The state could decide that your crime required a secret military trial. While under detention, good luck withstanding the routine practice of torture (think, not waterboarding, but electric shocks, drills, sodomy with a truncheon).

The Mubarak regime hounded political opponents. It targeted not only Islamists, but also secularists, threatening their families and intimidating them. One dissident campaigning for a secular Egypt (who has since left the country) told the story of sitting on the living room couch chatting with her best friend about their boyfriends. Weeks later, the phone rang in the middle of the night, but instead of speaking, the caller played back a recording of *that* innocuous private conversation.[13] It's what the caller didn't say that made the incident so menacing: *We can hide a listening device in your home, we can hear everything you say—so shut up.*

The Egyptian dictatorship resembled Saddam Hussein's dictatorship in Iraq (1969–2003), Muammar el-Qaddafi's manic domination of Libya (1969–2011), and the Assad family's hold on Syria (1971–ongoing). In the latter case, Bashar al-Assad assumed the role of dictator only after inheriting reins of power from his father, who died in 2000. Following that pattern, Egypt's Hosni Mubarak had groomed one of his sons to succeed him as dictator. But that never came to pass. In 2011, during the Arab Spring, tens of thousands of Egyptians gathered in Cairo's Tahrir Square. They demanded the end of Mubarak's regime.

Next came the brief rule of Mohammad Morsi of the Muslim Brotherhood, a group foundational to the Islamic totalitarian movement (from which, for instance, key Al Qaeda factions, Hamas, and sundry other groups spun off.) Mubarak's dictatorship was impious; Morsi sought to create a pious one, an Islamist tyranny.[14] Before long, however, the military establishment overthrew

Morsi. In the brutal crackdown that ensued, protesters in the streets faced soldiers with live bullets, while armored trucks rammed into crowds of people, crushing them. Following that coup the military installed as president one of its own, Abdel Fattah al-Sisi. Since Sisi assumed power in 2013, his regime has arrested "more than 40,000 people, killed more than 3,000 (including between 800 and 1,000 on a single day in August 2013), 'disappeared' hundreds more, and placed thousands in continuously renewable pretrial detention."[15] Call it Mubarak 2.0.

Islam, however, remains integral to Egypt's political system. We've observed, in the last chapter, Egypt's thought control, its censorship of film, TV, and books, its persecution of gays for "morality crimes." So, when the number of "blasphemy" cases went up markedly during Mohammad Morsi's brief proto-Islamist reign, it was unsurprising. But two years after the military unseated the Islamist leader and began purging his followers from society, the prosecutions for "insulting" Islam remained about the same.[16]

Islam encompasses a number of sects; Sunni and Shia are the major ones. Each regards the other as heretical. Most Egyptians are Muslims of the Sunni sect, and it's a measure of religion's role in the political system that the regime avidly persecutes religious minorities. There are some Shiite Muslims in Egypt, though perhaps not for much longer. The regime has hounded Shiites (along with Coptic Christians and atheists), and prosecuted them for contempt of religion.[17] Coptic Christians have been hit hard. With the regime's complicity, Islamist vigilantes have firebombed churches, brutalized members of the Coptic community, and slaughtered some who had yet to flee.[18] Egypt's security forces, moreover, have shot Coptic monks repairing churches (which the law restricts), and even "used their tanks to run over Copts peacefully protesting church burnings."[19]

The courts in Egypt, like those in Saudi Arabia, the Gulf states, Jordan, and elsewhere, heed the regime's agenda, rather than anything resembling the rule of law. In one case, an Egyptian court handed down a death sentence—not simply to one defendant found guilty of a crime based on the evidence presented in court, but summarily and *en masse* to six hundred and eighty-three people. Prior to that ruling, the same court held a one-day mass trial in which five hundred and twenty-nine defendants were sentenced to the gallows. All had been found guilty of the murder of one policeman. Did any of these individuals actually commit a crime? The court, evidently, cared nothing for facts or truth. Underscoring the politicization of the courts, it was revealing that one of the convicted was Mohamed Badie, the spiritual leader of the Muslim Brotherhood, which the regime had just outlawed.[20]

Equally, if not more, damning of the Egyptian legal system is the fate of the ousted dictator, Hosni Mubarak. After leaving office, he was detained and eventually the authorities—dense with Mubarak loyalists—decided to allow him to be tried in court. Initially, many of his victims nursed the hope that perhaps finally genuine justice would prevail. Over six years, several legal cases against Mubarak wound their way through the courts.

No objective accounting and evaluation of Mubarak's rule could end up with him being set free. But the whole thing, predictably, was a grim farce. By early 2017, Mubarak received little more than a slap on the wrist. He is a free man.

Although convicted for involvement in the death of protesters in the Arab Spring and sentenced in 2012 to life in prison, Mubarak appealed, and eventually he was exonerated. He managed to dodge various corruption charges, too. These crimes, although serious, are a drop in the ocean. To hold only these crimes against him is to trivialize the enormity of his dictatorial reign. In the end, for one charge that stuck (embezzlement) Mubarak was ordered to pay back some money and given three years in jail, but let go with time served. He will now enjoy the "privileges of a retired head of state."[21]

Behold "justice" under Egypt's politicized legal system. It's rigged to serve those in power.

Lebanon

Lebanon is neither a monarchy, nor a full-fledged dictatorship, but an authoritarian mash-up of two other forms of political domination: sectarian chaos and theocracy.

There was a time when Lebanon's capital city Beirut was known as the Paris of the Middle East. The city earned that title because of its cuisine, sophisticated architecture, and fashion-forward liberated women. Despite such Western influences, within Lebanese society there simmered long-standing religious hatreds. Then, in 1975, a civil war erupted among the country's religious factions.

That brutal conflict laid the country to waste. By war's end in 1990, Beirut's downtown channeled, not Paris chic, but post-apocalyptic hellscape. By some estimates, about a hundred thousand people were killed, perhaps as many maimed and left handicapped, thousands were "disappeared" by rival militias, and hundreds of thousands—out of a pre-war population of two and a half million—were displaced. Lebanon has struggled to rebuild itself, with modest success, but it remains fundamentally broken. For many years, Lebanon was essentially under the political control of the dictatorship in neighboring Syria.

Nowadays, Lebanon does have a parliament, with elected representatives, but that system is overlaid with a strict allocation of power among rival sectarian factions. The president has to be a Maronite Christian; the speaker of the parliament, a Shiite Muslim; and the prime minister, a Sunni Muslim. This fixed division of power reflects the three main religious groups within the Lebanese population, and the idea is to minimize sectarian wrangling within the government. So how goes it? Not so well. To give just one example: For two and a half years, the role of president remained vacant, because the political parties could not agree on who should fill the role, and elections were postponed twice. Eventually, the position was filled by a politician with strong ties to the Islamist regime in Iran.[22]

That development hints at the deeper problem in Lebanon. Many of its failings are typical of the region: to the extent the government functions at all, it is rife with patronage, its courts are politicized and corrupt, it censors news media, books, films, plays, and the internet—and, here as elsewhere, it's a crime to publicly criticize the president or foreign leaders. The government scours Twitter and Facebook and blogs to find anything remotely critical of political figures. It's also illegal to broadcast programs that are deemed to harm public morals, or insult religious beliefs. What's distinctive about Lebanon, however, is that the government lacks full sovereignty within its borders and bows to an Iranian-backed Islamist group, Hezbollah (literally, "party of God").

Any proper government must hold a monopoly on the use of retaliatory force (the police, the courts, the military) within its geographical limits, in order to do its job of protecting the lives and property of its citizens. Parts of Lebanon, to be sure, are under the jurisdiction of the elected government, but Hezbollah controls a patch of territory in the south, while in Palestinian refugee camps, various militias hold sway. So, if you find yourself arrested, the first question is not what have you been accused of, but *who* has arrested you. The country, in effect, has competing governments.

Within their dominions Hezbollah and the Palestinian militias carry out arbitrary arrests; they seize property at whim; they run their own "courts" of law; and they operate their own jails. The Palestinian and Hezbollah fiefdoms are essentially independent of the official police.[23] Consequently, foreign and local jihadists can find safe harbor within the Palestinian areas; Hezbollah is itself a prominent faction within the global Islamist movement.

Hezbollah's authority extends beyond the areas that constitute its Islamist state-within-a-state, and it has fought to capture ever more control over the country. In the mid-2000s, for example, Hezbollah threatened to topple the elected government. It summoned a vast crowd of protesters to the center of Beirut, and it demanded the power to veto cabinet decisions. Crowds blocked the streets. For months, the protestors camped out in the center of Beirut, while armed clashes flared up. Eventually, the beleaguered government tried to push back against the Islamist group. It shut down Hezbollah's vast telecommunications network and removed a video camera that the group had placed to monitor goings-on at Beirut airport. To this Hezbollah responded by venting its indignation: the gun fights that followed looked like the pandemonium last witnessed in Lebanon's horrific civil war. In the end, the government backed down. Lebanon bowed to the jihadists of Hezbollah.

Turkey

Turkey is an outlier of sorts, so it's worth pausing to consider its political system. The country lies at the edge of Europe, not only geographically but also, in a sense, politically. For many years Turkey was deservedly hailed as modern, secular, and pro-Western. Since the early 2000s, however, Turkey's political system has been steadily morphing: first, into a religious authoritarian regime, and now marching toward Islamist dictatorship. The man driving that transformation is the country's leader, Recep Tayyip Erdogan.

Since coming to power, Erdogan led an incrementalist campaign to remake Turkey's institutions. He appointed judges aligned with his Islamist agenda. And, openly subverting rule of law, he selectively refused to enforce uncongenial judicial rulings. Moreover, Erdogan prioritized Islamic over secular education, encouraging greater enrollment in religious academies, and seeded the universities and government posts with Islamists. With religious mores—notably public displays of piety and the subservience of women—becoming the new normal, women withdrew from the workforce in droves.

The ominous signs of Erdogan's religious authoritarianism were there all along. The signs became inescapable after a 2014 scandal, when secret audio recordings of Erdogan and senior officials were posted on YouTube. One recording apparently features "Turkey's foreign minister and spy chief discussing the viability of faking an attack by Syrian terrorists to justify armed intervention inside Syria."[24] With an election coming up, Erdogan was compromised. To contain the scandal and stymie an emerging protest movement, the regime ordered the blocking of dozens of websites.

> Twitter Inc. was banned for two weeks in late March and early April, and Google's YouTube video-sharing service has been dark since March 27. An opposition newspaper columnist and academic was sentenced Tuesday to 10 months in jail for a tweet that insulted the prime minister, while 29 defendants are on trial on allegations that include using tweets to organize protests and foment unrest last year.[25]

Despite the ban on Twitter and the government's spying and tight restrictions on Internet traffic, many people in Turkey still found ways to bypass the restrictions and criticize the regime. In doing so, they put themselves at grave risk. Critics of the regime have found that freedom of speech is a mirage. Challenge the regime's authoritarian control, and you risk being intimidated, detained, framed, and jailed.[26]

A couple of years after the Twitter blackout, Erdogan's regime decided to silence opponents. It seized control of *Zaman*, the country's most widely circulating daily newspaper, as part of a wider crack down on dissident voices.[27] Put in the hands of government trustees, *Zaman* began adhering to the regime's ideological line.[28]

Then in the summer of 2016, Turkey's accelerating slide from authoritarianism to dictatorship became glaring. Erdogan's regime faced a *coup d'état*, but managed to cling to power. The regime quickly began to carry out brutal purges. If you were a teacher, bureaucrat, or police officer suspected of disloyalty, you were fired along with tens of thousands of your colleagues. The government arrested untold numbers of university professors, political opponents, and journalists. Turkey has the horrifying distinction of imprisoning more journalists than any other country (more than China, more than Egypt); according to one report, in 2016 the regime had jailed at least eighty-one journalists and shuttered more than a hundred news outlets.[29]

Pushing the country further toward the Middle East's norm of subjugation, in 2017 the regime held a referendum—which was approved—to bestow on Erdogan even more dictatorial power.[30]

Theocracy

The Middle East is plagued by theocracies. Notorious examples are the Taliban of Afghanistan and the Islamic State in Iraq and Syria. Both (like Saudi Arabia) enforce piety through a "morality police," sharia courts, and barbaric punishments. They are totalitarian regimes under the banner of Islam. Long before the Taliban and ISIS became household names, however, the Iranian regime made itself the embodiment of Islamic totalitarianism.

Born of a violent revolution in 1979, the Iranian regime worked to realize the vision of a society shaped in *every* detail by religious law. Iran's particular version of Islamic totalitarianism reflects the theory of its founder, the cleric Ayatollah Ruhollah Khomeini. On that theory, one cleric—known as an ayatollah (literally, "token of God")—holds ultimate power. His official title is "Supreme Leader." The inherent menace of that title fits the regime's distinctive character.

Iran demands from its subjects total submission to its brand of sharia law. From its earliest days, the regime worked to reshape society according to its Islamist ideology. The clerics used every channel to push their agenda: radio, billboards, posters, school textbooks, postage stamps, currency.[31] The courts follow religious law. It's telling that (as we've seen) Iran—like Egypt, Saudi Arabia, the Taliban, and ISIS—has a "morality police." Moreover, since its revolutionary days Iran has had a peculiar institution called the Basij: a state-aligned vigilante militia that steps in to bolster the official police. Submission to state power is everything; the individual is nothing.

To better appreciate the role of religion in the Iranian regime, consider one grisly practice that emerged during Iran's drawn-out war with Iraq (1980–1988). Martyrs who die for the cause, according to the regime's official creed, end up in paradise. Along with its regular military forces, the regime deployed children and teenagers as soldiers, extolling their martyrdom on the battlefield. Their families were praised and congratulated. Streets were named after these martyrs. One of the most celebrated was a thirteen-year-old boy. In public speeches, Khomeini praised him for "attach[ing] grenades to his body and [throwing] himself under an enemy tank." The boy's portrait appeared on Iranian postage stamps and banknotes.[32] The Tehran regime adopted a tactic called "human wave" attacks, which cost thousands of lives. Some of these human waves, it appears, were children and youth sent to clear the battle-fields of landmines.[33] In the words of the scholar Matthias Küntzel, they had to "move continuously forward in perfectly straight rows. It did not matter whether they fell as cannon fodder to enemy fire or detonated the [land] mines with their bodies: the important thing was that [they] continued to move forward over the torn and mutilated remains of their fallen comrades, going to their deaths in wave after wave." This ghastly practice is today the source not of "national shame, but of growing pride."[34]

The Iranian regime's leaders and state-run media continue to sing the praises of "martyrdom" operations (translation: suicide attacks). "Today, more than ever," noted one Iranian president, "we must inculcate in the younger generation the culture of *shahada* [martyrdom]. This is a mission of supreme ideological [importance]…One who treads the path of martyrdom and brings himself to this extreme attains the pinnacle of human [achieve-ment]. It is a duty incumbent upon [each member of] the public to bring himself, as well as others, to this pinnacle."[35]

The flipside of this celebration of piety is the regime's hostility to nonbelievers and religious minorities. Iran is officially a Shia regime, and most Iranians belong to that sect. Accordingly, the regime persecutes members of religious minorities, particularly the Baha'i.

The Baha'i religion originated in Iran, but the Tehran regime regards this monotheistic faith as heretical and denies it any offi-cial recognition, which means (among other things) that adherents cannot own or inherit property. They've been blocked from getting into universities and holding jobs. The regime regularly locks up adherents of the religion, some of whom have been executed as apos-tates from—and conspirators against—Islam. Iranian government forces seized and then destroyed a number of Baha'i holy sites. To borrow a term from George Orwell's novel *1984*, the ayatollahs seem bent on making Baha'i citizens "unpersons"—eradicating them, along with any memory of their existence, from society.[36]

It is a striking measure of the Tehran regime's commitment to Islamic totalitarianism that it has always coveted the role of global leader of that cause (more on that in chapter four). In a twisted way, it makes sense: If Allah's word is the Truth—and Iran's leaders believe that—then all mankind must be brought under Its purview. How can there be any limits to where the Truth must reign? And so, because The Truth of Allah can have no geographical bounds, the regime has committed itself to exporting its ideology by force. While the Saudi regime (like certain Gulf monarchies, notably Qatar) has also backed jihadist groups and poured billions into proselytizing its own brand of Islamic totalitarianism worldwide, Iran's commitment to the cause is distinctively proud, militant, unrelenting.[37]

"The Iranian revolution," declared Ayatollah Khomeini, its founder and first Supreme Leader, "is not exclusively that of Iran, because Islam does not belong to any particular people. . . . We will export our revolution throughout the world because it is an Islamic revolution. The struggle will continue until the calls 'there is no god but Allah and Muhammad is the messenger of Allah' are echoed all over the world."[38] Iran's constitution commits the regime's forces not only to defend its borders but also to serve "the mission stated in the Book, of holy war in the way of God and fighting to expand the rule of God's law in the world." (Immediately following is a verse from the Koran [8: 60]: "Against them make ready your strength to the utmost of your power, including steeds of war, to strike terror into the hearts of the enemies of God and your enemies, and others besides.")[39]

Iran has made good on that mission. In the decade of the 1980s, while Ayatollah Khomeini's forces consolidated power domestically, "the principle of 'exporting the revolution' became a cardinal regime priority. Its importance was demonstrated in the fact that, despite the expense of a bloody, grinding eight-year war with Saddam Hussein's Iraq, the fledgling Islamic Republic sunk colossal resources into becoming a hub of 'global resistance.'"[40]

Iran built, trained, and funded jihadist groups. Its main proxy force is Lebanese Hezbollah, which has carried out attacks from Beirut to Buenos Aries, slaughtering Americans soldiers and diplomats in Lebanon and in Iraq.[41] Despite being subjected to (supposedly) biting economic sanctions in the 2010s, Iran funneled millions of dollars to support the murderous Assad regime in Syria and to provision Hamas, in the Gaza strip, with weapons and rockets. Year after year, the U.S. Department of State has described the Tehran regime as the world's foremost state-sponsor of terrorism. Iran is not merely a political regime; it's an embodiment of the jihadist cause.

Iran's theocratic regime answers only to Allah; for its own people's judgment and lives, it exhibits profound contempt. That was illustrated in a traumatic episode that took place after the country's 2009 elections.

The Iranian regime holds elections for a president, but the entire process is a grotesque pantomime. Only candidates blessed by the clerics can run, the outcome is basically a foregone conclusion, and ultimate power remains in the hands of the Supreme Leader. By itself, that is a caricature of representative government, and it is an affront to Iranians, conveying the message that they're unfit to make important decisions. But in 2009, the election results were so flagrantly rigged (far more so than usual) that *millions* of

Iranians marched in the streets. So, the Tehran regime unleashed its security apparatus to pulverize the dissenters.

During one of the protests, Neda Agha-Soltan, a college student, was out in the streets. She took a bullet. There's a YouTube video, taken by someone in the crowd, of Neda lying on the ground, her eyes vacant, bleeding to death. Neda is one more victim of a theocracy that treats human life as cheap.[42]

A Common Theme: Religious Subjugation of the Individual

When you look at the political systems of the Middle East, you can find marked contrasts between, say, Saudi Arabia and Lebanon, or Iran and Egypt, or Jordan and Turkey. But no matter how you juxtapose these regimes, their points of difference are overshadowed by what unites them. They are variations on the theme of religious tyranny.

Despite their differences in political form and institutions, these governments subjugate their people. What the ruler commands, the subjects must obey. Wielding arbitrary power and operating with impunity, these regimes put the holders of power above the so-called law. The politicized courts serve the government's agenda, mocking the principle of rule of law. And all of this oppression unfolds under the shadow of religion. Religion is woven into the political system and institutions not only of the region's outright theocracies and medievalist monarchies, but also of the nominally secular regimes.

One tragic effect of such religion-state unity is the concomitant hostility toward infidels, heretics, apostates, nonbelievers. Politically, it can be a deadly risk in the Middle East to be an atheist or to belong to the "wrong"—that is, the non-dominant—religious community (for example, the Baha'i in Iran; the Copts in Egypt).

To be a follower of Islam, however, provides no immunity from persecution. We've seen that a lot depends on which sect you belong to, and where you live. It's not only (mainly Sunni) Egypt that hounds its Shiite minority; they're also oppressed in (Sunni) Bahrain. And across the Middle East, belonging to the non-dominant sect can cost you your life. Religious subjugation of the individual is a salient political norm in the Middle East.

With one exception.

The Exception, Israel

Israel's political system differs fundamentally. One animating premise of Israel's government is that the individual is sovereign. The country's Basic Laws read, in part: "There shall be no violation of the life, body or dignity of any person as such. There shall be no violation of the property of a person.... All persons are entitled to protection of their life, body and dignity.... There shall be no deprivation or restriction of the liberty of a person by imprisonment, arrest, extradition or otherwise."[43] Your car, home, shop, patent, or copyright is yours. Israel's legal system borrows heavily from English common law. Consequently, Western legal ideas such as the venerable principle of *habeas corpus* are enmeshed in Israeli law. You are presumed innocent until proven guilty—a doctrine that we take for granted, but one that's seldom honored elsewhere in the region.

Emblematic of Israel's political vibrancy, its parliamentary system teems with a dizzying number of political parties, which sometimes splinter off or meld together. During the 2015 elections, for example, there were nine parties running candidates for seats; a coalition of four other parties formed a joint list.[44] Because Israel has a system of nationwide proportional representation, even tiny parties can win seats, but that also makes it difficult for one party to win enough votes to form a government. So for many years, Israel has been led by shape-shifting, fragile, coalition governments, with cabinet ministers from a hodgepodge of different parties. (Something similar has happened in Denmark. And in the United Kingdom a few years ago, the Liberal Democrats and the Conservatives, neither of which gained a majority of votes by themselves, formed a coalition government.)

Israel enables its citizens to set the direction of their society. If they're dissatisfied with the government, Israelis can replace it legally and peacefully. To anyone who lives in the United States or Western Europe, that may seem like a low threshold. Yet in the Middle East, like the rest of the Third World, leaders leave office not willingly after a poor showing at the polls, but typically because of coups and revolutions (Egypt 1952, 2011, 2013; Iran 1953, 1979; Iraq, 1956, 1969; Libya 1968, 2011; Syria, 1949, and several more times after that). The inverse problem is found among the monarchies, where power shifts only within the ruling family and only when the king dies.

Since Israel's founding in 1948, by contrast, every single transfer of power, from the incumbent to the next winning party or coalition, has been orderly and peaceful.

Israel's Rule of Law

Israel's political system upholds the principle of the rule of law. Courts that are insulated from the reach of political influence are essential for the rule of law—a principle upheld in Israel's judiciary, but, again, an exception in the region. Just ask those 683 Egyptians swept up in a political purge who were summarily sentenced to death. When Syria had a functioning government, practically all judges were members of the ruling Ba'ath party and beholden to the dictator. Courts across the Middle East are not tribunals of objective law and justice, but typically a tyrant's instruments of subjugation.

By contrast, Israel's Supreme Court serves as a check on parliament, and it is well known for overturning government policy. The Court serves both as an appellate high court and a "high court of justice." That means Israelis are able to "challenge governmental action directly to the highest court without first going through the lower courts," explains Pnina Lahav, a legal scholar. (For your case to reach the United States Supreme Court, you have to work through several lower courts, often waiting years.) "Israelis are fond of this mechanism and make extensive use of it."[45]

In one widely reported case, we can see how the direct petitioning of the court enables people to challenge government policy. In the early 2000s, Israel faced a wave of Palestinian suicide bombers. The government decided to erect a barrier to prevent (or at least greatly impede) Palestinian fighters and suicide bombers entering Israel from the West Bank. The barrier is an electrified chain-link fence, flanked by trenches and barbed wire; in some places, it is a cement wall, between twenty and twenty-five feet high. Surveillance cameras and underground sensors are used to keep watch.

The wending path of the barrier ignited controversy because the route in places bisected Arab villages. In the village of Beit Sourik, several land owners and the local council petitioned the Supreme Court, challenging the path of the barrier. The case was decided against the government, which was ordered to reroute the barrier.[46]

Is it conceivable that a Saudi or Iranian court would overturn laws because they violate freedom; say, the persecution of gays? The stoning of adulterers? Or the death penalty for apostasy? No, because in those regimes and elsewhere in the Middle East, the entrenched premise is that government exists to subjugate individuals, rather than protect their freedom.

The rule of law means that no one is above the law. One implication of that vital principle is that there can be no impunity for wrongdoing even—indeed, especially—by government officials. Moreover, it entails that particular laws and government practices be subject to judicial self-criticism and revision. Let's explore this issue by looking at two cases: wrongdoing by public officials, and the legality of torture.

Punishing Corruption

When an Israeli politician's wrongdoing is exposed, what happens? Every free country (alas) has city officials, mayors, politicians, ministers who commit wrongs or who are outright corrupt. Look up, for example, the scandals involving Rod Blagojevich, a former Governor of Illinois. (Among other brazen acts of corruption, Blagojevich tried to sell the Senate seat vacated when Barack Obama left Congress.) And Israeli politics is no stranger to graft and corruption. Consider one high-profile example.

Ehud Olmert, who had served as mayor of Jerusalem, was a rising star in politics. Olmert eventually became prime minister. Some years ago, he was accused of taking bribes in connection with a real estate development in Jerusalem. When the news broke, he stepped down from the leadership of his party. In 2014, he was convicted of two charges of bribery. He was fined and sentenced to six years in jail.[47]

Incidentally, notice how the rule of law interlocks with the freedom of speech, a principle so flagrantly violated elsewhere in the region. At the time of Olmert's verdict, the newspaper *Israel Hayom*—reputed to have the largest daily circulation in the country—published an op-ed that decried Olmert's corruption, lamenting how the government's regulatory power over the economy creates opportunities for officials to line their pockets.[48] Have the journalists who originally exposed Olmert, or the writer of that op-ed (hardly the only one to comment on the subject), faced any government persecution? No.

The fate of Olmert is particularly revealing. Whereas Olmert was punished, recall what happened to Egypt's former dictator, Hosni Mubarak, when he landed in court. It bears emphasis that Olmert's corruption—accepting envelopes stuffed with cash— pales in comparison with Mubarak's thirty-year reign of terror and massive looting of millions of dollars. Mubarak, who got a token punishment, benefited from a corrupt legal system and a muzzled press. Olmert, however, faced Israel's independent courts. In the depressing episode involving Olmert, there is nonetheless something admirable: it's the fact that in Israel corrupt politicians can be removed from power, held to account, and punished.

Judicial Self-Criticism: The Legality of Torture

We've seen that torture is common in Egypt, Jordan, Gulf states, Iran, and elsewhere in the Middle East. For decades, Israel has had to deal with national security crises—literal ticking time bomb scenarios. But it has also publicly grappled with the difficult question of when, if ever, torture may be permitted when interrogating suspected terrorists.

The Israeli Supreme Court heard a case brought by the Public Committee Against Torture in Israel against the government's agency responsible for safeguarding the country from terrorist attacks. That case led to a landmark decision. The court's chief justice, writes Nicolo Nourafchan, "ruled that the need to protect the democratic principles of the State of Israel obligated him to impose substantive protections for prisoners' human rights, even if that meant imposing limits on the [government's] ability to use an unfettered hand in fighting terror."[49]

The court explicitly prohibited the interrogation methods under consideration in the legal case, even though it viewed them as falling short of actual torture. Reflecting on that decision, Israel's chief justice wrote:

> We are aware that this decision does not make it easier to deal with [Israel's harsh] reality. This is the destiny of a democracy—it does not see all means as acceptable, and the ways of its enemies are not always open before it. A democracy must sometimes fight with one hand tied behind its back. Even so, a democracy has the upper hand. The rule of law and the liberty of an individual constitute important components in its understanding of security. At the end of the day, they strengthen its spirit and this strength allows it to overcome its difficulties. [50]

What's remarkable here is not only the fact of subjecting government practices to legal scrutiny, but also the court's ruling on the matter. Throughout the region, only Israel exhibits a commitment to the principle of the rule of law.

Religion and Israel's Political System

Israel is the self-defined "Jewish State." You might therefore suppose that Israel's religious character conforms to the perverse norms of the rest of the Middle East. In fact, religion's role in Israel's political system differs fundamentally.

Throughout its seventy years of independence, Israel has been ruled by secular governments; men and women, Jews and non-Jews, regardless of race or creed, have the same political rights. And although Israel has marked tensions over the influence of religion on politics, tensions rooted in its distinctive history, they're essentially similar to the religion/state conflicts we see in other free countries—and worlds away from the Middle East's prevailing unity of religion and state.

Before we explore the distinctive religion-state tension in Israel, let's take a brief look at the treatment of religious minorities in Israel, because it's a revealing marker.

Religious Minorities in Israel

Throughout the Middle East, it is only in Israel—with a preponderance of secular, non-observant Jews, and atheists—that we find freedom of thought and of religion extended to all citizens. Whereas Saudi Arabia harshly restricts the worship by Christians (and forbids proselytizing), whereas Egypt brutalizes its Christians, and whereas Christians throughout the region seem to be heading toward extinction, in Israel Christians freely worship in their own churches and monasteries. Whereas Iran makes the lives of Baha'i a living hell, in Israel the Baha'i—along with Muslims of all sects, and members of other religions—enjoy complete religious freedom. The Baha'i temple in the northern Israeli city of Haifa, flanked by lavish gardens, is a tourist landmark.

Whereas in Saudi Arabia all citizens are required to be Muslim, Israeli society encompasses citizens of all creeds: Muslim, Christian, Druze, Baha'i, and many others. Some members of the Druze community, whose secretive religion apparently spun off from Islam long ago, serve in Israel's armed forces. Salim Joubran, an Arab born to a Christian family, received a permanent appointment to the Israeli Supreme Court. Jamal Hakroush was the first Muslim to attain the rank of Deputy Commissioner in the Israel Police.[51] Rasha Atamny is an Israeli diplomat; she's not the country's first female diplomat, nor its first Muslim (or Christian) diplomat, but the first female Muslim one.[52]

Members of diverse religious and racial minority groups in Israel are often lumped together under the vague term "Arabs" (a term which we'll discuss in chapter three), and they consistently "make up more than ten percent of Israel's Knesset [parliament]," observes Joshua Muravchik, with "the largest number of them from Arab nationalist parties, some from a leftist party that also includes Jews, and a sprinkling from the range of Israel's major parties."[53] Arabic, along with Hebrew, is one of Israel's official languages, and there is an all-Arabic radio station and TV channel. The main networks have time set aside for Arab-language news, sports, and entertainment programming, while many shows in Hebrew have Arabic subtitles.[54] It's hard to imagine Egyptian TV airing a Hebrew-language version of *Sesame Street*.

Israel's Religion-State Tension

Let's now turn to consider the tension over religion's role in Israel's political system. To understand that tension, we need to flash back to an episode in Israel's founding. There were avowed secularists among the founders of Israel, but there was also opposition to the idea of separating religion from state.

To put that in a wider context, observe that the idea of secular government has been the exception, rather than the norm, in human history. The idea of separating religion from state is a comparatively recent innovation in political thought, an inheritance from the Age of Enlightenment. The first flowering of that idea occurred in the United States. The Founders of America, deeply influenced by Enlightenment thought, were well aware of the endless religious wars that tore Europe apart. They were committed to avoiding such destroyers of freedom. What the Founders did was to erect a wall of separation between church and state. For example, the First Amendment to the U.S. Constitution prohibits the Federal government from establishing an official, state-endorsed church. Our wall of separation—though chipped, battered, and undermined—remains mostly intact.

The founders of Israel were divided on the issue of religion's role in government. The most notable secularists among Israel's founders were Theodore Herzl and David Ben-Gurion. Herzl was the intellectual credited with galvanizing the Zionist movement, which sought to create the state of Israel. Ben-Gurion was a leading political figure at the time of Israel's founding.

In his manifesto *The Jewish State*, Herzl advocated for creating "the most modern [state] in the world,"[55] which for him meant respecting "the rights of the individual. Private property, which is the economic basis of independence, shall be developed freely and be respected by us."[56] Every person, regardless of creed or ancestry "should be accord[ed] honorable protection and equality before the law." Firmly opposed to "theocracy," Herzl argued that it was necessary to "keep our priests within the confines of their temples in the same way as we shall keep our professional army within the confines of their barracks."[57] There would be freedom of religion—and above all, "we shall make room for the immortal band of Freethinkers, who are continually making new conquests for humanity."[58]

Herzl's advocacy and writings inspired many, but some objected to his lack of emphasis even on Jewish culture, let alone religion.[59] Indeed, whereas Herzl himself was a secularist who admired science and commerce, the Zionist movement was ideologically variegated. Along with thinkers who put emphasis on Jewish cultural traditions, there were also religionists, and quite a few varieties of socialists.[60]

David Ben-Gurion, who became Israel's first prime minister, was a dyed-in-the-wool secular socialist. Described as "vehemently antireligious," Ben-Gurion scorned sacred rituals, he did not observe the Sabbath, and he refused to have a religious ceremony when he got married. Although he had respect for the Bible, "he did not regard it as a holy text and refused to swear with his hand on it."[61]

But at the formation of the state in the late 1940s, with threats of an Arab invasion looming (more on that in the next chapter), the secularists believed they had to reach a compromise with religionist political groups, if the new state was to be born. Under that fateful compromise, known as the "status quo agreement," the state ended up granting the Jewish religion privileges and subsidies that no private, voluntary association (whether a club, a business, or a spiritual group) should possess. The original "status quo" agreement, writes the scholar Ami Pedahzur, called for:

> ...declaring that Saturday would be the country's official sabbatical and a day on which Jews were forbidden to work; guaranteeing that only kosher food would be served at state institutions; determining matrimonial laws in accordance with the values of Orthodox Judaism; and certifying an autonomy that would allow the ultra-Orthodox to maintain independent educational frameworks for their children (where the state's authority would be limited).[62]

Ever since this compromise, secularists and religionists have clashed over Judaism's role in society. Decades ago, for example, one movie theater in Jerusalem took a stand by opening its doors during the Sabbath. That brought out two impassioned crowds: the secular Israelis eager to catch a movie, and a horde of religionists who protested outside. Some religionists have tried to deter their secular neighbors from driving on the holy day by throwing stones at passing cars. Nevertheless, beyond the city of Jerusalem the no-work-on-Saturday rule is widely flouted; the music at Tel Aviv nightclubs keeps pumping.

Many Israeli religionists are bent on imposing their dogma on other people. Thus they have continually sought greater political power and undeserved privileges. Through continual agitation, they managed to gain not only wider exemptions from military service, but also living stipends and family welfare handouts to men who study at Jewish seminaries. The journalist Bernard Avishai notes that religionist men "study virtually free of charge at yeshivot, protected religious schools, which are themselves funded largely by the education ministry."[63] Unlike regular government grants or scholarships for higher education, which are open to everyone, you can only get these benefits if you go to a seminary—a blatantly unjust privilege. Another source of friction are the wholesale military exemptions afforded to religionists, so they can avoid compulsory military service. Tens of thousands of them every year are let off the hook.[64] Seeing that, some Israelis have demanded what they regard as "equality in sharing the burden" of defending the country.[65] (It's worth adding that a military draft is profoundly at odds with the principles of a free society. For many Israelis, however, completing their military duty is a source of pride.)

And here are two more absurd consequences of religion's continued influence that impact almost every Israeli. To get married or divorced, you have to go through the Rabbinate, an officially sanctioned religious institution. You can still get a civil wedding, if you go overseas. Thousands of couples circumvent the Rabbinate by traveling to neighboring Cyprus for a civil wedding that Israeli authorities recognize as legal. The Rabbinate also has a legal monopoly over divorce, and in keeping with religious precepts, it's biased in favor of husbands and against wives seeking to end a marriage. Israelis across the political spectrum are outraged by the Rabbinate, and rightly so. According to one recent poll, fully 95 percent of secular Israelis are dissatisfied with the government's policy toward matters of religion, and 64 percent of the population endorse the idea of same-sex marriage.[66] The primeval idea of a state-backed religious institution deciding matters of personal law has no place in any free society, let alone one at the forefront of technological and scientific progress.

Religion-State Tension in Comparison

Israel's religion-state tension is a serious matter. But is it on par with the religion-state unity that prevails in the Middle East? No. The more apt comparison is to the situation in other free nations, which differ greatly on the issue of separating religion from state. To see that, let's widen our evaluative context, and compare the situation in two European countries, France and the United Kingdom. The point here is not to soft-pedal, let alone make apologies for, Israel's situation by noting shortcomings elsewhere. The point instead is to recognize that the problem facing Israel is far more similar to the problems afflicting the world's free societies— and vastly different from the religion-state unity prevailing in the Middle East.

France, along with the United States, admirably leads the way on the principle of separating religion and state. The French state is self-consciously and proudly secular. Under a doctrine known as *laïcité*, French law guarantees freedom of religious worship and legally separates church from state. Brought into force in 1905, the doctrine of *laïcité* aimed in part to block the interference of the dominant Catholic Church in the affairs of state.

Nonetheless, the church-state wall in France has chinks. Although the government cannot directly fund churches, mosques, synagogues, or other religious organizations, it can, and it does, afford religious organizations special economic privileges, such as loan guarantees, and it can exempt their places of worship from property taxes.[67] In France, as in other European countries, the public holidays largely mirror the days defined as holy by the Catholic Church, which remains a powerful national force. And despite the well-rooted doctrine of *laïcité*, there remain clashes over religion's role in public life. Recently, the French authorities were faced with having to adjudicate whether Nativity scenes in public buildings violate the principle of *laïcité*; one point at issue is whether such displays, honoring the birth of Jesus Christ, can be anything but religious symbols.[68]

The situation in the United Kingdom (where I lived for many years) is different. The church-state relationship is truly muddled. Practically, the government is secular, and there is complete freedom of worship. Yet Britain (like Denmark) has an established church, which enjoys special privileges and intrudes on life in many ways. The British monarch, though merely a titular head of state, is the "defender of the faith" and the Supreme Governor of the Church of England. The Church has some twenty-odd bishops to represent it in the House of Lords. The latter is the second chamber of the U.K. Parliament, and it is responsible for shaping law and serving as a check on the government.[69]

The Church has left a deep impress on British life. The Brits have been called a nation of shopkeepers, but until the Sunday Trading Act of 1994, it was illegal in England and Wales to open your shop on a Sunday.[70] On Sunday afternoons, if you flip the channel to BBC One you will find "Songs of Praise." This TV show, which has been on the air since the 1960s, features Christian hymns and "uplifting stories of faith." (The BBC is a government-chartered TV and radio broadcast network funded by a compulsory license fee; if you own a TV, you have to pay the fee—and thus help fund "Songs of Praise.")

Most mornings at the state schools that I attended, we had an assembly for announcements and collective prayer; any non-Christians (including me, an atheist, and my friend, a Jehovah's Witness) could get permission to sit it out. At one school, we were all made to say grace before tucking in to our lunch. Once a week, in elementary and high school we had a class called "RE"—religious education—in which we were taught Christian doctrine (along with a taste of Judaism, Hinduism, Sikhism, Buddhism, Islam, and a few other religions). Keep in mind: that's what I experienced attending *regular,* ostensibly secular, state schools. The government also funds at least seven thousand so-called faith schools aligned with particular religious orientations.[71]

From these comparisons, the point to take away is that while Israel's tension over religion's role in politics is distinctive, it fits a pattern among free countries. The religion-state tension is particularly acute in Israel, and religionist factions, like their counterparts in the United States, are zealous in seeking to inject their ideas into public life and arrogate special privileges for themselves. Israel (like every state) needs to figure out how to thoroughly wall off religion from the state in the name of upholding individual freedom. But without minimizing the importance of the issue, when you view it in this comparative context, you can see that Israel's religion-state tension belongs in a different category from the religious medievalism that pervades the rest of the Middle East.

Why Israel Stands Out

Throughout the Middle East, political power is an instrument of control and exploitation; the state stands above individuals as their master. The individual's life belongs to the government to command and dispose of. Your duty is to bow, obey, shut your mouth. But Israel's political system is fundamentally different.

Far from being a "shitty little country," Israel stands out for a political-legal system that aims not at subjugation, but at enabling individuals to live, think, produce, thrive. It enables individuals to shape their own society. It is predicated on the rule of law, with independent courts, and a supreme court that has distinguished itself for overruling government policies. It protects the freedom of individuals.

Israel's political system and institutions are crucial factors in explaining why life in Israel is far superior to the rest of the Middle East. The country's political system and institutions make it equal to the best among free societies—notably the United Kingdom, France, the United States—and, for the same reason, vastly superior to the Middle East's monarchies, dictatorships, theocracies. It is with this moral context firmly in mind that we must approach the Israeli-Palestinian conflict.

PART II

WRONGS, PAST AND PRESENT

What we've seen so far is that Israel is by far the best place to live in the Middle East, primarily because its political system aims at the protection of the individual's life and freedom. But there's a separate question of evaluating the Palestinian side of the conflict. The Palestinians are widely seen as victims lashing out in desperation. A natural question to ask is whether the Palestinians have legitimate grievances stemming from the founding and ongoing policies of Israel. It's possible, after all, that Israel is the best place to live *and* that Palestinians have legitimate claims against it. Justice requires that we consider seriously their claims. What are those claims? And what about the Palestinian movement, which says it is seeking to right those wrongs? These are the questions we explore in Part II.

People tend to think of Palestinian grievances and the Palestinian movement as inseparable. But there are distinct issues here that we need to separate out. First, for any given grievance, there's the question of whether it is warranted, and if so, how it might be redressed? Second, it's a vital but distinct question to judge the Palestinian movement itself in relation to the wrongs it has supposedly taken up arms to undo. We might conclude that the Palestinians have some legitimate grievances, but that the Palestinian movement does not speak for, or represent, the actual victims.

Exploring these distinct issues in turn, we start in chapter three by looking at four major, foundational grievances that Palestinians voice against Israel. In each case we ask: what are the claims, what's the historical context in which they arose, how should we evaluate them, and in cases of genuine wrongs, what might a reasonable solution look like? Next, in chapter four we turn to the Palestinian movement. What is the nature of that movement, what are its means and ends, and how should we judge it morally?

CHAPTER 3

PALESTINIAN GRIEVANCES

A Tale of Victims Lashing Out

In 1948, a thirteen-year-old boy living in what later became Israel "was forced to leave his home in the Galilean city of Safed and flee with his family to Syria. He took up shelter in a canvas tent provided to all the arriving refugees. Though he and his family wished for decades to return to their home and homeland, they were denied that most basic of human rights. That child's story, like that of so many other Palestinians, is mine," writes Mahmoud Abbas, a leader of the Palestinian movement.[1]

That movement took up arms in the name of avenging Israel's many victims. For decades, the public face of the Palestinian cause was Yasser Arafat. You can find covers of *TIME* magazine featuring Arafat, depicted as the idealistic leader of a "liberation" movement. Celebrated as the embodiment of that cause, in 1974 he was invited to speak before the United Nations General Assembly. Why were Palestinian guerrillas, or "fedeeyn" (in Arabic, "self-sacrificers"), fighting, and even martyring themselves? Arafat's answer: They were fighting to undo profound injustices, because no one else would. Standing at the podium of the U.N., Arafat explained that "When our people lost faith in the international community which persisted in ignoring its rights [sic] and when it became obvious that the Palestinians would not recuperate one inch of Palestine through exclusively political means, our struggle had no choice but to resort to armed struggle."[2]

This "armed struggle," across fifty-plus years, has cost the lives of thousands. During the 1970s, the Palestinian cause was synonymous with airliner hijackings, massacres, and random bombings. In recent years, the movement is inseparable from the tactics of suicide bombings, crowd-sourced stabbings, and rocket attacks. But all this brutality and bloodshed, we are told, should be seen as the actions of victims resisting injustice. "Stripped of its context, an act of Palestinian desperation looks like wanton murder," acknowledges the late Edward Said, an eminent professor at Columbia and champion of the Palestinian cause.[3] But in reality, argues Said, such acts of "desperation" are intended to impress the Palestinian claims upon a world inured to their suffering.[4]

Thus: Palestinians are victims lashing out in desperation. This notion has exerted a powerful impact in academia. Radiating out from scholarly books and seminars, it has become a fixture on the agenda of international institutions, and prominent advocacy organizations. It reverberates in the claims of advocates of Boycott, Divestment, Sanctions (BDS), the editorials of leading media outlets, and throughout political discourse.

Even if the Palestinian movement's resort to violence is not endorsed, it's a widely held view that the Palestinians are despairing victims. Empathizing with their plight, George W. Bush said that he "can understand the deep anger and despair of the

Palestinian people," and pledged to increase U.S. humanitarian assistance "to relieve Palestinian suffering." Why? Because, Bush explained, "It is untenable for Palestinians to live in squalor and occupation."[5] Barack Obama, who decried "resistance through violence," acknowledged that Palestinians "endure the daily humiliations, large and small, that come with [Israeli] occupation. So let there be no doubt, the situation for the Palestinian people is intolerable."[6]

If anyone deserves your sympathy and moral approval, many feel, it is surely a movement of weak, underdog victims fighting against oppression and injustice committed by the more-powerful. The question, then, is whether this evocative tale fits the facts.

Let's unpack this story. There are two intertwined threads to examine here. One thread has to do with the nature and goals of the Palestinian movement. This movement claims that it seeks to end the injustices afflicting Palestinians, deliver them from "occupation," and fulfill their national aspirations. Before we can turn to that, in the next chapter, we need to look at the other thread of the story, which comes first causally: the claim that the founding and ongoing policies of Israel have fundamentally wronged the Palestinians. Those grievances, evoked in Mahmoud Abbas's story of becoming a refugee, are wrongs that the Palestinian cause insists it is working to right.

What are the major grievances? In summary: Since the founding of Israel, Palestinians have been dispossessed; many have been expelled from their homeland, with hundreds of thousands exiled as refugees; many have been living under occupation; and they are continually denied their rights.

These broad charges—dispossession, expulsion, occupation, denial of rights—are crucial Palestinian grievances, they're widely known, and they're hard cases. You can hear these charges invoked by leaders of the Palestinian movement, its followers, and its sympathizers. In his influential book *The Question of Palestine*, for example, Edward Said articulates the claims of dispossession, exiling, and denial of rights.[7] And you'll find these points echoed in the demands of the global Boycott, Divestment, Sanctions (BDS) movement.[8]

In this chapter we'll examine these four grievances in depth, asking what, precisely, these claims mean—what actions, policies, historical facts they designate—and what assumptions they take for granted. Beyond these four, of course, there are other complaints, but which we need to put to one side. Our purpose here is not comprehensiveness, but rather to analyze major, foundational grievances on which so much hangs. (These analyses, by extension, indicate how one might think about and deal with other grievances.[9])

What, then, is the context of those historic and present grievances? How should we judge them? What do they imply for a moral appraisal of Israel's political system and of the Palestinian cause? And, ultimately, can these grievances explain, even justify, the Palestinian movement's resort to violent attacks across decades?

Who Are the Victims?

Some Israelis have long insisted that there are only *so-called* Palestinians. And, at my public talks and elsewhere, I keep encountering well-meaning folks who tell me that "there's no such thing as the Palestinians," because there was never a state called "Palestine," there's no "Palestinian" language, and anyway the people who lived there called themselves "Arabs" for the longest time. Well, I understand where this kind of objection is coming from, but I see the issue differently. *Today* there is a community of people who self-identify as Palestinian, they have discernible aspects of a culture, and they have shared experiences and history, which overlap largely, but not completely, with a political-ideological movement (about which I will say more in the next chapter). So in this book, when I say "Palestinians" I mean individuals in the community that self-identify with that label.

But it's true, and important for understanding the *Palestinian movement*, that the term "Palestinian" is politically charged. The Palestinian label was little known and politically dormant for decades, until the political-ideological movement associated with it took off in the late 1960s.[10]

Some historical background: At the beginning of the twentieth century, the area now known as Israel was part of the vast Ottoman Empire. The Ottoman Empire, centered in Turkey, spanned much of the Middle East, and its rulers viewed themselves as heading a "caliphate," an Islamic dominion. After World War I, the Ottoman Empire fell apart, and some remnants of it came under British control. The British governed the area that became commonly known as "Palestine" until 1947. The people living there—Muslims, Christians, and others—were mainly thought of, and most saw themselves as, "Arabs" (a nebulous term we'll examine later in this chapter). Who then is a Palestinian?

The Palestinian movement has labored to pin down what it means to be a Palestinian and to instill that vision among its followers. According to the Palestinian National Charter of 1968, a seminal document of the movement, the "Palestinians are those Arab nationals who, until 1947, normally resided in Palestine" whether or not they stayed there subsequently, and so is anyone born "after that date, of a Palestinian father," regardless of where that person is born. This identity—notably featuring "membership in the Palestinian community"—cannot be lost, nor negated. The Palestinian identity, the Charter states, "is a genuine, *essential*, and inherent characteristic; it is transmitted from parents to children."[Emphasis added.][11]

The pivotal term here is *essential*. Through birth, you are locked into this identity, you cannot change it, you cannot escape it, you cannot assume another. It defines you. Notice how this conception of identity ties who you are now to events and actions that occurred in the past, many if not all occurring before your birth. Your concern and focus are drawn away from your own life and future—from vital issues such as what kind of life should I build? What career should I pursue? What will it take for me to flourish?—and instead toward focusing on the group you're born into and *its* past.

There's a related aspect of what it means for this group identity to be *essential*. It means that individuals come to view themselves as interchangeable cells in the larger collective. Your identity derives, not from your choices, decisions, and accomplishments, but from your unchosen and unchangeable membership in the Palestinian community. And this collective comes first. Its needs and it values, its past injuries and its present wellbeing, take precedence over those of any individual member.

This collectivized outlook distorts how you think about justice. There's something warped about treating individuals alive today who were never personally affected by a long-ago wrong as, in fact, victims, solely because of their unchosen group-membership. The same logic means that we must hold children responsible for the sins of their parents (or their distant ancestors), which is unjust. But it's precisely this sort of collectivized outlook that the Palestinian movement adopts and fosters. Its leaders stoke collective hostility against the "Jews" now alive, for wrongs that occurred well before they were born. And it's precisely this collectivized outlook that gravely distorts our thinking about the Israeli-Palestinian conflict in general, and Palestinian grievances in particular.

When trying to understand and evaluate the grievances against Israel and identify the victims, what matters is not the so-called wellbeing of the Palestinian collective, but rather the particular, irreplaceable individuals. It is only their liberty and property rights that can be infringed. It is only their particular lives that should now be our primary concern. So, from this individual-first vantage point, what are we to make of the crucial Palestinian grievances?

1. Stolen Land: "Dispossession."

Consider the grievance of "dispossession." Starting in the late nineteenth century, European followers of the Zionist movement set out to create a Jewish national home in the area now known as Israel. The claim is that they came and took over the land of Arab farmers already living there, thus "dispossessing" them.

Ordinarily the idea of "dispossession" means to be *wrongfully* deprived of one's property, and so one understanding of this grievance is that the Zionists *stole* the land. But the claim of "dispossession" blends together two essentially different kinds of thing: voluntary trade, on the one hand, and theft and fraud, on the other. Morally, of course, we have to distinguish between these two categories. And the fact of the matter is that the incoming Jews acquired land by *purchasing* it.

The Zionists bought land individually, but also by setting up purchasing institutions (for example, the Palestine Land Development Company and the Jewish National Fund). Legal changes under the Ottoman regime during the mid and late 1800s had gone some way toward delineating property rights in land,[12] which meant that there were various sorts of legal claims you could have to land. For example, you could own the land outright; you could lease the land from the owner; you could have a limited kind of ownership called "usufruct," which meant you could use the land and keep the profits from it, but not sell it or borrow money against it without government permission.[13] Many peasant farmers were tenants in one form or another. Accordingly, because the Zionist purchasing agencies sought land that Jewish newcomers could easily settle and develop, they prioritized buying land that had few or no tenant farmers on it.[14]

During the first four decades of the twentieth century, the opportunities to buy land in Palestine were abundant.[15] Kenneth Stein, in a historical study of land acquisition in Palestine, reports that:

> ...the quantity of Arab land offered for sale was far in excess of the Jewish ability to purchase. Jewish buyers turned down purchase offers of small-tract land areas in the 1920s when it was in their interest and easier to buy larger tracts. Even during times of extreme tension between Arabs, Jews, and the British, the Jewish National Fund never lacked numerous offers though it suffered from severe shortages of funds.[16]

The same was true in 1940, after the British had imposed regulations to impede land sales: "the Jewish National Fund could not, because of financial constraints, effect all the purchase offers tendered."[17] Among the sellers were prominent Arab families. Ironically, quite a number of them were eager, in private transactions, to sell lands at skyrocketing prices to Zionists while, in public, voicing concern and objections about Jewish immigration. (Stein has a catalogue of Arab politicians and notables involved in land transfers to Jews, between 1918–45. He also notes that at least one quarter of the eighty-nine-member Arab Executive in 1920–28 can be linked to land sales to Jews.)[18]

What happened if someone bought a tract of land with tenants on it? Sometimes the contract of sale would require the existing landlord to ensure the tenants were no longer occupying the land. Commonly, they were offered an alternate piece of land or monetary compensation to relocate, finding work on farms operated in line with superior, more efficient techniques, or in newly opened factories. The monetary compensation could amount to a hefty sum, and, when offered, few refused it.[19]

But quite apart from, and predating, the purchase of land by Zionists, there were disputes over land, including friction between tenants and landlords.[20] Some disputes can be traced back to the perverse incentives that Ottoman land laws had created. Under the Ottoman regime, if you owned certain types of land, you were taxed on it and might also be conscripted into military service[21] (a fate that could mean serious hardship, possibly even financial ruin, for your family). So, some landowners either avoided formally registering their property, relying on unofficial records, or deliberately under-stated the size of their property when registering it. That creates a serious problem if you try to sell (or take out a loan against) land you've never registered, or if you want the buyer to pay you for more than is listed on a deed, because you underreported your land's size.[22] These kinds of problems, regarding the ownership and actual boundaries of land, arose when Zionists buyers sought to acquire land.

When the British took over after World War I, they imposed regulations on the sale of lands. These regulations in their own way added to some of the existing problems. The British regulations aimed to protect tenant farmers from their landlords; for example, after being a tenant for a set period of time, a farmer could gain certain claims to the land. Nevertheless, there were shady landlords who, eager to sell off their property unencumbered, found ways to get around the British regulations; for example, making tenants move to another plot of land, before they could qualify for certain protections.[23]

One other source of friction had to do with longstanding customs. Some peasants were accustomed to letting their flocks graze wherever they might roam, regardless of where the property lines happened to fall. (Often, property boundaries were vague; and in some places, land was held collectively by villages.)[24] That can be a problem, say, if your cattle trample over a neighbor's newly planted crops.

To put it kindly, the vital institution of private property was often little understood, if not openly resented. Clearly some peasants were upset about the sale of land to Jews, because their own ancestors had worked the land, and they themselves had an emotional attachment to it. For certain peasants, it was difficult to accept the new reality confronting them.[25]

What then are we to make of the grievance of "dispossession"? It may be that some, or even many, tenant farmers were unhappy at having to relocate or enter a new line of work, but the pivotal question is whether their individual rights were violated? It's helpful to look at a comparable scenario.

Suppose you rent an apartment and the landlord decides to sell off the building. You might well be upset about what the new owner decides to do with his property. Maybe you have to find a new place to live or pay more in rent. That's a tough situation; understandably you might feel upset. The need to find a new place to live, or the higher rent, may pose a hardship upon you. But have your rights been infringed? No.

The same sort of thing can happen in your workplace. The owner of the coffee house where you work decides to sell the business, and, under the new management, some or even all the workers end up being let go. However unpleasant that may be for you and the other folks affected, the new owner has neither stolen anything from you, nor defrauded you: your individual rights have not been violated.

By contrast, suppose one day you return home and find that it has been broken into. A bunch of dodgy people you've never met before have moved in. These squatters have ransacked your closets, thrown away what they disliked, and sold off your couch. They've gobbled up everything in your fridge. They refuse to leave, and they've changed the locks to keep you out. When you try to talk to them, they threaten to pound you with a baseball bat. This is a textbook example of being wrongfully deprived of your property—an egregious violation of your rights.

Circle back to the Palestinian claim of "dispossession." After a landlord sells a tract of land to Jews, a tenant farmer is required to leave farmland his family had plied for generations: were this tenant farmer's rights violated? No. He may, however, have a claim against the original landlord, if that landlord was required to give him advance notice, or an option to buy the land; or if the landlord was required to offer him compensation, but failed to do so, or refused. Or if the landlord in fact *coerced* him off the land.[26]

It bears emphasis that the claim of "dispossession" pertains to land transactions that unfolded roughly a century ago, involving people who are long dead. Here is a pivotal question: What does the claim of "dispossession" mean to someone alive today?

Meet Arwa, in her mid-thirties, born to parents who describe themselves as Palestinians. Let's say that Arwa's great-great-grandfather had every inch of the land he tilled lawfully sold off to Zionists. However unhappy her (now deceased) ancestors may have been about that transaction, it has no bearing on Arwa's ability today to pursue her goals and earn her own success in the world. Nor would it be rational for her to nurse a grudge against the Jewish buyer's great-great-grandchildren alive today.

But now take the argument one step further. Although the evidentiary paper trail is incredibly hard to reconstruct, let's suppose that Arwa's great-great-grandfather was a peasant farmer who *did* hold a legal title to the land, but that his property was coerced from him. Theft or fraud is a violation of his rights. *At the time*, the proper recourse was to a court of law, and back then the courts heard cases concerning land issues (for example, about the accuracy of the boundary lines of the land sold). But Arwa's great-great-grandfather never received justice.

What to do about it now, some hundred years later? Something like a statute of limitations should apply. For most legal wrongs, the principle of a statute of limitations defines a time limit for bringing legal action, because after a certain point, it becomes impossible to validate the objectivity of the evidence (it's difficult to adjudicate a case, for example, when neither the plaintiffs nor the defendants can take the stand). Another crucial reason for having a statute of limitations pertains to the rights of people now alive and their ability to plan and work. For example, suppose you've built a business on property that, four owners ago, was not justly acquired, but that you had no reason to suspect was wrongly taken. It would be a further injustice to use that century-old claim to the land to deprive you of your business and thus your livelihood. And the people who would be given your land, even if they are the great-great grandchildren of the century-old victim, should not want it.

For someone like Arwa living today and working toward a prosperous future, beyond a frank acknowledgment of the historic wrongs committed by any of the parties involved, the issue of "dispossession" can have no rational standing.

What can it mean that leaders of the Palestinian movement, and many of their followers, press the grievance of "dispossession," a term seemingly calculated to muddy the moral distinction between trade and theft? The slippery claim of "dispossession" encourages a mindset of collectivized victimhood and it stokes hostility against "the Jews" collectively, viewing every Israeli now alive as somehow responsible for long-ago deeds they had no part in.

2. Kicked Out, Kept Out: Expulsion, Refugees, and the "Right of Return"

Recall the heart-rending story of how Mahmoud Abbas, who, like so many thousands of others, was forced to leave his home during the 1948 war. What led to that outcome? And what are its implications? The prevailing narrative holds that the founders of Israel expelled hundreds of thousands of Palestinians, exiled them from their own homeland, and thus condemned them to the miserable, unending status of refugees. Palestinians broadly refer to this episode surrounding Israel's independence as the "Nakba" (catastrophe). And so long as there are refugees, their plight is taken as a stain on Israel's moral character.

Let's rewind that sound-bite version of history, and fill in key elements of the lead-up to the 1948 war, so we can assess the claims about expulsion and refugees.

The Run-Up to the War

The years leading up to the war are significant. When the Ottoman Empire crumbled in the wake of World War I, the British moved into the region and assumed control over Palestine. The British governed Palestine under an arrangement defined by the League of Nations (a predecessor of the United Nations) called a Mandate. Formulated in 1922 and in force until 1948, the British Mandate was created to pave the way for the "establishment of a Jewish national home" and "safeguarding the civil and religious rights of all the inhabitants of Palestine, irrespective of race and religion."[27]

In the decades following World War I, the number of Zionist immigrants grew considerably (particularly so with the rise of Nazism and the outbreak of World War II).[28] These newcomers had a profound impact. Electrical power plants began operating. New medical clinics and hospitals were built; training centers for doctors and nurses opened up. The ensuing financial investments in factories and businesses, the importation of scientific farming techniques, and the avid purchase of land by Zionists, resulted in a climbing standard of living.[29]

The effects were manifest throughout society. Economically, many people who were once peasant farmers gravitated to major cities in search of employment and the related benefits of city life: between 1930–39, the Muslim and Christian population of the port city of Haifa increased by eighty-seven percent.[30] Over all, the Muslim and Christian population, according to a British government report, saw massive growth (a "growth of over fifty percent in seventeen years").[31] What were key factors behind that population spike? The newly available health services, the combatting of malaria, the reduction in the infant death-rate, the improvement of the water-supply and public sanitation—all carried out by the incoming Zionists. Wages earned at Zionist farms and factories, and the profits from land sales, spurred the development of what British officialdom called "Arab industrial undertakings"—from soap and flour, to bricks and bedsteads, to alcohol and clothes—which nearly doubled between 1914–1933.[32] Such developments fueled progress and prosperity.

But from these advances, some people recoiled. The presence of outsiders, with their foreign ways; the reshaping of traditional society and customs; the acceleration of economic productivity on farms and in factories; the growth of industry and development of city life: Witnessing all of that, some inhabitants opposed continued immigration and land purchases.

The historians Baruch Kimmerling and Joel Migdal report that for some people, the opposition to outsiders tended to focus on the "port towns—seen as an insidious representation of the dislocation brought by the West—and on the open embrace of European manners and dress, and on an all-too-eager acceptance of byproducts of the Enlightenment and the Western Scientific revolution."[33]

Such opposition depicted outsiders as a corrupting force. Listen to the diatribe of one villager:

> Money is God [in Tel Aviv].… Must all Palestine become one day like this, including the Holy City of Jerusalem?… Tel Aviv is an ulcer eating into our own country. If it is what the Jews want to make of Palestine, I wish my children dead. We do not mind poverty, but we weep when our peace is taken away. We lived a modest and contented life, but what shall we do if our children grow up to ape the noisy ways of these new people?[34]

Stoking these anti-Western sentiments was Haj Amin al-Husseini, who held the post of Grand Mufti of Jerusalem, a kind of religious community leader and representative. The Mufti articulated that viewpoint even more forcefully. He railed against the "invasion of liberal ideas." Speaking in 1935, he explained: "The cinema, the theatre, and some shameless magazines enter our houses and courtyards like adders, adders, where they kill morality and demolish the moral foundations of society."[35] He also complained that the Jews have "spread their customs and usages, which are opposed to our religion and to our whole way of life."[36] Voicing a sentiment that would surely elicit nods of approval from the Taliban, the Ayatollahs of Iran, the clerics of Saudi Arabia, and the leaders of ISIS, the Mufti claimed that the "Jewish girls, who run around in shorts, demoralize our youth *by their mere presence.*" [Emphasis added.][37]

Hammering on these themes, the Mufti was integral to the riots and armed uprising that raged between 1936–1939. But soon this ferocious uprising became "primarily directed against the Mufti's Arab rivals and ordinary Palestinian Arabs."[38] The historian Howard Sachar observes that the "Mufti's offensive grew in scope and momentum, until by the end of 1939, his victims exceeded 3,000. Egypt and Lebanon were crowded with nearly 18,000 fugitives of the terror."[39] But all of this was in the name of what? A salient if not the principal factor in the Mufti's campaign appeared to be his lust for political domination.[40]

Here we can see two crucial, and related, themes that shape the 1948 war and that to this day continue to fuel hostility. Notice, first, how so much of the hostility toward the immigrants, and the nascent Israel, stemmed from a religious imperative. The Islamic self-image entails membership in a worldwide community of believers (the "umma"). Members of that vast collective in turn have a duty to show solidarity with their co-religionists against outsiders.[41] That collective religious imperative, present in 1936–1939, would move slightly to the background until the mid-1980s, but as we'll later discuss, it has surged to prominence again.[42]

Second, in the uprising of 1936–1939 we can see foreshadowed a key feature of the 1948 war that erupted when Israel declared its independence, the war that led to the refugee problem. A major if not the over-riding motivation behind the aggression in both cases was a desire for conquest and subjugation. Just as the Mufti attempted to seize power in the 1930s, so the invading Arab armies in 1948 hoped to enlarge their dominions.

A Scrimmage for Conquest

With the outbreak of World War II, the question of a future Jewish state in Palestine was postponed. During those war years, it's worth noting, the Mufti allied himself with Nazi Germany and relocated to Berlin. At a meeting with Adolf Hitler in 1941, the Mufti assured him that Arab countries were convinced Germany would win the war and that they shared common enemies, notably including the Jews. He also offered to raise a volunteer force eager to fight in coordination with the Nazi regime.[43] (While the full extent of his collaboration with the Nazi regime is unclear, he is known to have accepted payment from Germany's Foreign Office as late as April 1945.)[44] After the war's end, the Palestine question was finally put before the newly established United Nations.[45]

In 1947 the United Nations approved a compromise solution, known as the Partition Plan. Under that plan, the land would be partitioned into two states—one for the Zionists, another for the Arab (Muslim and Christian) population—but linked though economic union. The Zionists accepted the plan. Many Arab community leaders in Palestine opposed it, and they had the backing of an organization calling itself the Arab League. Its members at the time were Egypt, Syria, Lebanon, Iraq, Transjordan (now Jordan), Saudi Arabia, and Yemen. It rejected the partition.

The Arab League threatened war. Its Secretary General, Abdul Rahman Azzam Pasha, explained that "this will be a war of extermination and momentous massacre which will be spoken of like the Tartar massacre or the Crusader wars."[46]

What happened after the U.N.'s approval of the Partition Plan was the launch of a two-phase war against the emerging state of Israel, first from within Palestine, with backing by Arab states, and then in May 1948, from outside. The armies of Egypt, Syria,

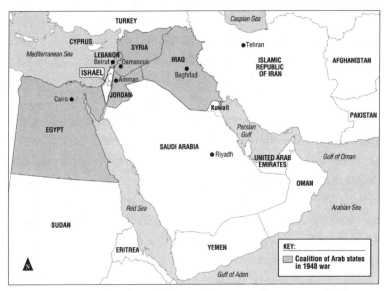

Map 1. Locating Israel in the Middle East. (This map is illustrative, rather than authoritative.)

Transjordan, Lebanon, and Iraq invaded (see Map 1). The aim was to obstruct the partition plan, prevent the creation of a Jewish state, and "preserv[e] Palestine as an independent unified Arab state."[47] That formulation of the goal was telling. It smacked of a pretext: *Palestine had never before been an independent state.* Nor was it credible that the invading forces of Egypt, Syria, Transjordan, Lebanon, and Iraq were intent on establishing a sovereign Palestinian regime.

Indeed, the appearance of Arab unity in the war "hid deep divisions that had little to do with ideological commitment and everything to do with personal ambitions and rivalries," observes the scholar Adeed Dawisha.[48] It was a scrimmage for conquest.

The spoils of war beckoned. To the conqueror would accrue not only the prestige of driving unbelievers out and expanding the dominion of Arab/Muslim power, but also a hugely desirable tract of land situated at the intersection of Africa, Asia, and Europe, offering ports on the Mediterranean Sea. It is telling that when the head of the Arab League, Azzam, promised to wage a "war of extermination" against Israel, he went on to note several distinguishing aspects of the war; one item in that list was that it "will be an opportunity for vast plunder."[49] And so, observes Dawisha:

> King 'Abdullah coveted the incorporation of Palestine into his domain, and preferably the creation of a Hashemite Greater Syria. The Syrians, eyeing 'Abdallah's enormous irredentist appetite "feared Jordan more than Israel." The Iraqis had no objection to Hashemite takeover so long as *they* became the senior partners; the Egyptians on the other hand were not about to allow the Hashemites to claim the spoils of war; nor would Ibn Sa'ud, whose Saudi Arabia was created only after defeating the Hashemites.[50]

In that war, Dawisha notes, the Muslim and Christian populations in Palestine and in neighboring regimes were "told to expect a swift victory," but in fact they were "witness to Arab armies and governments competing for their own slice of Palestine." The rivalry in pursuit of conquest was so bitter, that during the war against Israel they "went out of their way not to come to the aid of each other, and indeed, in some cases, sabotaged one another."[51]

Member-states of the Arab League could rally, for a while, against the hateful outsiders—the Zionists—but their aim in waging the war was not primarily, nor even secondarily (if at all) to realize any vague claims to Palestinian statehood. The invading states pushed political leaders within Palestine to the sidelines and instead vied for territorial self-aggrandizement. Like so many other tyrants throughout history, they sought to expand their dominion through conquest. Just as they had subjugated their own citizens, so they would do the same to the people on any newly captured lands.

Which brings us to the claims of expulsion and of the refugees.

What Triggered the Refugee Problem

Initiated by the Arab League, the war resulted in a substantial number of refugees. How many is difficult to say with precision, partly because it depends on how you define "refugee," partly because it's always difficult to count refugees, partly because the methods of tallying have been subject to error, fraud, and politicization. For decades, scholars have argued over the actual number. Even now, after prodigious historical research, the estimates range from about 609,000 to 760,000 refugees. The difference between these figures is hardly a rounding error.[52] What impelled so many people to leave?

Contrary to a widely accepted narrative, there's no evidence of a grand Israeli scheme to push them out, to effect some sort of "ethnic cleansing." The fundamental cause of the refugee problem lies with the forces that launched the war against Israel. What's more, those forces have prolonged and magnified the problem, with the aim of shifting the blame for the plight of refugees from themselves to Israel.

By word and deed, the insurgent forces and the invading armies bear the responsibility for initiating the war. Understandably, the residents of many villages abandoned their homes. Fear for their personal safety pushed many families to take flight from the shifting battlefront.[53] Such a reaction is an unavoidable fact of war. Look, for example, at the Syrian civil war that began in 2011: more than five *million* people—nearly a quarter of the country's pre-war population—have vacated their homes to avoid being caught in the crossfire.[54] In a study of the 1948 war in Palestine, the scholar Efraim Karsh has presented compelling evidence of cases wherein the Arab leadership instructed, sometimes bullied, residents to leave their homes (for example, in the city of Haifa, where Israeli town officials urged them to stay).[55] There's also evidence that the Arab leadership purposely spread rumors of Israeli massacres, rapes, and other atrocities, instilling profound fear in the hearts of those living in Palestine and thus triggering their flight.

Two questions remain. First, were there cases of Israeli forces also compelling villagers to leave? Yes, some; the historical record, however, points to ad hoc military rationales, rather than any systematic policy of "cleansing" the land of its inhabitants. For example, in the heat of battle, troops would seek to avoid having potentially hostile villagers at their flank, while fending off an advancing army.[56] The invading armies, however, exhibited a wholesale indifference to the lives of their supposed brethren. The "deliberate depopulation of Arab villages and their transformation into military strongholds," observes Karsh, "were marked corollaries of the Arab campaign from the onset of hostilities."[57]

Second, what about the allegations of Israeli atrocities? The most commonly mentioned allegations concern two villages, Lydda and Deir Yassin, where Israeli forces are said to have massacred civilians. Possibly someday, we'll have a definitive account of these incidents, but the debate among historians is ongoing. The analyses that I find compelling indicate that these notorious incidents were overstated to serve political ends and that they were exceptional deviations from Israeli policy, rather than the norm.[58] My read on that contested history is that there was no deliberate pattern of Israeli crimes on the battlefield.

What to Make of the Refugee Grievance

The Palestinian refugee grievance encompasses two major demands: to reclaim land and homes left behind, and to exercise a putative "right of return."

We should remember that untold numbers of refugees throughout history have been compelled by the perils of war to leave behind their homes, never to return, and their property, never to be reclaimed. Often they settle elsewhere, integrating themselves to their adoptive homes. That is what many Europeans did after World War II, a war which caused the largest refugee crisis of the last century. War, moreover, is inherently chaotic, and that limits the possibility of objectively establishing claims for redress. That slim possibility diminishes greatly with the passage of time.

Think back to Arwa, and consider her grandfather, Mustafa. In his pocket Mustafa carries a rusting key. It fits the lock of a home that, during the 1948 war, he left behind. And let's stipulate that Mustafa lived in a village that Israeli forces cleared out. Even if, somehow, it can be proven that the Israeli military's evacuation of the village was in fact wrong, today there is no way to right it, beyond a public acknowledgment of the circumstances and the culpability.

Leaders of the Palestinian cause, however, have led innumerable refugees like Mustafa to believe that one day they will reclaim their homes. Except that, as in so many other cases, the house no longer exists, destroyed in the original battles, fallen to ruin, or taken as conquered land and re-developed. Mustafa will never again walk through the doorway of his old house. This realization, if he is willing to entertain it, will surely cause him grief. But it is a gross injustice to encourage in him, and others, the unrealizable hope that someday, the outcome of the war will be undone, that a past irrevocably lost somehow awaits.

In the name of holding the perpetrators of injustice accountable, Mustafa *should* harbor ill-will. Some of it should be directed
at the Israeli forces, if they acted wrongly in 1948. But primarily,
Mustafa should blame and hold in contempt the instigators of the
1948 war and the corrupt goal for which they fought, as well as all
those who now stoke his grief, exacerbating it in the worst possible way. But Mustafa should also try to move on with his life, and
cooperate with peaceful people wherever he can find them.

For Arwa, whose own parents had yet to be born, the grievance can have at most the significance of one thread in a family
history—in the same way, for instance, that I look back on my
grandparents' departure from what is today Iraq. They left their
home, fleeing to Palestine, in fear for their lives, their children, and
their future. Even if their loss had been greater in economic terms
than, say, Mustafa's home, and even if it had been an incontestable case of injustice, neither of these facts separately or combined
would be a grievance that I have any reason to shoulder, nor hold
against anyone now residing in Iraq. The same is true for Arwa.

Now consider Arwa's other grandfather, Ali, who as a result
of the war also became one of the Palestinian refugees. Throughout history, once the emergency context of war has ended, many
refugees eventually resettle, plant roots, build their lives in other
countries (and resettlement of the Palestinian refugees was, for
some time, a favored solution by certain members of the international community).[59] But this largely has not happened with the
Palestinian refugees, and their plight is distinctive in two revealing ways.

First, with the partial exception of Jordan, the neighboring
Arab regimes refused to absorb Palestinian refugees, and in many
cases treated them harshly. For example, those unlucky enough to
end up in Lebanon were banned from working in many professions

and ineligible to become citizens. By opposing the resettlement of the Palestinian refugees, by leaving them suspended in limbo, by confining many to squalid camps with inadequate facilities, Arab regimes perpetuated the misery they had caused, so as to exploit the continuing existence of unsettled refugees. Treating the refugees as pawns, these regimes fingered Israel as the cruel agent inflicting their suffering. (It should be noted that Israel has at various points offered to allow some, though not all, refugees to return.)[60]

The other distinctive feature of the Palestinian refugee problem has to do with their number. Earlier I mentioned that defining the category of "refugee" is surprisingly difficult. Perhaps the least controversial example of a refugee is someone who, because of a war, is unable to return to his home, in another country. But what about nomads (like the Bedouin tribes of southern Israel) who, after the war, can no longer roam on certain lands? What about migrant workers who, after the war, can only offer their labor to a smaller number of farm owners, because some of their former employers are on the other side of an armistice line? And there are still other hard cases.[61]

You would expect that the number of refugees would dwindle over time, simply because of human mortality. That is true of the tens of millions of refugees from World War II. But the number of Palestinian refugees has in fact ballooned. The United Nations has an agency—United Nations Relief Works Agency (UNRWA)—dedicated to the Palestinian refugee community, and it keeps tabs on the size of that population. While there were as many as 760,000 refugees at the war's end, the U.N.'s agency claims that today—some seventy years, and nearly three generations later—there are approximately five million.

The U.N. agency defines Palestinian refugees as "persons whose normal place of residence was Palestine during the period 1 June

1946 to 15 May 1948, and who lost both home and means of livelihood as a result of the 1948 conflict"—but the descendants of male
Palestinian refugees, including adopted children, are also eligible for
registration as "refugees."[62] Think back to Arwa and her family. The
U.N., it seems, would count as refugees not only Arwa's grandfather,
who actually lived in the war-torn area; not only his son (Arwa's
father); not only Arwa and her brother, Samy; but *also* Samy's five-
year-old son—and eventually, *his* sons. And on. And on.

If that boggles the mind, consider this parallel: I have a friend
whose Polish grandparents were refugees from World War II.
Neither my friend (born in 1975), nor his daughter, has ever set
foot in Poland. Yet if we applied the U.N. agency's logic to his
family, that would make my friend's baby-boomer father, my
friend himself, and his daughter all refugees.

You can see why a bureaucracy such as United Nations Relief
Works Agency would engage in dodgy accounting to ensure a
growing number of needy Palestinian refugees, thus justifying
its own reason for existing. But there's also a political and moral
advantage for leaders of the Palestinian movement, who can point
to an ever-growing community of victims whose suffering is
blamed on Israel. Thus the refugee problem not only persists, but,
if the number of victims is a measure of its severity, the problem
is worsening. And while the U.N. agency and Palestinian leaders
stand to gain from inflating the problem, where does that leave
the refugees themselves? Many have been consigned to a life of
ongoing dependence, with all of the moral degradation and resentment that so often go along with it.[63]

Leaders of the Palestinian movement, furthermore, demand
a sweeping "right of return" for everyone considered a refugee.
What would that entail? If the refugee population is ever-growing,
rather than naturally dwindling, the "right of return" is a demand

for the return of a population *more than six times larger* than the one that fled, seventy years ago. It is a population that has been indoctrinated for three generations to blame Israel for their suffering, rather than the actual culprits. It is a population replete with individuals deeply hostile to Israel's continued existence. That cannot end well.

If we re-conceive a "right of return" in a rational context, what might it look like? It's far from obvious that individuals have such a moral, or political, right. And if such a claim for return were to be granted, it would have to be conditional. Two obvious conditions: it would have to be time-limited (e.g., applicable to actual refugees still living) and highly selective. Not every refugee would qualify for return. They would need to demonstrate that they did not support and cooperate with the Arab regimes, that they blame those regimes for their plight, that they seek a peaceful life in Israel, and that one of the reasons they seek to return is precisely because it is by far the better place to live in the Middle East.

Moreover, if such a hypothetical "right of return" were to be implemented, it would be necessary to expose and hold accountable the Arab regimes for their continued victimization of the refugees and their descendants, and for distorting the issue beyond any credible position. Ali, a refugee who is still alive, has a well-founded grievance against the regimes that initiated the war. It is conceivable that he might lodge a claim for some form of restitution, assuming that compelling evidence can be pulled together. But it is fantastical to think that his grandchildren, Arwa and her brother, Samy (let alone Samy's children), are victims of an identical wrong that unfolded long before they emerged from the womb.

Can we solve the refugee problem by snaring successive generations into the ranks of U.N.-certified refugees, and instilling in them an irrational hope of reversing the outcome? No. But doing so can mass-manufacture victims and hostility. It's telling, therefore, that leaders of the Palestinian movement demand—as an article of faith—a wholesale, nonselective "right of return."

3. "Occupation"

The Israeli "occupation" ranks high on the catalogue of Palestinian grievances. The term is sometimes used as a catch-all epithet for practically all Israeli wrongs, past and ongoing, as well as claims over land. By its nature, we hear, the occupation victimizes and oppresses. It frustrates Palestinian aspirations. It kindles resentment. It magnifies desperation. Look to the occupation, in other words, if you want to explain Palestinian violence. So let's begin by asking: What is the occupation? What is its nature? What are its effects?

How Egypt's Climactic Battle Led to the Occupation

The natural place to start is with the occupation's origin and scope. Recall that the 1948 war—promised as a "war of extermination"—was intended to abort the newly formed state of Israel. In fact, the Arab League's secretary general had vowed at the time that "Should the Jews defeat us in the first battle, we will defeat them in the second or the third battle...or the final one."[64]

Stepping forward to launch the next battle was Gamal Abdel Nasser, the military dictator of Egypt, who took up the challenge of "liquidating" Israel. Nasser cast himself as a quasi-secular prophet and promised to redeem the collective honor of the "Arab nation." Nasser's vision called for "Arab unity." This entailed Arab political dominion throughout the Middle East.[65] By its sheer existence, Israel stood in the way of that goal.

Nasser inveighed against Israel. "Arab unity," Nasser claimed, "means the liquidation of Israel." Listen to the vitriol that emanated from Cairo Radio:

> The Arab people will pronounce the death sentence against criminal Israel, namely disappearance.
> Israel is the cancer, the malignant wound, in the body of Arabism, for which there is no cure but eradication.[66]

What Nasser portrayed as a climactic battle unfolded in June 1967. On the eve of war, Egypt had mobilized its forces and concentrated troops in the Sinai Peninsula, on Israel's southern border. Egypt also closed the Straits of Tiran, an important shipping route in the Red Sea, to Israeli vessels. In a speech Nasser said:

> Recently we felt we are strong enough, that if we were to enter a battle with Israel, with God's help, we would triumph. On this basis, we decided to take steps.... We will operate as one army fighting a single battle for the sake of a common objective—the objective of the Arab nation.... The battle will be a general one and our basic objective will be to destroy Israel.[67]

Even as Egypt and its Arab allies, notably Syria and Jordan, were preparing for attack, however, the Israel Defense Forces launched a daring preemptive response that crippled the Egyptian air force before it was airborne. The Arab militaries were driven back, utterly humiliated, again. The major fighting lasted merely six days.

The pivotal result of the Six Day War was that Israel took control of several territories beyond its pre-war borders, territories critical to its security. These included:

- the Golan Heights, in the northeast, formerly under Syrian control;
- the eastern portion of the city of Jerusalem, and the West Bank area, both formerly part of Jordan;

- the Gaza Strip, in the south along the Mediterranean coast, formerly under Egyptian control;
- the Sinai Peninsula, in the south, formerly part of Egypt.

Following the war, Israel complied with the customary norm of putting the conquered territory under military administration, which we'll examine in a moment (see Map 2). But we should go down that list of territories one more time to note where things stand today, a half-century later.

Israel ceded the Sinai Peninsula to Egypt in stages, under a 1979 peace deal known as the Camp David Accords. By 1982, Israel had withdrawn from the Sinai, and the area was back under Cairo's sovereignty. Israel formally annexed the eastern part of the city of Jerusalem. In 1981 Israel annexed the parts of the Golan Heights under its control (eight years earlier, during another major war, Syrian forces had used the area to mount their attack).[68] And the West Bank remained under Israeli occupation through the early 1990s, until the onset of the so-called Oslo Peace Process. That diplomatic agreement led to an interim, quasi-state, the Palestinian Authority, which assumed progressively more control over the West Bank areas (because of ongoing Palestinian attacks, however, Israel has had to re-assert more control over parts of the West Bank). The Palestinian Authority also assumed responsibility for portions of the Gaza Strip until 2005, when Israel withdrew every last one of its citizens and soldiers, handing it over entirely to the PA. Hamas has ruled that coastal enclave since 2007, while subject to an on-again, off-again Israeli blockade, due to the three Hamas-Israel wars (see Map 3).

What's left? The scope of the "occupation" itself is disputed. The Palestinian movement has a staggeringly expansive view, evident in its public statements, maps, flags, and school textbooks.

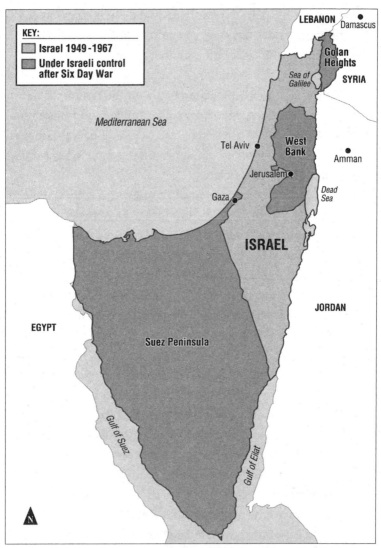

Map 2. Israel Following the 1967 War. (This map is illustrative of borders and armistice lines, but is not meant to be authoritative.)

Map 3. Contemporary Israel. (This map is illustrative of borders and armistice lines, but is not meant to be authoritative.)

Essentially it claims not just the territories that fell under Israeli control post-1967, but every last inch of Israel to be "Palestinian" land that must be "liberated." This definition of the "occupation" is revealing of the movement's goals, a point we'll explore in the next chapter. But beyond that tendentious, maximalist definition, today it is reasonable to count Israel as "occupying" the Golan Heights, which is a patch of ground along the Syrian border;[69] and the parts of the West Bank territories outside of the PA's remaining purview.

Nature of the Occupation

What was the "occupation" like in the most populous territories, the West Bank and Gaza Strip? Let's evaluate the quarter-century period between 1967 and the early 1990s, from the end of the war until Israel began ceding land to the Palestinian Authority. This was the most geographically comprehensive and longest period of uninterrupted Israeli control of those lands.[70]

The abstract thought of "occupation" may activate sinister connotations in people's minds, and the Palestinian narrative pushes a malignant view of Israel's occupation. The facts tell a different story. During the two-plus decades when they lived under Israeli authority, the Muslim and Christian residents of the occupied territories actually saw their standard of living rise and their economic opportunities multiply.

But before we turn to that, it's necessary to note that Israeli policy toward the occupied territories had, and still has, numerous problems. Israel's control over the territories was viewed as a temporary situation, but it has continued, in varying ways and with an evolving scope, for five decades. It has been riddled with unclear, often conflicting, aims. This has led, for example, to convoluted legal and administrative arrangements.[71] Some of the problems reflect the tendency of Israeli officials to temporize. But, no less important, the problems besetting Israel's policy also reflect the fact that while Israel won the 1967 war, it then found itself in control of populated territories formerly under the power of hostile regimes. Recall that it was following a war of self-defense that Israel assumed control of the Gaza Strip (previously ruled by Egypt, the initiator of the 1967 war), and the West Bank (previously ruled by Jordan, an ally of Egypt). That's a difficult situation. And it would be facile to suppose that the ideal way of handling such a situation is easily defined or implemented.

One major issue Israel faced was the Palestinian attacks that emanated from the territories. Although the war had ended decisively, the occupied territories were honeycombed with potential, and real, threats. Gamal Abdel Nasser, the dictator of Egypt, had spent several years backing Palestinian guerrillas targeting Israel, and prior to the 1967 war, his regime formally aided them in establishing their operations in the Gaza Strip. These forces operated in coordination with the Egyptian authorities, which imposed a special tax on the inhabitants of Gaza to fund the guerillas.[72] And particularly in the West Bank, the institutions of city and local government had answered to the Jordanian monarchy, which had repeatedly waged war on Israel. Palestinian guerrillas, moreover, worked to build cells within the West Bank area. For Israel, then, one proper goal would have been to render the Gaza Strip and West Bank territories non-threatening by (at minimum) rooting out institutionalized authoritarianism and hostile Palestinian groups, and to encourage the inhabitants to adopt political and cultural values that enable human flourishing. But what Israel actually did fell short of that goal, and in fact, as we'll see, it left the door open to the Palestinian movement to proselytize for its cause and to launch violent attacks.

To understand the nature of Israel's occupation and evaluate its consequences, we need a benchmark for comparison. For a paradigm case, take a look at the American-led military occupation of Japan after World War II.[73] This is a good benchmark, for two reasons. First, the United States (like Israel) is a free nation that fought in a war of self-defense. Having prevailed, the United States (like Israel) faced the prospect of assuming control over a foreign populace. We can put aside the many historical examples of occupations following wars initiated by dictatorial regimes, with the undisguised goal of imperialist domination and looting (see: Nazi Germany in France, Poland, Austria, etc.; the 1990 Iraqi invasion of Kuwait). Because such cases differ fundamentally from America's occupation of Japan, and Israel's in the West Bank and Gaza Strip, they're unhelpful as comparisons. The second reason to look at the post-war occupation of Japan is that it was culture-wide and profound. Aiming to pacify the defeated nation, the occupation's impact was designed to be (and has been) permanent.

The case of Japan, then, offers a benchmark for what it looks like when a free nation, the United States, assumes control of a non-Western culture and refashions that society into one that is non-threatening. So let's compare America's occupation of Japan with Israel's in the West Bank and Gaza.

Washington's "Initial Post-Surrender Policy for Japan" articulated broad goals. The "ultimate objectives" were to "insure that Japan will not again become a menace to the United States or to the peace and security of the world," and to bring about a "peaceful and responsible government" in Tokyo that "will respect the rights of other states and will support the objectives" of the United States.[74] Japan had to be pacified. For good. In the directive given to Gen. Douglas MacArthur, who was in charge of the military occupation, he was instructed (among other things) to make clear:

...to all levels of the Japanese population the fact of their defeat. They must be made to realize that their suffering and defeat have been brought upon them by the lawless and irresponsible aggression of Japan, and that only when militarism has been eliminated from Japanese life and institutions will Japan be admitted to the family of nations.[75]

For the sake of lasting peace, Japan had to be not only comprehensively demilitarized, but also purged of the collectivist-militarist ideology that led it to wage war. People who had been "active exponents of militant nationalism and aggression," or "who have been influential members of any Japanese ultra-nationalistic, terroristic or secret patriotic society, its agencies or affiliates" were to be barred from holding public office or other positions of influence. School curriculums had to be reformed to excise traces of the former regime's militant ideas.[76] The United States had set as a goal to encourage Japan to embrace a "desire for individual liberties and respect for fundamental human rights, particularly the freedoms of religion, assembly, speech and the press."[77] And, indeed, these ideals were incorporated into Japan's post-war Constitution.

The occupation not only demolished Japan's war machine, but also thoroughly remade the society's institutions and culture. The Japanese had to re-think their former beliefs, the ideas that had brought them economic ruin and defeat. Deliberately, the occupation of Japan had an enduring psychological impact.[78]

Now consider Israel's post-1967 occupation in the West Bank and Gaza.

Whereas the Americans openly declared their aim to defang Japan and articulated a clear vision of what long-range success looked like, the Israeli government approached its occupation without a clear conception of its long-range aim.

Whereas the American forces sent a thundering message by their conspicuous presence, Israel started by adopting the principle of "non-presence." They wanted to be as unobtrusive and inconspicuous as they could. This meant removing signs of Israeli rule such as the flag, military patrols, and military headquarters (which were to be located away from main streets).[79] Israel's minister of defense explained, "we have to make it a goal of our military administration that a local Arab can live a normal life as long as he has not violated the law, without needing to see or interact with any Israeli representative of our military occupation administration."[80]

Whereas the Americans removed from power leaders of the former Japanese regime, Israel's military command—including representatives from the ministries of health, justice, agriculture and education—discreetly worked hand in hand with the pre-war Arab civil service.[81] The aim was that "the population should lead its own life undisturbed" by Israeli involvement, except for problems (such as sanitation, the economy) that had a direct bearing on Israel.[82] Moreover, for years the political ties between the West Bank and the former ruling power, Jordan, remained strong. Indeed, after the war, Israeli authorities asked certain members of prominent families in the West Bank to open channels for talks the Jordanian regime.[83]

Whereas American policy had required the flushing out of Japan's militant ideology and the wholesale re-molding of cultural values, the Israeli policy of non-presence aimed to leave the political culture of Palestinians unchanged—notably including their hostility to Israel. So long as the local leaders refrained from inciting violence against Israel (an obviously illegal act), they were left to espouse whatever ideology they wished. They could cross the border to meet with the Jordanian regime, and many community leaders (often called "notables") "continued to receive their salaries in dinars from the Hashemite government [of Jordan], even as others shared at least indirectly in the political life of Jordan."[84] Even though Egypt and Syria remained openly hostile toward Israel, some Muslim and Christian leaders living in the occupied areas "maintained contact with Nasser, with the Ba'ath regime in Syria, and with a variety of Arab parties, institutions and organizations in neighboring countries."[85]

Israel disallowed residents of the territories to open new TV or radio stations, but they had access to the Arab-language newspapers published in east Jerusalem and elsewhere in the region. The Arab-language press within the territories, like Israeli media, was subject to the military censor.[86] The publication of editorials supporting the Palestinian movement's leading organization, the Palestinian Liberation Organization (PLO), was permitted in local newspapers, and "anti-Israel activities by PLO supporters were tolerated so long as they did not involve overt incitements to violence."[87] Even more astonishing, for a time Israel allowed PLO-controlled funds to stream in to the occupied territories. The Minister of Defense, Ezer Weizmann, argued that: "It does not matter that they get money from the PLO, as long as they don't build arms factories with it."[88]

Israel's initial policy was vastly different from America's (largely) successful approach in post-war Japan. It was clear that some elements of the Palestinian population remained hostile, and the policy of "non-presence" was hard to sustain amid sporadic, then more frequent, terrorist attacks.[89] And yet, as Shlomo Gazit, who served in senior leadership roles in Israel's occupation, writes: Israeli policy had aimed to "nurture the feeling (and perhaps the illusion) among the Palestinian residents that the Arab military defeat in the [1967] war and the presence of Israeli forces on the ground hardly changed anything at all in the[ir] daily life."[90]

One major exception was a policy of integrating the economy of Israel with the territories, which had tremendously positive results. When the occupation began, Israel lifted the wartime road barriers and travel restrictions (it came to be known as the "open-bridges" policy).[91] This meant that tourists from neighboring regimes (which were essentially still at war with Israel) could visit friends and family in the occupied areas. Many also visited vacation spots, particularly coastal cities, including Tel Aviv and Jaffa.[92]

The freedom of movement between Israel and the newly occupied areas led to considerable economic integration. When the Egyptian military ruled the Gaza Strip, observes Gazit, many residents had no "legal status or internationally valid identity papers, and therefore could not travel to or enter any other place."[93] That isolation changed under Israeli rule, and it opened up the possibility of working in Israel. Laborers were able to find work in construction, factories, shops, hotels, commuting from their villages to Israeli towns and cities. Farmers were able to sell their produce in Israeli markets.[94]

Egypt's rule in Gaza and Jordan's in the West Bank had been marked by economic stagnation. Under Israel's post-1967 administration, that changed dramatically.

> The opportunity to work in Israel gave the population of the territories the means to fund a considerable improvement in their standard of living, whose signs were everywhere. The number of telephone subscribers multiplied sixfold, the number of tractors ninefold, and the number of private cars tenfold. Compared to the pre-1967 era, there was a steep rise in the purchase of electrical appliances, in the standard of health, and even in the popularity of leisure activities; many Gazans, for example, frequented the nightclubs of Ashkelon [a city on Israel's Mediterranean coast].[95]

Efraim Karsh reports that during the 1970s, the West Bank and Gaza:

> ...constituted the fourth fastest-growing economy in the world—ahead of such "wonders" as Singapore, Hong Kong, and Korea, and substantially ahead of Israel itself. Although GNP per capita grew somewhat more slowly, the rate was still high by international standards, with per-capita GNP expanding tenfold between 1968 and 1991 from $165 to $1,715 (compared with Jordan's $1,050, Egypt's $600, Turkey's $1,630, and Tunisia's $1,440). By 1999, Palestinian per-capita income was nearly double Syria's, more than four times Yemen's, and 10 percent higher than Jordan's (one of the better-off Arab states). Only the oil-rich Gulf states and Lebanon were more affluent. [96]

Compared with their circumstances prior to 1967, under Egyptian and Jordanian rule, and even compared to life elsewhere in the Middle East, the people in the occupied areas saw their standard of living climb. They had more opportunities for work, greater freedom, and the real prospect of a better life.

Consequences of the Occupation

Israel's occupation, however, failed to uproot hostile Palestinian forces, to counter the legacy of Egyptian and Jordanian authoritarianism, and to foster in the local population the embrace of better ideas and values. So much so that the Palestinian cause exploited the openness of the occupation to stoke anti-Israel sentiment and launch deadly terrorist attacks. The Palestinian Liberation Organization, which spearheaded the cause, tried to foster "revolutionary" zeal among the people of the territories. The PLO's initial attempts to ignite a bottom-up "people's war" flopped.[97] But the PLO persisted, and so did the Islamists, whose influence grew. The Israeli policy of allowing foreign money into the occupied territories proved unwise (and it was suspended). The activists of the Palestinian movement used that money to arm themselves. Then they deployed those weapons. They inflicted devastating harm and suffering within Israeli towns and cities.

Facing the persistent threat of Palestinian terrorism, the Israeli government tightened its security controls. In the past, many of the Muslim and Christian workers living in occupied areas (and later under the Palestinian Authority) had been able to commute to jobs in Israeli cities, but that became more difficult. Travel and trade likewise were stymied. The lowest point, during this span of Israel's occupation, was probably the "intifada" (in Arabic, "shaking off"), or uprising.

The intifada began in 1987 with Palestinians in the territories rioting, holding strikes, and mounting violent attacks. The upheaval, which became increasingly coordinated, persisted through the early 1990s. The Israeli government was ill-equipped to respond to the intifada. Israeli forces were trained to deal with conventional war, cross-border attacks, and terrorist groups, not teenagers roaming the streets throwing rocks and hurling Molotov cocktails. At the outset, the Israeli "army began to debate the use of punitive measures as a way of quelling the unrest without causing physical injury," an approach that proved unsustainable. Then Israeli's military "found itself resorting to tactics that ranged from cutting off phones and electricity to placing extended curfews on villages, towns, and whole cities." During the intifada, perhaps the most controversial punishment meted out was the sealing or demolishing of houses (emptied of their occupants) belonging to suspects involved in the violence; it's doubtful if these measures were effective.[98]

While an exploration of the intifada's origin, nature, and causes is outside the scope of this book, it's centrally relevant that the men, women, and particularly children who went into the streets to riot had been marinating, for at least two generations, in the ideology of the Palestinian movement (we'll discuss that movement in detail in the next chapter). Moreover, rival factions of the Palestinian movement (especially the Islamists) championed the intifada and jockeyed to set its direction.[99]

It was near the end of the intifada that the nature and scope of Israel's occupation changed considerably. In 1993, Israel and the Palestinian Liberation Organization entered into the so-called Oslo peace process, leading in the following year to the creation of the Palestinian Authority. Israel ceded to the PA control over areas of the West Bank and the Gaza Strip. We'll explore the subsequent quarter-century, from 1993 to the present, in the next chapter, but it's important to note briefly what happened next, and Israel's response to it.

The crucial point is that, following the creation of the Palestinian Authority and its control over some of the territories, Palestinian violence continued and even worsened. In reaction to flare-ups, Israel further tightened its security measures. For Palestinians, going through Israeli security checkpoints became a daily frustration. They chafed at being stopped, searched, delayed. These interactions fueled mutual distrust and resentment.

By the early 2000s, Israel faced a growing menace of Palestinian suicide bombers. To protect its citizens from such attacks, Israel was compelled to erect a security barrier (see chapter two). Although largely effective, the barrier became hugely controversial, both within Israeli society and internationally. Pointing to the barrier, the leaders of the Palestinian movement and their Western surrogates insist that here, in the form of concrete and chain-link fencing, is the symbol of the injustice of Israel's occupation.

But for anyone who seeks freedom and a better life, living under Israeli rule was objectively superior to what came before, under Egyptian or Jordanian authority—and superior to whatever degree of Palestinian self-rule was permitted to take hold later (as we'll see in the next chapter). Who bears the responsibility for the economic hardships, political constraints, and tightened security—the lineups at checkpoints, the security barrier, the curfews, the travel permits—under the occupation and since its partial dissolution? Fundamentally, the Palestinian movement and its state sponsors, who have backed guerrilla forces, and who have encouraged, fomented, and funded terrorist attacks. They, not Israel, are the ones who have made life worse for every individual in the occupied territories who truly seeks peace and a better life for himself and his loved ones.

The "Settlements"

Inseparable from the occupation grievance is the issue of Israeli "settlements." If you've ever heard about "settlements" at all, odds are that you heard them being vilified—by Palestinian leaders; by United Nations agencies; by European governments; by the White House[100]—as yet another way Israel subverts Palestinian hopes for a homeland. The controversy over "settlements" is bewilderingly complex, because it cuts across Israeli law, domestic policy, and international diplomacy.[101] Fully untangling it would require a whole other book; instead, our aim is to understand the essentials of the issue and its moral significance. What matters here is how the "settlements" impact the lives and freedom of particular individuals.

What, then, are the "settlements"? Why are they regarded as inimical to Palestinians? How should we evaluate them?

"Settlements," basically, are existing and new neighborhoods under Israeli jurisdiction, but located on contested land. Nowadays, that means principally in the West Bank and around the city of Jerusalem. (There are some in the Golan Heights; and there used to be some in the Gaza Strip, until Israel withdrew in 2005, leaving behind every last one.) From the way that the term "settlements" is invoked, you might expect it to refer to some uniform phenomenon. Not so. Some are urban neighborhoods. Some are villages. Some are tiny outposts. A few are no more than a handful of shacks on a hillside. And whereas some are not only reasonable, legal, and moral, others are immoral, illegal, and subversive of the rule of law. So it's crucial to keep these distinctions in mind when thinking about the "settlements."

The suburban "settlements" began after the 1967 war. The Israeli government worked to fortify its security along the armistice lines. That entailed holding the conquered territories and encouraging their development, with homes, schools, businesses, factories, and military installations. A significant impetus was national security, along areas of vulnerability.[102] Another salient rationale was a political goal of having Israelis populate more of the land. That goal was, and continues to be, controversial in Israel. Probably the most vocal group agitating for that goal are Jewish religionists, some of whom not only lobby for it, but also advance it illegally (more on that in a moment).

Many people, within Israel and in the international community, oppose the settlements on the basis of international law (mainly the Fourth Geneva Convention and the Hague Convention). The doctrines of international law tell us, for example, that a country that gains territory in war cannot properly hold onto it, regardless of whether it was fighting in self-defense or initiated the war. So one kind of objection is that Israeli settlements flout provisions of international law.

But this point is far from settled. One argument is that the Fourth Geneva Convention is inapplicable. Some hold that the doctrine might apply if, prior to 1967, the Gaza Strip and the West Bank were internationally recognized as (respectively) Egyptian and Jordanian territory.[103] But they were not. Egypt and Jordan had taken over those territories in 1948 following a military invasion; in other words, they had seized those lands as a result of initiating a war. Since then, neither Egypt nor Jordan had attained wide international recognition for their possession of those tracts of land.[104] Another argument is that even if the Geneva Convention does apply to the territories, the settlements do not constitute a breach of its provisions. And there are still other arguments.[105]

The legal scholars Abraham Bell and Eugene Kontorovich have argued that a *different* international-law doctrine could be invoked (it is known as *uti possidetis juris*). If it were applied, they write, it would entail recognizing Israel's "territorial sovereignty over all the disputed areas of Jerusalem, the West Bank, and Gaza, except to the degree that Israel has voluntarily yielded sovereignty since its independence."[106]

If you delve into that debate, whichever view you find compelling, it's necessary to appreciate the limitation of arguments predicated on international law. The limitation stems from the fact that "international law" is fundamentally unlike English law, or the U.S. Constitution, or Israel's Basic Laws, or the laws of France. Instead, international "law" is based on the consent of sovereign nations that sign on to it. International "law" is at most customary.

Practically, it's an opt-in arrangement, with some countries choosing to abide by some international norms, some of the time. And, unlike, say, American law—which the U.S. courts and police enforce—there's no equivalent world agency that enforces international law. To call it "law" is an overstatement.

Keep in mind, moreover, that even actual laws can be morally right (e.g. laws prohibiting theft) or morally wrong (e.g., government censorship of the media). Notice also that certain actions can be legal but morally wrong (e.g., Jim Crow restrictions), while other actions can be morally right but illegal (e.g., drinking alcohol during Prohibition). From these observations, there is a fundamental lesson to draw. The lesson is that even laws—and certainly conventional "international laws"—must be subject to moral judgment.

Israel fought to defend its citizens from enemy forces that initiated war—more than once. Given the geographical path that invading forces took in the past, the land Israel acquired is vital to its ongoing territorial security. So it is reasonable to put that land to use through cultivation and development. And on those grounds, Israel is well within its moral right to permit and encourage the productive use of those lands in the form of building homes, schools, and businesses.

But there are at least three factors that greatly complicate this picture: 1) Israeli land-use policy; 2) the government's taking of private lands; and 3) the campaign of certain religionists to establish unauthorized settlements.

For many years, Israeli law enabled the state to take over private property in land under its control (that's similar to the U.S. government's power of "eminent domain" to take property for "public use"). In 1950, in the aftermath of Israel's war of independence, the government passed the Absentee Property Law which transferred to a government custodian abandoned real estate (fields, orchards, houses) that had belonged to Muslims, Christians, and others defined as "Arabs." Land records were incomplete, which made it difficult for returning owners to reclaim their property. Applying laws akin to eminent domain, the Israeli government continued to take lands belonging to Arabs and transfer them to the administration of quasi-governmental organizations, the Jewish National

Fund and The Jewish Agency. The government's taking of property in these ways should be subject to legal scrutiny. In cases of unjust takings, the owners should be able to seek damages if not also the restoration of their property.

A second compounding factor is the fact that so much land fell under the administration of a government agency and allied non-profit organizations, such as The Jewish Agency and the Jewish National Fund. This presents a host of difficulties. For example, between them, the government and these quasi-private, quasi-state organizations exerted control over most of the land in Israel, and these organizations followed a policy of allocating and selling land exclusively to "Jewish" people. This unjust practice was challenged in Israel's Supreme Court. An Arab couple with two children wanted to live in the settlement of Katzir, but their request was denied because they were Arabs. In a landmark ruling in 2000, the Supreme Court invoked the principle of equality under the rule of law, and it held that:

> ...the State may not discriminate directly on the basis of religion or nationality in allocating state land. From this it follows that the State is also not permitted to discriminate indirectly on the basis of religion or nationality in the allocation of land. Consequently, the State cannot enable such discrimination by transferring land to the Jewish Agency.[107]

Adalah, an Israeli nongovernmental organization, estimates that as much as ninety-three percent of land in the country remains under the control of the state and a non-profit organization, the Jewish National Fund. Adalah has argued that JNF-owned land was being allocated through bids open only to Jews, and it mounted a legal challenge to this unjust practice. In 2005 Israel's attorney general decided to disallow such discrimination in the marketing and allocation of JNF-owned land.[108]

The third compounding factor is the ongoing campaign of some Jewish religionists to proliferate settlements in disregard of property rights and the rule of law. When the occupation began, recall, Israel had pursued a policy of non-presence, hoping to administer the territories unobtrusively. But some religionists flouted that policy: they moved in to create unapproved—therefore illegal—settlements. Often they squatted on land belonging to Palestinians, until the Israeli army showed up to evict them.[109] They also lobbied the government to use its power to expropriate private land belonging to Palestinians, for the purpose of building new Israeli neighborhoods. Even though many Israelis repudiate that agenda, the religionist factions have found politicians who sympathize with, sometimes avidly endorse, their goal.

This policy of expropriating Palestinian landowners is immoral, because it's a clear violation of property rights. And it (rightly) met with considerable opposition. During the 1970s, Israeli courts heard several cases brought forward by Palestinians whose land was taken to create settlements. The turning point came in 1979. In the Elon Moreh case, the Israel Supreme Court decided in favor of the petitioners, the Palestinian landowners. From then on, the government was effectively prohibited from taking private land for use in settlements. The government decided, writes Shlomo Gazit, "that future settlements would be built only on state and public lands," and it encouraged private buyers to purchase land surrounding an existing or planned settlement.[110]

Nevertheless, certain Jewish religionist factions regularly break the law in seeking to create illegal—and immoral—settlements. Typically such unauthorized outposts pop up and then grow incrementally: a handful of zealots drag a mobile home to some patch of land, often land belonging to a nearby Palestinian family. Then, they bring another mobile home, and a few more people to establish a presence, sometimes putting up some shacks. Once situated, they demand police protection, though in reality, many of them have proven to be the real menace. Some of these messianic squatters beat up their Muslim or Christian neighbors, seeking to drive them off the land and out of business by vandalizing olive trees and burning crops.[111] They exhibit contempt for the rule of law.

Of course, this phenomenon has no place in a free society. No proper government can allow one citizen to violate the rights of any other citizen. Like all criminal acts, the deeds of these religionists must be brought before the courts and punishment meted out to the guilty. The landowners are entitled to the state's protection of their lives and property. They deserve compensation for any property damage and any land stolen from them. (A worrying sign: a new law is making its way through the Israeli parliament that would recognize certain unauthorized outposts and in effect reverse the prohibition on the taking of private land.[112])

The Israeli government, it should be noted, has often worked to dismantle such outposts, forcibly removing squatters and demolishing their makeshift homes.[113] But part of what keeps the phenomenon going is that activists collude with sympathetic officials in regional councils and within various ministries. The scale of the problem—going by the number of illegal outposts—may be small, but it cannot be permitted to continue.[114]

Let's sum up our discussion of the intertwined grievances about the occupation and settlements. First, when we consider the years from 1967 through the early 1990s (when Israel began ceding some of the territory to the Palestinian Authority), we see that residents of the occupied territories in general saw their standard of living greatly improve. Second, Israeli errors—in failing to make the territories non-threatening—and Israeli moral breaches—in its land-use policy and the taking of private property—are real, and they're important for understanding the Israeli-Palestinian conflict. Third, we've seen cases wherein some Palestinians have current, legitimate grievances about Israeli government policy and practices.

Without excusing any of these wrongs or injustices, we've also seen that it is only under Israel's legal and political system—notably its Supreme Court—that Palestinians and advocacy groups working on their behalf have the chance of eventually getting justice through the law. If they lived in Saudi Arabia, Egypt, Iran, or elsewhere in the Middle East, and some comparable wrong were done to them, they would have no reason to expect justice in the courts, and worse, by speaking up against their government's policies, they risk having the government inflict further injustices against them.

When looking at Israeli errors and moral failings here, one crucial point comes through. Even the most serious of the grievances pertaining to the occupation, settlements, and land-use cannot explain the view advocated by leaders of the Palestinian movement, its patrons, state-sponsors, and supporters: that the Israeli government *per se* is illegitimate, and that the state of Israel must be scrubbed from the map. The disparity between the wrongs and the putative remedy is so vast, so incommensurate, that it points to an ulterior, preexisting motivation. And it is particularly revealing that the fundamental hostility toward Israel long predated the occupation, and it actually became more ferocious when Israel began ceding control of some of the occupied territories (as we'll see in the next chapter).

4. Minority Rights: "Second-Class Citizens"?

Finally, let's turn to the grievance about Israel's denial of Palestinian rights. This broad complaint bundles together at least two distinct things: one, Israel is accused of blocking the realization of

Palestinian statehood (which we'll consider in the next chapter); and two (our subject here), the Israeli government is charged with mistreating about twenty percent of its citizens who are lumped together under the cloudy term "Arabs" (or, more confusingly, "Israel's Palestinians"). Owing both to government practices and social factors, members of this minority are said to be "second class" citizens.[115] To unpack this issue, let's begin by asking: who are Israel's "Arab" citizens?[116]

Who are Israel's Arab Citizens?

The broad term "Arab" attempts to designate a particular identity. There are various communities of people who view themselves as Arabs, but the term "Arab" is impossible to define, because it blends together culture, language, shared experiences, ancestry, or race, often religion, sometimes ideology. These features overlap in important ways, but with so many variances that there is no essential.

Is it, for example, supposed to refer to religion? Well, not quite, because while most Arabs are Sunni Muslims, there are also many Shiite Muslims who are Arabs. Some Arabs are Roman Catholics, Greek Orthodox Christians, Greek Catholics, Maronites, and Coptic Christians. And—strange as it may sound—some Arabs are Jewish,[117] like my grandparents, who were born and raised in Iraq.[118] Among Arabs, there are still many more differences in dialect, cultural practices, political outlook.[119]

So, it's unresolvable who should be counted as an "Arab." Thus, when we try to use this concept, it impedes our thinking. For an illustration of that, consider two individuals, both self-identified "Arab" citizens of Israel, whose families, coincidentally, were originally from the town of Nazareth. One is a journalist, the other a politician. Note the contrasts between them, and consider what it means in your own mind to group them both under the concept "Arab."

Azmi Bishara, a longtime member of the Israeli parliament (the Knesset), served as head of the Balad party. Born to a Christian family, Bishara was strongly influenced by Marxism. He earned a Ph.D. in East Germany, and then taught at a university in Israel. Throughout his career in parliament, he campaigned on behalf of Israel's Arab citizens. But his actions and statements also reveal that he shared common ground with Israel's enemies, having met with some of them in Syria (thereby flouting Israeli law). "Return Palestine to us," he scolded Israelis "take your democracy with you." In 2006 Israel fought a war against the jihadists of Hezbollah in Lebanon (and their ally Hamas): after the war, Bishara went to a Hezbollah-controlled area of Beirut and exhorted the anti-Israel forces to "keep the pressure on Israel."[120] Of course that kind of travel and engagement is prohibited. Moreover, Bishara allegedly helped Hezbollah during the war, accepting money from the group and offering advice on optimal targets for their long-range rocket attacks on Israeli population centers.[121]

Now consider Lucy Aharish, a well-known news anchor on Israeli television. Born to a Muslim family, she recalls fasting during Ramadan but also, like many Israeli kids, getting dressed up in costume during the Jewish holiday of Purim. Aharish attended Hebrew University in Jerusalem and then journalism school. Some excoriate her for assimilating into Israeli society— for selling out her Muslim, "Arab" identity—while some Jewish religionists have questioned her loyalty to the state. When in 2015 she was picked to light a torch at a ceremony marking Israel's Independence Day celebration, some critics felt it was an undeserved honor. Aharish told a reporter that she was proud to be an Arab and an Israeli citizen.

"People tell me you shouldn't be here, it's not your place, go live in Gaza, you have 22 other [Arab] states. I say no, no, no. This is my country, I am a citizen. You have to give. me. my. rights. as. a. minority!" she says, banging the table again.

She is also highly critical of Israel's Arab lawmakers, and skeptical about whether the election alliance of Israel's four Arab-dominated parties will help the Arab minority. "It's impossible to put all the Arabs under one umbrella, it's like you're saying all Arabs think the same, and they don't," she says.[122]

During a wave of Palestinian knife attacks and car-rammings that began in 2015, Aharish appeared on a TV news program and unleashed an articulate, impassioned denunciation of Palestinian leaders. Far from trying to quell the murderous knife attacks, she argued, "you are inciting thousands of young people to go into the streets. You are destroying their future with your own hands." Neither religion nor frustration, she insisted, can justify stabbing innocent people.[123]

Lucy Aharish and Azmi Bishara are both Israeli citizens—but whereas Aharish relies on her Israeli passport when traveling, Bishara proudly traveled to aid and abet Israel's would-be destroyers. What sets them apart fundamentally are their sharply contrasting political-ideological outlooks, which are the result of their choices (and thus changeable). While there are contexts in which we can say both Bishara and Aharish are Arabs, we have to be wary of that fuzzy category, because it can our warp our thinking. It can suggest to us that these two people have something essential or fundamental in common, when they don't.

The danger here is to adopt a collectivized perspective that assumes "Arabs" somehow "all think the same," and thus to fail to evaluate them as individuals. That means, in effect, condemning Lucy Aharish for Azmi Bishara's conduct, or else putting him on moral par with the fiercely independent, courageous Aharish. Either would be irrational and unjust. While you can certainly find "Arab" citizens in Israel aligning themselves with the Palestinian movement (adopting the ideologically freighted Palestinian identity; publishing manifestos; marching in solidarity with the cause, etc.), there are many "Arabs" who reject that movement and simply want to live the best life they can within Israel.

Before turning to look at what life is like for these citizens of Israel, we should keep in mind two takeaways. First, because the category "Arab" nudges us toward a collectivized perspective, it can impede our thinking. Second, we ought to take an individual-first perspective, putting weight on the choices and beliefs of individuals, rather than the group membership they're born into.

What Life Is Like for "Arab" Citizens

Citizens of Israel—Muslims, Christians, Druzes, Jews, atheists, and members of all minority groups—have equal political rights. We've seen that they are free to form political parties; or work for the government; free to serve in the police force; free to run for public office; free to hold seats in the parliament; free to serve in the judiciary; free to publish books, newspapers, and websites; free to operate businesses; free to study and teach in schools and universities; free to file legal cases, all the way up to the Supreme Court; free to worship (or not). They live in the only country in the region that upholds the rule of law and protects individual liberty.

They are all in a position to benefit from Israel's economic progress. Speaking broadly of minority communities, the scholars Ilan Peleg and Dov Waxman report that members of these communities have over the years "gone from being farmers and unskilled laborers to becoming industrial workers, small business owners, and professionals (especially teachers, lawyers, doctors and pharmacists)."[124] Their communities have undergone a "process of modernization," having been:

> ...transformed from an impoverished mostly rural and feudal society dependent on subsistence agriculture to a more modern, industrialized, individualistic, and mobile society. [Their] living standards have substantially improved, as their levels of education, employment, health, housing and income have steadily risen.[125]

Peleg and Waxman note two spectacular illustrations of material progress:

> One clear indication of the gains that have been achieved is the increase in life expectancy for Arabs—life expectancy for Arab women increased from an average of 71.9 years in the period 1970–1974 to 77.4 years in the period 1994–1998; and for Arab men from an average of 68.5 years in the period 1970–1974 to 74.2 years in the period 1994–1998.[126]

Turning to another indicator, infant mortality, Peleg and Waxman note a dramatic decline, from "24.2 deaths per 1,000 births in 1980 to 8.2 deaths per 1,000 in 2003."[127] Relative to their counterparts elsewhere in the Middle East, citizens of Israel—especially Muslim, Christian, secularists, atheists, and members of various minorities—are freer and much better off economically.

Why then do some argue that Israeli "Arabs" are "second-class citizens"?

Peleg and Waxman summarize the problem: Israel's "Arabs" "suffer from numerous inequities, tacit discrimination, government neglect, and social prejudice."[128] This bundle of problems, moreover, is linked to "extreme socio-economic inequality between Jews and Arabs," which Peleg and Waxman regard as "one of the biggest, if not the biggest, problems that affect majority-minority relations in Israel."[129] These socio-economic gaps, however, "cannot be attributed to a single cause"; indeed, they are "the result of multiple factors," and so the Israeli government "cannot be totally blamed" for all these problems.[130]

To untangle these issues, it's helpful to distinguish between two *kinds* of factors, which can get blurred. One kind of factor pertains to the government's policies and practices. Another stems from the decisions and actions of private individuals, business, and associations. Let's start by looking at government policy and practices.

Government Neglect and Discriminatory Policy

A major government report in 2003 noted that the state's "handling of the Arab sector has been primarily neglectful and discrimina-tory."[131] Advocacy groups echo that claim.[132] Earlier we saw how government policy prevented those deemed Arabs from leasing and buying land. Here are two other significant examples of poli-cies that unfairly favor the majority "Jewish" population: schools and municipal budgets.

At the time of Israel's independence, the founders felt it was an urgent priority to provide universal, compulsory schooling. "From the start," writes the scholar Jacob Landau, "the state authorities campaigned to persuade the Arab population of the importance of education (a matter not always taken for granted in some villages and among the Bedouin). Separate classes were opened for boys and girls with women teachers for the latter, whenever parents insisted on such separation."[133] Over the years, however, these schools fell short of parity with the parallel system of Hebrew-lan-guage schools. The problems—a shortage of classroom space, of computers, of labs, of sports equipment, of guidance counselors—all betokened an ongoing lack of adequate funding.[134] For example, by one reckoning, in the academic year 2000–01 the government spent about three times more per student in "Jewish" schools than in "Arab" schools.[135]

Zoom out from the school system, and the data seemingly point to a similar pattern at the level of cities and towns. I say *seemingly*, because there are inbuilt challenges to accounting for how government funding is spent: do you account for a newly paved road as investment in a "Jewish" or "Arab" neighborhood, when the locality includes citizens of various ancestries and ideological beliefs? There's no clear answer.[136] Nonetheless, let's posit that the government does spend more on areas where the citizens are regarded as "Jewish." The state budget allocates money for developing industrial zones throughout the country, on the premise of stimulating businesses to grow and add jobs. Here again, more of those industrial zones are earmarked for "Jewish" towns than elsewhere.[137]

What to make of these disparities? Such channeling of financial resources to benefit one constituency at the expense of another is unjust. Today this kind of practice is a deplorable commonplace in the world's free societies, notably including the United States, and it reflects their decay. You can see it play out in favor of both economic pressure groups and ideological ones. For example: note the vast subsidies and tax breaks that flow to corn- and ethanol-producers in Iowa—at the expense of all other taxpayers. Or: the blocking of Uber and Lyft from offering ride-sharing services in a particular city to protect the taxi industry. Or, to take an ideological example: consider the efforts of anti-abortion politicians in Texas to impose extraordinarily stringent medical requirements on abortion clinics, with the intention of causing dozens of clinics to shut down.[138] In all such cases, regardless of which side you favor or oppose, the use of government power to advance or block particular groups or agendas is a fundamental problem, and the conflicts it engenders can only multiply.

In Israel's case, the government tends to privilege the major-ity "Jewish" population, the largest voting constituency (many of whom are secular, non-observant, or atheist). That's unfair. And it happens not only because politicians have more and more power over economic matters, which allows them to dispense favors.

Israel's distinctive conception of itself as a homeland and refuge for the world's persecuted Jews leads to other difficult legal issues. For example, Israel's immigration laws give precedence to "Jews." In contrast with the immigration policy of the United States and the UK, which are notably restrictive, Israel opens its doors in welcome to Jewish immigrants. Under The Law of Return (1950), if you meet the official definition of a "Jew," you can rapidly become a citizen. You'll also be offered Hebrew lessons and help settling down. Other would-be immigrants can obtain residency and citizenship, but it is nowhere near as easy or quick.

To be sure, these are difficult issues that need to be addressed. More broadly, the state's unjust discrimination and neglect should be remedied through the legal process and advocacy campaigns.

Social and Economic Factors

Quite apart from warped government policy and practices, in Israel as in every society, you will find irrational people who in their own lives, relationships, and work cling to prejudices and act on racist beliefs. Many Israeli minorities face prejudice, and they are treated with suspicion in their daily lives and work. Of course, there's no place for such prejudice in any society, and it should be combatted and marginalized by individual citizens.

This brings us to another element of the argument that Israeli "Arabs" are second-class citizens, the claim of socio-economic "inequality." While acknowledging the elevated standard of living of Israel's "Arab" citizens, Peleg and Waxman (along with other critics) underscore the "material disparities between Arabs and Jews." [139] Members of the "Arab" minority "still mostly occupy the lower rungs of the occupational ladder."[140] According to a report by the advocacy group Adalah, "Arab families are greatly over-represented among Israel's poor: over half of Arab families in Israel are classified as poor, compared to an average poverty rate of one-fifth among all families in Israel."[141] Within the workforce, they are "sorely under-represented" in civil service jobs. The "representation of Arab citizens" as employees in government ministries, "falls far short of their proportion of the population."[142]

It's important to acknowledge that these claims about economic inequality point to a complex phenomenon, involving numerous causal factors and data that lend themselves to conflicting interpretations.[143] An in-depth exploration of this phenomenon is well beyond our scope here. There are, however, two important points that help clarify the issue. First, it's true that government policies (such as lackluster state-run schools) can impede an individual's ability to rise economically. A second, under-appreciated point is that a lot rides on an individual's choices and values. Because of that fact, it's deeply problematic to set economic equality as an ideal.

Equality is not, nor can it be, an ideal economically. What any proper government must provide is *political and legal equality*; in other words, the protection of individual freedom under rule of law. It is a fact that individuals are unequal in many respects—strength, size, intelligence, beauty, perseverance, risk-taking, work ethic, frugality, moral character. The principle of political-legal equality has a natural consequence. Left free, some people will produce small amounts of wealth while others will create more.

Such freedom also opens up differences in opportunity, observe Don Watkins and Yaron Brook, and it is "obviously true that some people will find the struggle to succeed harder than others. If you're born to loving, educated, and affluent parents, you will likely find it easier to achieve your aspirations than someone born in less desirable circumstances."[144] There's every reason to expect people's economic circumstances and outcomes to be unequal.[145]

What does it mean to talk about a particular minority group being under- or over-"represented" in a given profession or sector of the economy? The objection itself presupposes a collectivized outlook, treating individuals as if they were interchangeable members of their unchosen (racial, tribal, ethnic) group. We've already seen how the nebulous term "Arab" groups together people who differ in innumerable ways. That fact casts doubt on the notion of reaching collective assessments about that group.

At the same time, notice the depreciation of a truly consequential factor: the *chosen* cultural values and ideas individuals accept and *choose* to live by. It may well be true, by some definition of "Arab," that they are "one of the poorest groups in Israeli society" but so also are Jewish religionists and Ethiopian "Jews" living in Israel.[146] What accounts for this commonality? A significant part of the explanation stems from the cultural values and ideas that these groups choose to live by.

Primacy of An Individual's Choices and Beliefs

Notice that many Muslim ("Arab") families and many Jewish religionists hold certain beliefs about the world that shape their actions, thereby subverting them economically. Because of their religious and cultural ideas, they tend to have many children; statistically, the fact that they have larger families impacts the data on per capita income. Because of their respective religious beliefs, fewer Muslim and Jewish religionist mothers enter the work-force.[147] They are often expected to be child-bearing vessels and kitchen-bound housewives. By taking that path in life, a woman—whether a Muslim ("Arab") or a religionist Jew—severely limits her future career options and ability to contribute to household income.

Education is another pivotal factor. For anyone who's grown up in a middle-class family in North America or any advanced European country, it is easy to take for granted today's world of heli-copter parenting. It's practically a cliché: mom and dad expect their kids to deliver straight-A's, ferrying them to after-school tutoring, enrichment programs, prep courses for getting into university. But not every family chooses to put such emphasis on education, nor invests equally in it, if at all. Though education in Israel is state-funded and compulsory, some students drop out. Some families, particularly in villages, have held the view that modern education is a waste of time.[148] In religionist Jewish households, it is common for daughters (like their mothers) to marry young and stay at home to raise children—rather than pursue higher education and a career. A lack of education and training, especially for women, is a serious handicap that some families inflict upon their own chil-dren. Some religionist Jewish families go a step further by sending their sons to schools that focus on scripture to the exclusion of math, science, and basic skills.[149]

So, no simple tally of over- or under-"representation" by members of some collective can serve as evidence of discrimina-tion, precisely because it disregards the choices and values of the individuals involved. And given the fact that individuals differ in their abilities and choices, there's reason to expect differences in people's economic outcomes—and certainly no reason to expect equal outcomes.

To summarize: when considering the situation facing Israel's "Arab" citizens, we find real challenges. We find government neglect and discrimination, and we find other, private sources of prejudice. The unjust discrimination they face is repugnant, and it should be uprooted. It is a distinctive feature of Israel's political system, however, that citizens are free to campaign, advocate, and work through the courts of law to undo wrongs stemming from government policy and practices. Socially, the uprooting of prejudice and unjust discrimination requires arguing and changing minds and instilling better, more rational views in the culture. Individuals are free to do that in Israel, but elsewhere in the region, they can do so only at the risk of severe peril. The characterization of Israel's "Arab" citizens as "second-class" citizens is an overstatement.

What the Grievances Cannot Explain

Dispossession. Expulsion and Refugees. Occupation. Minority Rights. When you consider these foundational Palestinian grievances as a whole, something just does not add up.

The grievances cannot justify the vociferous condemnations of Israel. None comes remotely close to the actual "gender apartheid," nor the incontestable violations of individual freedoms, nor the daily atrocities that are the norm throughout the Middle East. None of the grievances comes remotely close to warranting the conclusion that Israel *per se* is an illegitimate state.

And once you winnow down to grievances implicating the rights of individuals and actual injustices, one conclusion is unavoidable. For anyone who seeks freedom and justice, it is under Israel's protection of freedom of speech that you can advocate politically and culturally to have your grievances heard and taken seriously. And it is under Israel's political system, its rule-of-law institutions, its independent courts, that you would stand the best chance of having wrongs righted.

Indeed, the more intensely you desire to see actual injustices addressed, the more you would want to preserve, reform, and improve Israel's political system and institutions.

What does it mean to take up arms against Israel? You would take such a momentous step if and only if you were convinced of the necessity to repudiate and break completely with the existing society and government. But the foundational grievances we've looked at are not the kind of wrongs, nor at a degree of severity, that would warrant such a complete rupture with Israeli society and law—particularly considering the institutionalized brutality and oppression elsewhere in the Middle East.

Put another way, these grievances cannot explain (let alone justify) the "armed struggle" carried out in the name of the Palestinian cause. They fail to explain what animates the Palestinian movement.

What does animate it?

CHAPTER 4

THE PALESTINIAN CAUSE

The Palestinian movement claims to speak for the Palestinian people. It fights to right the wrongs against them. It champions their cause, their claims for justice, their political aspirations. What is this ideological-political movement's origin? How did it rise to prominence? What steps has it taken in championing the Palestinians? What has it done to redress injustices? What would the fulfillment of its ideological-political cause look like? In short: What animates it?

In this chapter we'll explore the nature, goals, and actions of the Palestinian movement.

The Movement's Origin

Meet the godfather of the Palestinian movement. Gamal Abdel Nasser, Egypt's dictator, had come to power in the mid 1950s following a military coup. Recall that Nasser championed "Arab nationalism," an ideology calling for the political unity of all Arab peoples. Israel's sheer existence was an obstacle to Nasser's quest for domination (and a convenient scapegoat for all manner of ills). Israel was viewed as an illegitimate presence on Arab land. Egypt and its allies were still smarting from their military defeat in the war of 1948. Remember: the neighboring Arab regimes had instigated the war. Eyeing the spoils of war and expecting a swift victory, the combined forces of five Arab countries invaded the nascent state of Israel. But they were humiliated on the battlefield.

By the early 1960s, one advocate of Arab nationalism explained the situation in these words.

> *The existence of Israel* nullifies the unity of our homeland, the unity of our nation and the unity of our civilization, which embraces the whole of this one region. Moreover, the existence of Israel is a flagrant challenge of our philosophy of life and the ideals for which we live, and a total barrier against the values and aims to which we aspire in the world. [Emphasis added.][1]

For Nasser, war to "liquidate" Israel was a necessity; the question was not if, but *when* to attack. Nasser was adamant that the war should not be initiated until "we have completed building our military force to decisive superiority."[2] This came to mean the combined forces of Egypt and her allies (notably Syria and Jordan).

Something more was needed, however, to position this clash in the minds of Arab publics as a moral cause. Fighting to overcome a despised "outsider" (non-Arab) enemy, Israel, in the name of realizing the glory of "Arab unity" could certainly capture the imagination. But that's fairly abstract; much more compelling is the added claim that in waging such a war, the "Arab nation" would be avenging specific, sympathetic victims of Israel. Nasser's strategic innovation was to entwine the Palestinians with his region-wide goals. By associating his agenda with the redemption of Palestinians, Nasser found a source of moral legitimacy for his militant campaign for conquest and domination.

The slogan encapsulating Nasser's logic, and a rallying cry for Arab nationalism, was: "Arab unity is the path to Palestine."

Thus, at Nasser's instigation, in 1964 the Palestinian Liberation Organization was born. The PLO was an umbrella group intended to corral a host of rival guerilla factions, which had begun launching attacks on Israel. The guerilla factions called themselves "fedeeyn" (in Arabic, "self-sacrificers"). Nasser saw value in their efforts (he believed that militarily they served to "trouble the enemy's rest"[3]) but doubted that their tactics would ever be sufficient. Pulling these gangs into the Palestinian Liberation Organization had two major benefits.

First, Egypt and the other state-sponsors of the PLO thus gained a mercenary force. Each state-sponsor backed its own favored factions within the PLO. From its main backers—Egypt, Syria and Iraq—the PLO received funds, military training, weapons, and radio air time for propaganda. Radio was that era's most powerful communication medium, reaching an audience of millions, from illiterate peasants to the intellectuals and everyone in between. The Egyptian regime's own media outlets lionized the "fedeeyn." Syria served as one base of operations; it was also a logistics hub and arsenal for weapons and military equipment that arrived from such patrons as Algeria, communist China and the Soviet Union.[4] The PLO factions, linked to their state-sponsors in complex webs of shifting loyalties, served as instruments of their patrons.[5] Egypt and Syria explicitly viewed PLO guerrillas as adjuncts to their traditional military troops.

The second, and more significant, benefit was that the PLO's state-sponsors could exert some control over the guerrilla groups. Such control was important, because after the failed 1948 attempt to destroy Israel, the guerrillas wanted to accelerate the march to another war: the new tactic was to use sporadic attacks to push

Israel and the neighboring states into a decisive final battle.[6] Nasser, however, wanted to decide the timing himself.

Among the factions and their state-sponsors, there was also friction over who was more militantly committed to the goal of liquidating Israel. This jockeying over militancy continued long after the PLO's formation (and, as we'll see later, it persists to the present day). Since its inception the PLO was dogged by the criticism that it was too close to its state-sponsors and "inadequately militant or revolutionary."[7] It is telling that one of the guerrilla groups, Fatah (led by Yasser Arafat), rose to prominence because of its ardent commitment to "armed struggle." While other factions talked, Fatah took up arms against Israel. By distinguishing itself through militancy, many saw it as heroic, and Fatah eventually took over leadership of the PLO.[8]

Nasser had promised that Arab "unity" was the path to "liberating" Palestine. Stripped to its essence, here was a campaign by a militant dictator (Nasser), his tyrannical allies in Syria and Iraq, and their mercenary brigades (the PLO factions) to initiate a war of conquest against a free, Western state reviled as a malignancy to the region because of its non-"Arab" identity. To call Nasser's invocation of Palestine a pretext is a monumental understatement. The aim of Nasser's scheme was to destroy Israel, not to seek any semblance of (genuine) justice, let alone make Palestinians better off. Notice the conspicuous absence of any serious attempt to address their putative grievances. Furthermore, the miscellaneous Palestinian guerrilla groups, allying with Nasser and the nationalist-fascist Ba'ath regimes in Syria and Iraq, were themselves would-be dictators seeking an equal footing with their vicious sponsors.

But the climactic battle that Nasser and his allies had envisioned was yet another humiliation. In the 1967 war, recall, Israel defeated its adversaries in six days. This defeat was a turning point.

Israel had proven to be so strong militarily, that another conventional war to "liquidate" it seemed implausible. But the Palestinian factions, with their guerrilla warfare and terrorist tactics, seemingly offered an effective alternative to the conventional armed forces of the Arab states.

There was another, even more compelling selling point for shifting to the PLO's tactical approach. Israel was strong; the guerrilla forces were materially weaker. Here was a prime opportunity to repackage the conflict in a way that exploits the Underdog Premise. Shift the numerous Arab regimes (with their considerable military arsenals and oil reserves) into the background, push the guerrillas to the foreground, and you could reframe people's understanding of the conflict. In 1948 and 1967, the fledgling state of Israel reminded people of a virtuous David defending itself against a brutal Goliath—the combined forces of multiple Arab regimes. Now that picture would be flipped: The PLO fighters, passing themselves off as scrappy "freedom fighters," would come to be seen as the underdog David fighting against the towering military force of an Israeli Goliath.[9] This recasting made a mockery of justice, but over time, it stuck.

The trauma of defeat in 1967 opened the way for a distinctly Palestinian movement (richly funded by state-sponsors) to succeed where its forerunners had failed. Deploying a different model of warfare for the same objective, the Palestinian movement promised to wage a "people's war" of "liberation" to overthrow Israel. The front man was no longer Nasser, but the "chairman" of the PLO and co-founder of Fatah, notorious for its militancy: Yasser Arafat.

On November 13, 1974, Arafat was invited to address the General Assembly of the United Nations. Keep in mind three facts that were at this point incontestable: Arafat was committed to destroying Israel, he himself was a killer, and, under his command,

Palestinian fighters were committing murderous attacks. Indeed, one of the worst attacks (up until then) targeted a school in the northern Israeli town of Ma'alot just *six months* prior to his U.N. speech; *TIME* magazine, among other prominent media outlets, reported on it. Among the dead students at the school were ten girls "each with a bullet in the neck."[10]

But at the U.N., Arafat was welcomed with a standing ovation. He delivered a lengthy speech denouncing Israel, justifying "armed struggle" against it, and presenting himself as leading a "revolution" to realize the dream of a "liberated" Palestinian state. Arafat told the audience: "I have come bearing an olive branch and a freedom-fighter's gun." Then he leaned in to the mic, wagging his finger menacingly,

> Do not let the olive branch fall from my hand.
> Do not let the olive branch fall from my hand.
> Do not let the olive branch fall from my hand.[11]

A few days later, the U.N. bestowed upon the PLO formal "observer status," which entitled it to participate in certain U.N. sessions and conferences.

The Palestinian movement had arrived, center stage.

The Palestinian Movement: Ends and Means

Whereas Nasser had promised that "Arab nationalism was the path to Palestine," over time the PLO put emphasis on a narrow, specific form of "Palestinian nationalism." They pushed their agenda by inverting Nasser's shopworn slogan: now conquering Palestine was the path to "Arab unity."

The PLO encompassed numerous, sometimes splintering, factions. They embraced a mixture of the doctrines of Marxism-Leninism, watered-down socialism, and variations on Arab nationalism. They found inspiration in the writings of Mao Zedong, whose totalitarian communist regime in China had inflicted man-made famines killing between twenty to forty-three *million* people.[12] They revered Che Guevara, whose face you'd recognize from ubiquitous t-shirts emblazoned with his iconic portrait, or from adoring movies about him. Mostly evaded today is the butchery that he orchestrated during and after the Cuban revolution. One of the PLO's major financial and military patrons was the Soviet Union, a regime that enslaved its people and thinned out the population through purges and engineered famines that claimed the lives of tens of millions.[13] In the 1960s and 1970s, members of Fatah, the leading PLO faction, had met some of their political heroes, notably Guevara, leaders of Chinese and Vietnamese communist factions,[14] and Cuba's dictator, Fidel Castro. It's revealing of the nature of the PLO that its leaders admired and emulated such dictators and mass-murderers.

Just as there's conflict within every ideological-political movement, so the factions of the PLO had their disagreements, and given their dictatorial nature, they engaged in often brutal, at times murderous, infighting. For example, a persistent question had to do with which faction was, in fact, truly faithful to the theory of Marxist class struggle; some were judged to be overly Marxist; some insufficiently loyal to Arab nationalism.[15] These ideological disputes, however, were swamped by what united the factions: their common goal. In its foundational 1968 document, the Palestinian National Charter, the PLO extolled "armed struggle" with "fedeeyn" actions at the core of the "popular liberation war." The "armed struggle," according to the Charter, constituted "the overall strategy, not merely a tactical phase."[16]

The PLO's charter emphasizes the need for thought control. It is a "national duty to bring up individual Palestinians in an Arab revolutionary manner. All means of information and education must be adopted in order to acquaint the Palestinian with his country in the most profound manner, both spiritual and material, that is possible."[17] When that kind of indoctrination succeeds, the outcome is someone who is "prepared for the armed struggle and ready to sacrifice his wealth and his life in order to win back his homeland and bring about its liberation."[18] To "liberate" Palestine entails reclaiming it as an "indivisible territorial unit" and the "elimination of Zionism in Palestine."[19]

There's no way around it: to realize the latter goal entails overthrowing the institutions of Israel's government. It entails putting untold numbers of people to death. It entails, in short, destroying a free society.

Initially, the PLO deployed the tactics of guerilla warfare against Israel. The "essential features of guerilla warfare," notes the scholar John Nagl, "are avoiding the enemy's strength—his main fighting forces—while striking at outposts and logistical support from unexpected directions."[20] But for the PLO this approach, coupled with random acts of sabotage and destruction of property, had its limitations. The PLO embraced the tactic of terrorism, deliberately. The scholar Barry Rubin notes that it sought to "wage war against Israel's civilian sector, to bring about the collapse from within of a country [that the PLO] appraised as a fragile, artificial entity." The aim, according to a PLO magazine, was to "destroy [the enemy] in order to take his place . . . not to subjugate the enemy but to destroy him."[21]

Observe the self-identified champion of the Palestinian people. Instead of working through Israel's legal system and political process to right whatever legitimate grievances Palestinians had at the time, the PLO sought to terrorize Israelis into submission, with the ultimate aim of wiping the only free country in the Middle East off the map.

Before Al Qaeda and ISIS, the PLO Blazed the Trail of International Terrorism

The Palestinian movement's violent attacks became a scourge not only within Israel's borders, but also outside it. Long before Hezbollah, Al Qaeda, and ISIS went global, the Palestinian cause was synonymous with international terrorism. One rationale for going international was to demonstrate that the PLO could strike Israelis *anywhere*, thus heightening the pressure on Israel to submit. For countries friendly toward Israel, such attacks sought in part to induce them to stop supporting it, even though Israel was, and remains, the only free society in the Middle East.

For example, at the 1972 the Olympic Games in Munich, Germany, a team of Palestinian fighters took Israeli athletes hostage. Journalists from around the world, at the scene to report on the Olympics, swarmed around the building where the hostages were held, and transmitted a video feed of the crisis as it unfolded. Eventually the German authorities attempted to rescue the hostages, but they failed; every last hostage was killed.

PLO factions pioneered hijacking airliners, notably on international flights. So audacious did these attacks become that on a singled day in September 1970, a faction of the PLO hijacked *four* flights simultaneously. One of the hijackers, Leila Khaled, was captured. So her brothers-in-arms hijacked *another* flight three days later to extort her release.[22]

The Palestinian movement claimed the lives of American victims, too. Among the first were Curtis Moore and Cleo Noel, two diplomats working in Sudan, who were tied up and shot to death in 1973.[23] Nor were they the last Americans to fall victim to the Palestinian cause. In 1985, Leon Klinghoffer and his wife were vacationing on the cruise ship *Achille Lauro*. Off the coast of Egypt, a team of Palestinian hijackers seized the vessel and took the passengers hostage. After the standoff, it was discovered that Leon Klinghoffer, who got around on a wheelchair, had been shot and then dumped overboard along with his wheelchair.[24]

Through hostage-taking, hijackings, bombings, and mass murders, the Palestinian movement sought to inflict punishing blows on Israelis, aiming to break their will (and scaring off some of the country's friends, into the bargain). But there was yet another rationale behind such terrorist attacks.

Within the PLO and among its followers, militancy became an index of moral standing: the more militant, the greater the honor and legitimacy. Factions within the Palestinian movement "competed in staging spectacular actions to gain recruits and prestige. The smaller the faction, the more it needed to use terrorism to seize headlines in a grab for a share of power and glory."[25] Essentially, the factions jockeyed to prove who is more murderous.

They competed to take credit for particular attacks, with several factions asserting that their cadres were, in fact, responsible.[26] Factions would hype their accounts of the number of attacks they carried out and the casualties they inflicted on Israel—far beyond what was plausible.[27] Some claims were outright fiction.[28] Earlier, I noted that Fatah had initially distinguished itself as the most militant of the PLO factions, but that reputation had to be maintained. Soon it was being out-done by rival factions. In order to vindicate its militancy, Arafat and his Fatah faction put together its own specialized terror brigades, Force 17 and Black September.[29]

This more-militant-than-thou dynamic was an echo of what we've seen in the emergence of the Palestinian movement from behind the shadow of Arab regimes. A major impetus for the factions had been their disgust with the Arab regimes for (repeatedly) failing to destroy Israel. Such defeats betrayed evidence of disloyalty to that goal. So the vanguard of Palestinian "armed struggle" saw itself as embodying a *total* commitment to the cause.

This phenomenon of "outbidding" rival factions with demonstrations of ever-greater ferocity has at least three audiences: Israel's government; its public; and the community that is sympathetic, or already committed, to the Palestinian cause. It is within that latter audience that the attacks are meant to gain an ardent following, loyalty, and new recruits.[30] It worked, and it still does today.

What Palestinian Statehood Actually Looks Like

When Yasser Arafat gave his landmark speech at the United Nations in 1974, he stated that the Palestinian movement seeks a secular, "democratic" state, one that would embody progressive values. This, he claimed, was the political end for the sake of which all of the romanticized "revolutionary" "armed struggle" was the means. Arafat received thunderous applause, and many people today demur at the movement's violent attacks, but support the idea of Palestinian statehood. So much so that, it is not only the leaders, but also the surrogates and supporters of the Palestinian movement who rail against Israel for (allegedly) thwarting their national aspirations. We encountered this claim in the last chapter; it's part of the grievance about the denial of Palestinian rights, specifically their desire for a homeland.

But if one cares about justice and the rights of individual, living human beings, here is a crucial question that is too seldom asked. What would such a Palestinian state actually look like?

No need to speculate; there have been *four* Palestinian quasi-states that furnish ample data. The first was in Jordan (1968–1970); the second, in Lebanon (1970–1982); the third, the Palestinian

Authority in parts of the West Bank and Gaza (1994–present); and the fourth, the Hamas regime in Gaza (2007–present). Each of these mini-states was celebrated at the time as a leap forward on the path to realizing the movement's national aspirations.

When the Palestinian movement achieved its declared goal of a self-governing homeland, even to a limited degree, it subjugated the people under its dominion and waged war against Israel. Reflecting the horrific political-cultural norms of the region, the Palestinian cause embodies the same lust for power, the lust to dominate people, that we have observed in the monarchies, dictatorships, and theocracies of the Middle East. The Palestinian movement is a roving dictatorship in search of territory to dominate.

Jordan, 1968–1970

The location was perfect. Being situated near the Israel-Jordan border was a boon for Palestinian fighters who used it as a staging area for attacks. Arafat boasted of having as many as thirty-six thousand rifles under his command.[31] That base of operations swelled into a mini state. Although the area was officially under the jurisdiction of the Jordanian monarchy, the PLO built up shadow government institutions in all spheres—military, political, social—that were autonomous.

The Palestinian factions ran their own "police" forces and courts of law. They arrested people and punished them at will. They imposed taxes, erected their own roadblocks, and swaggered through Jordan's capital city Amman, flouting the regime's authority. Some guerrillas began extorting "donations" at gunpoint. One faction sought to build local "soviets" (revolutionary councils) of workers and peasants. Invoking an analogy with the Vietnam war, Fatah called for turning Amman, the capital of Jordan, into the

Palestinian "Hanoi" to be used as a base for attacking Tel Aviv, the Israeli "Saigon."[32]

The situation grew tense. Fearing the encroachments on its authority, the Jordanian regime moved to rein in the Palestinian factions. It prohibited the factions from bearing arms and wearing uniforms in town, impounding vehicles, arresting Jordanian citizens and drafting fighters, or recruiting deserters from the Jordanian military.[33]

Clearly the PLO desired to expand its dominion within Jordan; some openly called for supplanting the government in Amman. The monarchy feared that the Palestinian forces were poised to launch a *coup d'état* (something that certain factions had tried to do in the past). So, in September 1970 the Jordanian regime ordered its military to liquidate the nascent Palestinian mini-state. "Full warfare ensued; using heavy armor, artillery, and air attacks, the Jordanians inflicted a shattering defeat." By the end, around three thousand Palestinians had been killed.[34] Evidence pieced together afterward validated the suspicions of a planned coup.[35]

Chased out of Jordan, the vanguard of the Palestinian movement re-established themselves in Lebanon. But in a move typical of street gangs, mobsters, and dictators, the PLO took its revenge against Jordan: it dispatched a hit squad to assassinate three of Jordan's ambassadors.[36]

Lebanon, 1970–1982

In southern Lebanon, along the Israel-Lebanon border, the PLO built for itself another mini-state. Within the camps of Palestinian refugees, the PLO established its dominion. It imposed taxes, operated its own "courts," conscripted men of fighting age, and revised the school curriculum to indoctrinate a new generation of warriors. The PLO provided military training and put emphasis on the cultivation of a "revolutionary" culture. The widows and orphans of "martyrs" to the cause (terrorists and regular PLO fighters killed during attacks on Israel and Arab states) received special pensions and benefits.[37]

Beyond that mini-state, which some dubbed "Fatah-land," Lebanon was already seething with sectarian conflicts. The weak government was unraveling. Amid the chaos, the PLO leapt at the opportunity to expand its dominion. The PLO "enforced its will with an iron hand," taking over the municipal governments of the coastal towns of Tyre and Sidon along with "branches of the national administration." For a while, PLO operatives "virtually ran Beirut's international airport." Members of the organization asserted exclusive control over several parts of the capital city Beirut, usurping the authority of Lebanon's police force, and even clashing with the Lebanese army. PLO cadres set up roadblocks, and expropriated cars and whole buildings for their use—again, as in Jordan, erecting a shadow authoritarian government complete with "revolutionary" courts.[38]

What deserves special emphasis here is the Palestinian movement's fundamental, wanton contempt for the lives, property, and freedom of individuals—for Palestinians, Israelis, Lebanese: for *all* individuals. Lebanese citizens were understandably frightened by what one scholar (in a highly euphemistic phrase) characterizes as "the guerillas' tendency to showmanship and weak discipline."[39] What that meant: The PLO factions took part in looting, extortion rackets, and smuggling (activities central to many Lebanese militias). One PLO commander in Nabatiye "collected his own tax from every truck that drove into the town's open-air market." His counterpart in Tyre "murdered a local soccer player for refusing to join the 'Palestinian team,'" while among the lower ranks, "rape and robbery reached epidemic proportions."[40] This general climate of lawlessness, exploitation, infighting among factions, and the military friction from PLO cross-border attacks on Israel was so awful that it became known with a generic term: the "excesses" (in Arabic, "tajawuzat").[41]

But by asserting brutal control over more Lebanese territory, the PLO was better able to wage war on Israel. It assembled a significant military infrastructure in southern Lebanon. By 1982, reports the scholar Yezid Sayigh, PLO forces:

> ...numbered 5,000 full-timers backed by a loosely structured reserve of up to 20,000 part-timers and militia, fielding dozens of artillery pieces and rocket-launchers, several dozen obsolete tanks and light armoured personnel carriers, and hundreds of anti-aircraft and anti-tank weapons (including portable guided SAM-7 and Sagger missiles).[42]

Deploying a tactic that Hamas would later adopt in its warfare, the PLO used Lebanese homes and civilians as shields in its military campaign against Israel. Speaking to a reporter from *The New York Times*, one Lebanese landowner explained how the PLO showed up one day and "set up rocket launchers in his orange groves; crates of ammunition were stacked nearby." They filled a small outbuilding with boxes of explosives and ammo, and as the weeks passed, the *Times* reported:

> ...barns became armories, fuel drums appeared, jeeps and trucks arrived, 130-millimeter artillery pieces were deployed among his 100 acres of orange groves and vineyards.
> The guerrillas finally began to move into his main house, an elegant stone building on a hilltop.[43]

Because of how the PLO exploited civilians and their homes, Israeli retaliation in self-defense unavoidably resulted in significant casualties.

The PLO, moreover, behaving like an authoritarian Arab state among equals, embroiled itself in Lebanon's civil war, pouring gasoline on the flames. The conflict spiraled into a catastrophic war, from which Lebanon is still struggling to recover. Israel became involved in the Lebanon maelstrom. The Israel Defense Forces invaded from the south in 1982 on the premise of uprooting the Palestinian forces.[44] The PLO was seriously bloodied, but thanks to a diplomatic plan to end the fighting, Palestinian forces were able to leave Lebanon unbowed. Under the protection of mainly American and French troops, Palestinian leaders and guerillas were evacuated to Syria, Iraq, Tunisia, and elsewhere. The PLO's leadership eventually set up a base in Tunisia.

The Palestinian Authority, 1994–Present

Next came the quasi-state known as the Palestinian Authority.[45] By now you might be thinking, hey, I've seen this movie before, and I know how it ends. And you'd be right, mostly. This time the outcome was even worse.

The two previous mini-states, in their own ways, were painful impositions upon the host regimes. But the Palestinian Authority was different. It was the fruit of a widely hailed peace negotiation, sometimes called the Oslo peace process (for the Norwegian city in which the talks began). The peace deal was supposed to culminate in a fully sovereign Palestinian state. The Palestinian Authority, which took over most government functions in parts of the West Bank and the Gaza Strip, was designed as a transitional, interim step toward full self-rule and political sovereignty.

This new quasi-state was handed to the Palestinian movement on a silver platter—by Israel, the United States, and the rest of the international community. The Palestinian Authority enjoyed formal recognition—from practically everyone, Israel included—and it had far, far more autonomy. By contrast with the mini-states in Jordan and in Lebanon, the Palestinian Authority had greater power—and it was correspondingly more oppressive and militant. (If you're wondering why anyone thought it was a good idea to give the Palestinian movement its own mini-state, great question. We'll get to that in chapter six.)

Dictator of Palestine

The first "president" of the Palestinian Authority was Yasser Arafat, and predictably, he emulated his state-sponsors and patrons. The PA—like Saddam Hussein's Iraq, Hosni Mubarak's Egypt, King Hussein's Jordan—was Arafat's dictatorship. To be sure, it had many of the trappings of a regular state: an elected president, legislative assembly, courts. And of course, a security force. Actually, not one but *eight* (perhaps more) "security agencies," with competing agendas, that are loyal, not to the law, but to various Palestinian factions.[46] The Palestinian Authority's security apparatus specialized in the "intimidation of political opponents," while "Arafat alone made all major decisions" of the executive branch. The regime distinguished itself by the pervasive "intimidation of the media and human rights organizations, to the point that it became virtually impossible to transmit any message other than one personally approved by Arafat."[47]

You've likely heard people on TV shows and in B-movies talk about "signing a death warrant," but in dictatorial regimes *that kind of thing actually happens.* Arafat's signature appears on documents, found in the offices of the Palestinian Authority, approving payments to terrorist groups and individuals launching particular attacks against Israel. Some documents are like invoices seeking reimbursement for expenses already incurred. Wrap your mind around that: this was such a mundane, run-of-the-mill thing, that

hit squads, mercenaries, and terrorists would literally file paper-
work to have their fees and costs paid. (The documents also show
that the Fatah-led Palestinian Authority was apprised of the operations of rival factions; little happened that escaped the notice of
Arafat's dictatorial state.)[48]

Just like the Palestinian mini-state in Lebanon, the Palestinian
Authority doled out pensions to the families of fighters killed in
attacks or imprisoned in Israel—a practice that continues to the
present day. In 2016, for example, it disbursed about three hundred
million dollars to thousands of families;[49] the 2017 budget called
for spending 344 million dollars in such payments. (That's about
49 percent of what the Palestinian quasi-state receives in foreign
aid, and more than it gives in actual welfare handouts to families
on the poverty line.)[50]

The Law and the Courts

Under Arafat's rule, Palestinian courts were a travesty. The legal
system—as in Egypt, Iran, Saudi Arabia, et al.—lacked any
semblance of judicial independence. According to a 1996 report
by two human-rights organizations, many people who faced trial
were never informed of the charges against them, and the security forces tortured people in custody. To extract a confession, they
would sometimes exert pressure on the accused by taking their
family hostage. The State Security Court, established in 1995, held
its "sessions secretly, often late at night. These sessions are very
brief, often only lasting a few minutes, in which time the defendant in [sic] accused, tried, convicted, and sentenced." Those
condemned to death "were not given the chance to defend themselves in court."[51]

Such court proceedings are horrific, but even getting as far
as facing a judge in a courtroom was something of a privilege.

For some, the most they could expect was street "justice": being accused, convicted, and punished on the spot. That practice long predated the Palestinian Authority and persists today. Probably the worst transgression was to "collaborate" with Israel.

The term "collaboration" proved to be an all-purpose accusation, when rival Palestinian factions decided to mete out "justice." In the years predating the Palestinian Authority, sometimes "collaboration" applied to actual or suspected informants for Israel, but it was commonly flung at anyone you might have a grudge against or at individuals seen as flouting "traditional social norms, including adulterers and homosexuals."[52]

The practice of summary execution has a long history. In the late 1980s, for instance, Palestinians launched an uprising known as the "intifada," and during that period, various armed factions, much like medieval warlords asserting a fiefdom, arrogated to themselves the authority to police some patch of ground, from which Israeli forces had pulled back. People accused of being collaborators were commonly executed on the spot "without interrogation or any preliminary proceedings." The suspect was killed "either in a premeditated or a spontaneous fashion, at home or in the street, by shooting, normally in the head, knifing, axing or using some other sharp instrument." Lynching was another favorite means of putting "collaborators" to death.[53] The persecution and arbitrary punishment of "collaborators" continued under the newly formed Palestinian Authority, but now with a significant difference.[54] The Palestinian quasi-state, an internationally recognized polity, lent this practice the cover of moral legitimacy.

Economic Exploitation

From the start of the Palestinian Authority, officials of the regime built up vast racketeering and extortion networks, collecting thousands of dollars in kickbacks. This brings to mind the mafia-like practices of the Palestinian leadership during its mini-state in Lebanon. Meanwhile, if you were a well-off businessman, you risked being subjected to false arrest in order to extract a ransom (or bribe) for your release.[55] A report published in 1997 analyzing the Palestinian Authority's finances found that about three hundred and twenty-six million dollars of the PA's annual budget of eight hundred million dollars "had been squandered through corruption or mismanagement."[56] By another reckoning, between 1995 and 2000 Arafat had "diverted $900 million of the [Palestinian] authority's tax and business income to personal bank accounts."[57] That may well be a low-ball estimate.

At the inception of the Palestinian quasi-state, many people in the international community hoped that it would one day blossom into an economic dynamo. Such hopes were soon dashed. The story of Issam Abu Issa, an entrepreneur from Qatar, is illustrative. Hoping to bolster the newly created Palestinian quasi-state, Issa founded the Palestine International Bank in 1996, which became the largest bank in the territories. The Palestinian Authority made it difficult for Issa to grow the bank. Then Issa was pressured to surrender control of the bank to a member of Arafat's inner circle. Issa refused. In 1999, the PA took over. Issa reports that:

> ...in direct breach of the law, Arafat issued a decree dissolving the Palestine International Bank's board of directors. The state-controlled Palestine Monetary Authority took over the bank, and with Arafat's blessing and written approval, formed a new supervisory board of directors, including at least one convicted and Interpol-wanted felon. The unlawful takeover was a confiscation of my own, my shareholders', and my clients' private assets for Arafat's personal use. At the date of seizure, PIB total assets amounted to $105 million. [58]

Worse was still to come:

Arafat's staff confiscated my private belongings, including my car, which Arafat took for himself. My brother Issa accompanied a Qatari Foreign Ministry delegation to Gaza in order to resolve the stalemate. But, upon his arrival, Palestinian police acting on orders from Arafat arrested him. *The PA said they would trade his freedom for mine. Only after the State of Qatar threatened Arafat with financial sanctions and severing of diplomatic ties did the PA give us free passage to leave Gaza for Qatar.* [Emphasis added.][59]

What made Arafat and his cronies worse than mere gangsters is that their looting was now done under the moral cover of the Palestinian quasi-state, an institution that supposedly was to enforce the rule of law and to protect individual freedom.

Censorship

We've seen how the muzzling of dissent, pervasive throughout the Middle East, is one of the unmistakable characteristics of dictatorship. The Palestinian Authority distinguished itself in controlling the press and silencing opponents.

Under Israeli rule, the Arabic-reading inhabitants of the West Bank and Gaza enjoyed considerable freedom of the press. After the Palestinian Authority was established, Arafat moved quickly to shutter newspapers that operated during Israel's authority, especially those aligned with rival factions. Arafat ordered the *Al-Nahar* daily newspaper to be closed, for instance, because its editorial positions were supposedly friendly to King Hussein of Jordan. The paper did re-open—once it began to mouth the official Palestinian line.[60]

Reporters and editors even mildly critical of Arafat would find themselves in the crosshairs of the regime. After reporting "the exact size of a rally" held by opponents of Arafat, the editors of several newspapers were summoned to a meeting and "officially informed that henceforth they were authorized to publish only those texts and statistics given to them by Wafa, the Palestinian news service." What if they refused? The PA security forces (read: thugs) beat up journalists and burnt down their offices.[61] To intimidate journalists into compliance with official propaganda, the Palestinian Authority routinely arrested, interrogated, and jailed journalists.

Incidentally, the notion that Arafat was the chief problem is refuted by the fact that such repression has continued long after his death. Arafat was succeeded by one of his inner circle, Mahmoud Abbas. Abbas is now nearly nine years past his legal term as president, which expired in 2009. And under Abbas's rule, the PA still brutally silences critics. In 2013, for example, a court in the Palestinian Authority sentenced a journalist, Mamdouh Hamamreh, to a year in prison for "insulting" Abbas on Facebook.[62]

Manufacturing New Generations of Martyrs

Censorship under the Palestinian Authority reflects the movement's deep commitment to enforcing thought control. The regime seeks intellectual control over the minds of its subjects, particularly the young.

Just as it had done in Jordan, Lebanon, and wherever it has held sway, the Palestinian movement continued to invest heavily in molding a "revolutionary" mindset in its followers. Now with the PA, it had both the opportunity, the (ample) means, and a large audience. Palestinian media, an organ of the regime, features an unending stream of articles, TV shows, and documentaries extolling the goal of eliminating the hated enemy, Israel. Palestinian TV, for example, has aired a program glorifying the "heroes of special operations" that featured a poster of the three PLO fighters responsible for the 1974 slaughter at the school in Ma'alot. In that tribute, which was broadcast more than ten times, they were shown alongside the photos of dozens of other terrorists.[63]

Many schools run by the Palestinian Authority are named after revered cultural figures, which means: many are named after mass murderers and terrorists. But not only schools. Kindergartens, streets, buildings, neighborhoods, sports facilities, summer camps, athletic teams, sports tournaments and events: all of these have been named in honor of admired "martyrs" to the cause.[64] For example, in 1978 Dalal Mughrabi led an attack involving a hijacked bus near Tel Aviv. In one of the most deadly attacks in Israel's history, Mughrabi and her team killed thirty-seven civilians (twelve of them children). She has had "summer camps, schools, graduation ceremonies and sporting events named for her, as well as many TV documentaries honoring her."[65]

Sometimes the faces of such "martyrs" are depicted in murals and in school insignia. Inside the classroom, students are assigned textbooks that deny Israel's legitimacy, and they are sometimes shown maps that deny its present physical existence. Such books are calculated to instill a hatred of Jews and of Israel.[66] Beyond the classroom, the PA created a network of summer camps to carry on the work of instilling the virtues of martyrdom and to impart military training.[67]

By indoctrinating the populace and particularly the young, the PA molds subjects loyal to the cause. It creates a self-replicating culture of hostility to Israel, and it fosters a population willing to sacrifice its young for the destruction of a free nation.

War Machine

Bringing peace was the essential rationale for establishing the Palestinian Authority. The diplomatic agreement that gave birth to the PA occurred in 1993, on the tail end of the intifada, a grim period marked by Palestinian violence. Many people—within Israel, in the United States, throughout the international community—hoped that the interim, quasi-state would mature into a fully sovereign state committed to peaceful co-existence with Israel. But in the first years of the Palestinian regime, the ferocity and lethality of attacks climbed, surpassing even the intifada. Even with only limited self-rule, the Palestinian Authority provided space and abundant resources to foment and carry out attacks on Israel.

To the extent that the Palestinian movement came close to realizing its aspirations, what it built was a dictatorial war-machine. That's bad enough, to put it kindly, and if we stopped here, our moral verdict on the Palestinian cause would be straightforward. It is a movement seeking to eradicate freedom and contemptuous of human life. But over the last couple of decades, the dictators who led the cause for so long—the aging PLO peddlers of Marxist-Leninism, Arab nationalism, Palestinian nationalism—have been eclipsed. Again, the more-militant-than-thou dynamic has asserted itself. What moved to the foreground was a group that's even more vicious, one with global ambitions.

Islamists.

The Palestinian Movement Goes Jihadist

To understand the emergence of Islamists in the vanguard of the Palestinian movement, we need to look at two major factors and their interplay. One factor was regional. For the Middle East, the success of Iran's Islamist revolution in 1979 was a fundamental turning point. It jolted the political landscape and galvanized the broader Islamic totalitarian movement. The other factor was local. Within the Palestinian movement, the failure of the (quasi-secular) factions of the PLO to destroy Israel was an indictment of their militancy, their basic fidelity to the cause.

The Islamists came to fill the void left by the fading, bankrupt ideology of Arab nationalism. Consider the path of Fathi al-Shaqaqi, who was a founder of one Islamist faction, Palestinian Islamic Jihad. Until 1967, Shaqaqi was a follower of Gamal Abdel Nasser, the champion of Arab nationalism. The crushing defeat of the 1967 war, however, led Shaqaqi (like many others) to abandoned that ideology, which was declining as a cultural force. Instead he joined the Muslim Brotherhood. By the mid 1970s, he gravitated toward the views of Ayatollah Khomeini.[68] Indeed, Shaqaqi went on to write a book extolling Khomenei's ideological vision (which at one point "could be found on every street corner in Cairo").[69] The success of Islamists in Iran's 1979 revolution galvanized Shaqaqi. In his eyes, their victory "demonstrated that even against an enemy as powerful as the Shah [of Iran], a jihad of determined militants could overcome all obstacles."[70]

The rise of Islamists fed off and reinforced the religiosity of the Middle East. The Palestinian territories were a case in point. The burgeoning number of mosques in the West Bank and Gaza, writes the scholar Ziad Abu-Amr, is an "indication of the rise in Islamic influence. In the period between 1967 and 1987, this number nearly doubled in the West Bank, rising from 400 to 750." In Gaza during that period, the number of mosques "had tripled, rising from 200 to 600."[71] This trend worked to the advantage of Islamists.

The doctrines of Islamic totalitarianism resonated with widely shared historical accounts and beliefs. Islamists could evoke the glory days of Mohammad and his successors who built a vast empire under the shadow of the sword, conquering much of the Middle East, North Africa and parts of Europe. Fighting to conquer Palestine was now, not some vague "class struggle," or a nationalist campaign, or a step toward fulfilling the exhausted vision of Arab "unity." It was something more resonant: a sacred duty commanded by Allah.

Islamists in Palestine agreed with Khomeini's vision that Muslim states, along with Muslims everywhere, should strive to put an end to the element of "corruption," Israel.[72] To do so is to follow in the path of righteousness. Here's how one Palestinian group of Islamists put it: "The day that enemies usurp part of Moslem land, Jihad becomes the individual duty of every Moslem. In face of the Jews' usurpation of Palestine, it is compulsory that the banner of Jihad be raised."[73]

Aftershocks of Iran's Islamic Revolution

The most established Islamist group among the Palestinians was the Muslim Brotherhood, which had pursued a long-term, incrementalist strategy focused on preparing the culture for jihad.[74] After the 1979 Iranian revolution, however, a newly energized cadre of Islamists felt that the time to launch the jihad was *now*. Anything less would pointlessly delay the eventual triumph. It was in part this tactical dispute—initiate the jihad later, or now—that led Fathi al-Shaqaqi in the early 1980s to splinter off from the Brotherhood to form Palestinian Islamic Jihad, which the Iranian regime took under its wing and nurtured. PIJ was an early adopter of the tactic of suicide bombing. The formation of Palestinian Islamic Jihad amped up the more-militant-than-thou dynamic.

The Brotherhood was under intense pressure to vindicate its militancy. Thus emerged the jihadist group Hamas, an outgrowth of the Brotherhood. Hamas is an acronym for Islamic Resistance Movement (fittingly, the acronym spells "zeal" in Arabic).

Giving voice to the global ambitions of the Muslim Brotherhood and other Islamic totalitarian groups, Khaled Mishal, one of the leaders of Hamas, explained that "Hamas is not a local organization," but rather "the spearhead of a national project, which has Arab, Islamic and international ambitions as well."[75] The group's founding document, the Hamas Covenant, states in Article Two:

> The Islamic Resistance Movement is one of the wings of Moslem Brotherhood in Palestine. Moslem Brotherhood Movement is *a universal organization* which constitutes the largest Islamic movement in modern times. It is characterised by its deep understanding, accurate comprehension and *its complete embrace of all Islamic concepts of all aspects of life, culture, creed, politics, economics, education, society, justice and judgement, the spreading of Islam, education, art, information, science of the occult and conversion to Islam.*" [Emphasis added.][76]

And whereas Palestinian Islamic Jihad was a small if lethal splinter group, Hamas drew upon the Brotherhood's moral authority within the community. It was a bastion of piety that people looked up to.

Hamas has a deep-rooted social, educational, and charitable network, which is integral to its jihadist goal. Hamas invests heavily in inculcating its totalitarian doctrine through an integrated network of charitable and social organizations, which not only "fund the families of Hamas suicide bombers, they finance important health, education, and welfare projects." Such projects, framed in Islamist terms, build sympathy, expand grassroots support, and create loyalty.[77] The scholar Matthew Levitt reports that "charity committees, mosque classes, student unions, sports clubs, summer camps, and other organizations run by Hamas are places where recruiters (usually themselves dawa [outreach] activists) recruit Palestinian youth into Hamas—whether into other dawa positions, or for suicide and other terror attacks."[78]

Just as the Palestinian Authority, run by the rival faction Fatah, methodically indoctrinates its subjects, so does Hamas. On TV, in print, on radio, at the mosque, the Islamists hammer on the theme of holy war against Israel. In a program for kids broadcast by Hamas, a bunny called Nassur chats with a girl in the studio and viewers who call in by phone. One segment concerns this topic: how to rid the land of Israelis. Bottom line: unless they leave on their own, they'll have to be chased away, and, the cheerful bunny adds, "we'll have to [do it] by slaughter."[79]

Here's what you would find in the Hamas children's magazine *Al-Fateh*. It features stories, riddles, poems and puzzles—about jihad and the glories of suicide bombing. It presents holy warriors as role models. According to a report by the Middle East Media Research Institute:

> Some issues feature stories with martyrdom themes, including characters who express a wish to die in battle and meet the virgins of Paradise, and parents who rejoice at their son's death in a jihad operation and celebrate by uttering cries of joy and handing out sweets. . . .
>
> The 60th issue of *Al-Fateh* features a story about Sa'id Hassan Hutari from Qalqilya, who carried out the June 2001 suicide bombing at a disco near the Dolphinarium in Tel Aviv, killing 21 people, mostly teens. The magazine presents Hutari's last message, in which he says: "I shall turn my body into pieces and bombs that will pursue the sons of Zion, blow them up, and burn the remains [of their bodies]." He then addresses his parents, telling them not to weep over his death, saying, "There is nothing greater than to give one's soul for the sake of Allah on Palestinian soil. Mother, utter cries of joy; Father and brothers, hand out sweets. Your son is awaiting his betrothal to the Virgins of Paradise."[80]

Triumph of the Pious and Steadfast

Which brings us to the second factor behind the rise of Islamists within the Palestinian movement. The narrative that Islamists peddle goes like this: we Muslims deserve to dominate, but we're poor and weak—precisely because of the impiety that runs through our land. The solution? Restoring piety through a totalitarian society defined in every last particular by Islamic law, sharia. Viewed from this framework, the leading quasi-secular factions of the Palestinian cause must be judged as abject failures. Why have they failed to destroy and supplant Israel? Precisely because of their irreligious ideology and impious behavior.

The PLO leaned toward socialism and communism, it was nominally secular, and its ideas were Western; "Arab" nationalism, even of the Palestinian sub-type, traces its origins to German philosophy. Practically, the PLO cadres allied themselves with un-Islamic regimes (Egypt, Syria, Iraq, the Soviet Union). They lined their pockets through rampant graft. They were indistinguishable from the region's impious dictatorships and monarchies, regimes that Islamists believed had to be overthrown. The Islamists objected to the PLO's charter, not because it called for the destruction of Israel, but because of what it did *not* call for: "the establishment of an Islamic state in place of that entity."[81] The Islamists' damning critique was that the PLO was "an organization that does not serve God."[82]

Further, over time the PLO had supplemented its "armed struggle" with a "phased strategy": extracting diplomatic concessions from Israel in order to re-conquer Palestine incrementally, taking small steps toward the ultimate goal of liquidating Israel.[83] Although this ruse worked up to a point in duping many Westerners, PLO officials were clear (when speaking in Arabic) that this incrementalism was a subterfuge, not the abandonment of their over-arching goal. But the combination of these factors—that Israel thrived while the PLO seemed to sell out on the shared goal of destroying it—enabled the Islamists to make a credible argument that the PLO was morally bankrupt.

By contrast the Islamists vaunted their piety and self-sacrificing dedication to the cause. In the community, they commanded enormous moral clout, precisely because they lived their religious ideology. For example, scores of Palestinians visited the home of a leader of Hamas, seeking his advice and counsel.[84] Leaders of the group "settled disputes without receiving personal payment," and applied Islamic law as their justification. The fact that Hamas depends for much of its funding on "zakat" (a religious tax, like a tithe) sets it apart: the Islamists appear to owe allegiance to their local constituents, rather than state sponsors, thus seeming incorruptible.[85]

The Islamists' hallmark is an uncompromising commitment to the destruction of Israel in the name of Islam. Here is the official slogan of Hamas: "Allah is its target, the Prophet is its model, the Koran its constitution: Jihad is its path and death for the sake of Allah is the loftiest of its wishes."[86] In its founding document, Hamas states that it "strives to raise the banner of Allah over every inch of Palestine." And the jihadist group insists that:

> ...the land of Palestine is an Islamic Waqf [endowment] consecrated for future Moslem generations until Judgement Day. It, or any part of it, should not be squandered: it, or any part of it, should not be given up. Neither a single Arab country nor all Arab countries, neither any king or president, nor all the kings and presidents, neither any organization nor all of them, be they Palestinian or Arab, possess the right to do that. Palestine is an Islamic Waqf land consecrated for Moslem generations until Judgement Day.[87]

Anything less would be to treason to Allah.

More Militant Than Thou

In the emergence of Islamist factions, we see (again) the playing out of the more-militant-than-thou dynamic. That dynamic was a significant factor in their adoption of the tactic of suicide bombings. It was Palestinian Islamic Jihad and later Hamas that led the way in deploying suicide bombers. Where these groups led, others soon followed.

The scholar Mia Bloom observes that more Palestinian factions "jumped on the suicide-bombing bandwagon," including newly formed groups. Moreover, "previously secular groups" began using the "language of religious holy war (*jihad*) to bandwagon onto Hamas's popularity." After a suicide bombing, Palestinian factions were known to issue competing claims for responsibility.[88] Recall that the leading PLO faction, Fatah, had gained prominence by setting the bar for militancy. Now, Fatah too formed the Al Aqsa Martyrs Brigade, which carried out suicide bombings.[89]

Pause to let that sink in. For the leaders and many followers of the Palestinian movement, the source of glory, the standard of one-upmanship here, is to take one's own life while also taking the lives of strangers.

Gaza: An Islamist Palestinian Mini-State, 2007–Present

By 2006, the George W. Bush administration had launched its "forward strategy for freedom" in the Middle East, and as part of that policy, it demanded elections in the Palestinian Authority (more on this in chapter six). The Hamas candidates won. By a landslide.

Theoretically, Hamas would now have a role in running the Palestinian Authority, which until then was dominated by the PLO's Fatah faction. By June 2007, however, Hamas had launched a military campaign to wrest total control of the Gaza Strip from Fatah. Thus was born one more Palestinian mini-state, this time predicated on the Islamist worldview shared by the Taliban, Al Qaeda, the Islamic State, Saudi Arabia, and Iran.

The Islamist takeover of Gaza was predictably gruesome. In one incident, reminiscent of how the Islamic State executes men accused of being gay, Hamas fighters pushed two members of Fatah from the roofs of tall buildings. The Islamists also "abducted and executed some political enemies. Reportedly Hamas even killed [Palestinian Authority] supporters who were already injured, or shot Fatah fighters at point-blank range to ensure permanent wounds." There were attacks against "private homes and apartment buildings, hospitals, ambulances, and medical crews associated with the Palestinian Authority." In this six-day civil war some one hundred and sixty-one people died; seven hundred were wounded.[90]

Islamization of Gaza

True to form, the Islamists pursued their totalitarian agenda within their new mini-state. That meant enforcing religious orthodoxy. Bear in mind that under the Palestinian Authority, minorities—particularly gays and Christians—were, and continue to be, viciously persecuted, so much so that some gay Palestinians have fled to Israel.[91] To this kind of persecution, the Islamists brought their signature zeal. On television, Hamas announced that its takeover would mark "the end of secularism and heresy in the Gaza Strip."[92] At the outset, they hounded the minority Christian community, for being non-Muslims, and attacked churches. Hamas fighters fired rocket propelled grenades at the main entrance of one church and its related school, stormed inside, and destroyed almost everything inside.[93] Furthermore, writes the scholar Jonathan Schanzer, Hamas tightened its grip on the media, intimidating journalists, and exerting control "over all electronic media in Gaza, except one radio station linked to the Palestinian Islamic Jihad."[94] Sharia courts "became the primary arbiters of disputes," presided over by Hamas-appointed judges.[95]

One priority for the newly formed Hamas regime was the enforcement of Islamic moral values.[96] From what you know of the Taliban, the Islamic State, Saudi Arabia, and the Iranian regime, you can project some of what that meant. For Hamas, writes the scholar Yezid Sayigh, it included enforcing a "proper" dress code on women, "separating unmarried men and women on the beach, banning women from riding motorcycles, requiring female lawyers to wear the hijab in court, and preventing male hairdressers from working in women's salons." You can also throw in bans on "witchcraft, sorcery, and charlatanism."[97]

The fear of being caught out was enough to make many inhabitants of Gaza comply with these Islamist dogmas. But there were also members of Hamas's proselytizing activists who went door to door instructing people on what's expected of them. "One of the most visible signs" of fear-induced compliance, writes one analyst, "is the increasing number of bearded men, and women wearing hijab and veil in the streets of Gaza. Some of [the men] grow beards for religious reasons, but women simply do not want to be harassed by Hamas 'morality police' and dawa [proselytizing] groups."[98] Such squads of morality enforcers had patrolled Hamas-controlled neighborhoods in Gaza and the West Bank for years, but under Hamas rule in Gaza, observes Jonathan Schanzer, "they began to operate in wider territory and with impunity."[99]

Waging Jihad on Israel

Having seized control in Gaza, Hamas was far better positioned to pursue its jihad against Israel. They trained fighters, many of them teens, and amassed weapons. Using tunnels to bypass Israeli border controls on the passage of goods in and out of Gaza, they smuggled in weapons and rockets. One study estimated that after taking over in Gaza, Hamas had secretly brought in rocket launchers; anti-tank devices; at least 80 tons of explosives; and factory-produced rockets with a longer range (likely sourced from Iran). Adopting a well-practiced technique, pioneered by the PLO in Lebanon in the 1970s and early 80s, the Islamists concealed their arsenal in densely populated neighborhoods,[100] particularly inside mosques and schools.[101]

What began as sporadic rocket attacks from Gaza climaxed into a full-scale war. From 2007 to 2008, more than 5,700 rockets had been fired at Israeli neighborhoods and towns.[102] To quell such attacks, Israel deployed air and ground forces in Operation Cast Lead, or what became known as the Gaza War of 2008–09. By 2012, the Islamists renewed their attacks, triggering another, briefer war. Then in 2014, amid continuing rocket and mortar attacks, Israel retaliated with air strikes and ground forces. During that 50-day war, Hamas and its allies fired more than 4,500 rockets and mortars—many of them longer-range missiles, putting most of the country within range.[103] They had built a network of tunnels designed for smuggling weapons in—and for launching armed raids on Israeli neighborhoods. The aim of Israel's Operation Protective Edge was to halt the rockets, impair the Islamists' military infrastructure (launching sites, munitions factories, arms warehouses), and destroy the tunnel network.

How the two sides waged war is deeply revealing. Islamists often proudly tell us that they love death like we in the West love life.[104] They really do mean it.

Israel's retaliatory campaign abided by conventional norms of warfare, which require self-imposed restrictions intended to

minimize harm to noncombatants. In keeping with its longstanding policy, the Israel Defense Forces dutifully went out of its way
to warn of impending strikes. It dropped thousands of leaflets in
Arabic warning Gazans to avoid certain areas that may be targeted.
It phoned and texted people residing in apartment blocks where a
rocket is about to hit, giving them time to evacuate. Often it fired
"a knock on the roof" warning rocket, before leveling the building.
It aborted missions if civilians were spotted nearby the target.[105]

By the war's end, the IDF succeeded in destroying thirty four
known tunnels, and the missile defense system known as Iron
Dome knocked out more than 700 rockets mid-air, which less-
ened the casualties and damage to residential areas within Israel.
Nevertheless, the Israeli death toll reached 70: six civilians and 64
soldiers.[106]

But those numbers fail to capture the full, gut-wrenching
story of how the jihadists of Hamas waged war. Essential to their
campaign was a profound contempt for human life, not only the
lives of Israelis, but especially the Palestinians who live under their
dominion.

Consider eyewitness testimony of Israeli soldiers who fought
in Gaza. After the war, their experiences were transcribed, and
members of the Israeli parliament (Knesset) read aloud from those
accounts.

> "The [Israel Defense Forces] followed all the rules to clear areas
> of civilians, but Hamas cynically forced some to stay," MK Dani
> Atar (Zionist Union) said, reading the testimony of a Golani
> soldier. "[Palestinians] were killed by explosives they didn't
> know were there that Hamas planted."
>
> "We lost our element of surprise, the best of our sons, to
> make sure we wouldn't kill civilians that the enemy used as
> human shields," he added.
>
> . . .

MK Merav Ben-Ari (Kulanu) read a testimony by Dror
Dagan, who was injured while arresting a terrorist, and listened
from the visitors' gallery, sitting in his wheelchair.

"When we burst into the house and quickly scanned the
rooms, the wife of the terrorist, a senior Hamas member,
fainted. As a medic, I did not hesitate and started taking care of
her," Dagan wrote. "Not two minutes passed and it turned out
that it was a trap. It was all pretend, a trick to gain time so the
suspect could get organized."

"I was injured, because I was taught the values of the IDF,
to take care of anyone who is injured, even if it is the wife of a
terrorist," Dagan added.[107]

Israel's devotion to the conventional norms of war was a tactical gift for Hamas and its allies.

One Hamas spokesman, in an interview on Al Aqsa TV
during the war, had called on the inhabitants of Gaza to climb to
their roofs to serve as human shields against Israeli bombardment.
Some Gazans were doing precisely that.[108] This captures the essence
of the Hamas regime, now at the vanguard of the Palestinian cause.

A Contempt for Human Life

That Hamas openly summoned, and got, volunteers to act as
human shields is a sign of how far the Palestinian movement has
succeeded in molding a culture that reflects its ideological-political
vision. Every dictatorship and totalitarian movement has worked
to enforce thought control. At that goal, the Palestinian movement
has excelled. From the outset, leaders of the Palestinian movement
have indoctrinated their avid followers—along with innocent
children and unwilling adults—in the nobility of slaughter and
destruction and martyrdom. This perverse inversion—the valuing
of death over life—has become a distinctive feature of Palestinian society. By instilling a reverence for martyrdom and murder,

leaders of the Palestinian movement have cultivated a population that not only offers up its sons and daughters as human shields, but also as human bombs—and then celebrates the massacres their sons and daughters commit.

Here is one example of many. Consider the adoration of Izzadin Masri. What did he do? How was he lionized?

One day in August 2001, Masri strolled through Jerusalem's downtown, and stepped into the Sbarro restaurant on the corner of Jaffa Street and King George. The pizzeria, popular with young families, was busy with the usual lunchtime crowd. Masri had brought with him a bag. It contained a bomb, packed with nails. The explosion gutted the restaurant. Lying in the wreckage were strollers and baby carriers.

> Among the critically wounded, with uncertain chances of surviving, was a baby only a few months old.
>
> Naor Sharabi, a young Israeli soldier, happened to be passing by when he heard the explosion, which blew out the front of the restaurant and sent bodies flying across the street, along with shattered glass and twisted metal. He turned and saw a girl on the ground. She was 2 or 3 years old. She was dead.
>
> "Someone took her mother to a store and tried to calm her down," the soldier said. "But she was looking at her dead baby. She could see her girl was dead, and she was screaming hysterically."[109]

Some days earlier, Izzadin Masri had posed for a photograph. The bearded twenty-three-year-old stood gripping an automatic rifle in one hand and a copy of the Koran in the other. His green headband and the banner hung on the wall behind him both testified to his membership in Hamas, which had released his "martyrdom" photograph when claiming credit for the bombing.[110] It killed fifteen. Among the dead were seven children. About one hundred and thirty people were injured. Such survivors can look forward to a lifetime with nails and shrapnel lodged in their lungs, spine, or brain.

What makes this attack doubly horrific was the reaction of people living in the Palestinian territories. Upon hearing about the Sbarro attack, some number of Palestinians reportedly celebrated in streets.[111]

Nor was this an aberration; typically after such attacks people come out of their homes, hand out candy, and fire pistols and rifles into the air to express their jubilation.

Try to imagine hearing that someone you love had just committed mass murder, by blowing themselves up, in a crowded pizzeria. It's difficult even to project what that would be like. *This* is what Masri's own mother, appearing on television, said: "I congratulate him: Congratulations, my son, on your Martyrdom, praise Allah...."[112]

Nor was she the first mother to extol her child's "martyrdom" for the sake of the Palestinian cause.[113]

Far from being a shameful memory, something people would wish had never happened, and perhaps could forget, in fact the Sbarro massacre—like many other murderous attacks—was publicly extolled. About a year later, students at Al Najah University in the West Bank put together an exhibit commemorating the anniversary of the "second intifada." It featured:

> ...a mock-up of the Sbarro restaurant in Jerusalem where 15 people were killed in a suicide attack in August including not only gnawed pizza crusts but bloody plastic body parts suspended from the ceiling as if they were blasting through the air.
>
> . . .
>
> Inside are toppled stools, pizza crusts, police tape, broken glass, as well as photographs of the actual scene of carnage and of the young Palestinian, Izzeden Masri.[114]

Mia Bloom, the terrorism scholar, offered this disturbing account of Palestinian attitudes toward suicide bombings in the early 2000s (the Sbarro attack happened in 2001). "Violence has become *the* source of all honor among Palestinians," and esteem for an individual "is bound to group status, physically and symbolically." The "martyrs" are lionized.

> The portraits of the bombers have become symbols of resistance as political groups vie to claim responsibility for the individual martyrs. The martyrs' posters covering the storefronts of West Bank towns pay homage to the *intifada* dead. With each incident, new posters cover over the tattered remains of the previous photos, proclaiming the Koranic slogan, "the martyr is not dead, but lives on," and displaying the martyrs' political affiliation prominently. The martyrs become the main topic of conversation. People discuss how they were killed, assess the posters for the kinds of weaponry displayed around them, and occasionally deride the political factions who vie for the right to claim the dead as members of their organizations.[115]

Consider one final marker of the popular sentiment toward those who fight and die for the cause. Beginning in late 2015, Palestinians carried out a growing number of random-seeming stabbings and car-ramming attacks in Israel. This upsurge of violence was celebrated in popular music.

> Spend any length of time walking in the main streets of East Jerusalem and the West Bank, and you'll hear [the song] "Lovers of Stabbing"—by far the most popular of a series of such hits— as well as similar songs calling for the killing of Israelis, blaring from cars, stores, and restaurants. Publicly, and without any embarrassment, individuals and businesses are playing songs whose lyrics blatantly call for the murder of Israelis via stabbing, vehicular attacks and other brutal means. [116]

The casualness of a song glorifying murder, heard in stores and from passing cars; the public adulation for suicide bombers, on television and on posters in the street: these examples illustrate the success of the Palestinian movement in inculcating its ideological vision upon the Palestinian community.

Put another way, some of the Palestinian movement's victims are individuals living under its rule; specifically, those individuals (however few remain) who genuinely want peace, justice, and freedom for themselves and everyone else—emphatically including for Israelis.

What Animates the Palestinian Cause

The Palestinian movement claims to fight for freedom, justice, and the well-being of the Palestinian community. But that's a fraud.

Instead of seeking to protect the freedom of individuals, the movement has worked to eradicate it. What enabled its rise to prominence and has nourished it is the backing of the region's dictatorial regimes, bent on liquidating the Middle East's only free society, Israel. That common goal has animated the movement, even as it marched under varying ideological banners. And wherever the movement has come close to realizing its political aspirations, it has subjugated and exploited the people within its dominion.

Instead of seeking justice, the movement inflicts injustice. There is no genuine Palestinian grievance, no past or present wrong, that it has worked to right. There is no genuine grievance, moreover, that can be righted by the creation of a nationalist dictatorship or an Islamic theocracy.

Instead of seeking a better life for Palestinians, the Palestinian movement exhibits an utter contempt for human life.

When a movement seeks not to undo injustice but to commit it; when a movement seeks not progress and individual flourishing, but the destruction of the only free, progressive society in the region; when a movement is nurtured by, reveres, and allies itself with, dictatorships and theocracies; when its fighters boast about their kill rate and compete to take credit for murder; when they jockey to out-martyr each other: we pollute our language, corrupt our thinking, and betray that movement's many victims when we deny the fundamental evil of that movement and its cause.

PART III

THE WAY FORWARD

We have observed the stark, consequential differences between the adversaries in the Israeli-Palestinian conflict. Is it even solvable? What would it take to advance America's interests in this conflict and the region broadly?

Yes, the conflict is solvable, and, yes, America's interests can be attained—but only if we take seriously the demands of justice.

Chapter five spells out the answer to the book's central question, What does justice demand of us in the Israeli-Palestinian conflict? Building on that moral verdict, in chapter six we consider how America should act in the conflict (and the region, broadly), in contrast to how the United States has actually behaved. This comparison will underscore the necessity of applying rational moral principles to guide our foreign policy. Finally, that chapter outlines some of the first necessary steps toward a truly just resolution of the Israeli-Palestinian conflict.

CHAPTER 5

WHAT JUSTICE DEMANDS

When you compare Israel with the Palestinian movement, what you find is not a matter of subtle contrasts. It's a fundamental difference. There is a profound moral inequality between Israel and its adversaries, which was thrown into even sharper relief with the ascendance of Islamists.

Israel is basically free. Like the United States, Canada, the United Kingdom, France and so many other free nations, a basic premise of Israel's government is that it exists not to dominate people, but to protect their lives and freedom. From its origins as an agricultural backwater of the Ottoman Empire notorious for malarial swamps, Israel has become a leader in technological and scientific advances and a dynamo of human progress. In Israel—a tiny strip of the Earth's surface engulfed by barbarism and savagery and tyranny—there now flower medical research institutes, symphony halls, computer-chip factories.

The Palestinian movement, by contrast, is hostile to human life and freedom. We've observed how this movement was born as a tool of the region's dictators, who sought to wipe out the lone free country in their midst. The leaders of the Palestinian cause are cut from the same cloth: they themselves are power-lusting tyrants and theocrats. To the extent they have attained some modicum of political power, they have exploited and dehumanized their own subjects, disposing of them as pawns. They have indoctrinated them in a mindset of unresolvable grievance and fostered in them an adoration of martyrdom and mass murder. They have prosecuted a decades-long war of aggression against Israel.

What, then, does justice demand?

On Principle

What justice demands of us in the Israeli-Palestinian conflict is *a principled stand in support of Israel—along with everyone else in the region who seeks genuine freedom, including among the Palestinian population—and a stand against the Palestinian movement and its cause.*

But what, exactly, does it mean to be "pro-Israel" on principle?

Let me explain what that means—and what it doesn't mean—by addressing a number of questions and objections that will likely come to mind.

A Stand for Freedom—and Everyone Who Seeks It

By a principled stand, I do not mean an endorsement predicated on Israel's ethnic-religious character, nor on biblical commandments. Instead, it is an endorsement of Israel's distinctive character as a free society. We should recognize and celebrate the momentous achievement of any country that actually protects individual freedom. Freedom is a rare and precious political value that we, like all other nations, need to live up to and champion.

To embrace the ideal of freedom as a principle means that we uphold it consistently across time, in every situation—rather than haphazardly, or only when it suits us, or only in some cases. Thus we should stand alongside *everyone* who genuinely seeks to live in freedom, who desires peace, who seeks human progress—elsewhere in the Middle East and particularly within the Palestinian population (these latter are among the Palestinian movement's unrecognized victims). Because of their ideas and values, such individuals are at odds with the prevailing norms of religious subjugation in the Palestinian Authority, in Gaza, and the rest of the Middle East.

We should stand alongside these brave souls—however many or few they may be—lending them our moral endorsement. We should encourage all who seek to break their chains and pursue a free society—and we should shun, ostracize, denounce, thwart the world's monarchs, dictators, authoritarians, and theocrats.

A Commitment to the Facts, Not Dogmatism

To be "pro-Israel" is often equated with a kind of dogmatic, regardless-of-the-facts support of Israel—an "uncritical," "unconditional," even blinkered support. A principled stand requires that we be fact-based.

No objective moral appraisal—whether of an individual, an organization, a regime, or a nation—can lead to a blanket, one-time-and-never-to-be-reconsidered endorsement. That's a caricature of moral judgment, and it certainly cannot serve our interests. People, organizations, countries are subject to change across time, and unless you revisit your moral appraisals, you'll miss relevant data, and quite possibly end up supporting those hostile to your values (or fail to recognize and appreciate new friends). Nor can you disregard present shortcomings or flaws, which must be discouraged and reformed.

By calling for Americans to be "pro-Israel," I mean that we should recognize Israel's fundamental virtue as a free society, and lend it our moral endorsement *so long as* that remains a defining feature. The same applies to our view of any other country. Should the UK or France, say, devolve into a dictatorship (following the example of Turkey, or worse), that fact would necessarily alter our appraisal—and relations—with that country. And if, say, the UK were to become beleaguered by hostile, tyrannical forces seeking to eradicate it, if it were a battle front in the conflict between free societies and Islamic totalitarianism, it would be an abdication of moral judgment to ignore that context and its implications for policy. That description, of course, captures Israel's actual situation.

Money and Military Aid

When people hear that the United States provides huge amounts of financial and military aid to Israel, two questions come up.[1] First, does a principled pro-Israel stand just boil down to material support, measured primarily in dollars and bullets? Second, is it in America's interest to be giving such support at all?

It's a misunderstanding of justice to think that support for Israel (or any free nation) is essentially material. In fact, America's *moral* support for freedom (and all who seek it) is far more consequential than people imagine, and it's greatly under-appreciated by our own policymakers. The vocal, serious endorsement and championing of freedom should be a defining feature of a rational foreign policy. It should be the resounding theme permeating everything we say and all of our policy decisions, not only toward the Israeli-Palestinian conflict, but everywhere—and emphatically including the Middle East. (In the next chapter we'll see that, contrary to what you might suppose, that's not what our foreign policy looks like.)

Which brings us to the question of when if ever American support should take the form of financial and military aid. Over the decades, the United States has provided considerable financial aid to Israel. Foreign aid, however, is inconsistent with the principles of a free society (regardless of who the beneficiaries are). You may disagree with me on that point; nevertheless, it's worth bearing in mind that in practice foreign aid is detrimental to the receiving countries, resulting in various economic distortions. By advocating principled support for Israel, I do not mean that the United States must provide an endless stream of financial support.

What it does mean, however, is that we should be willing to lend, share with, and sell Israel military technology, intelligence, and hardware. Doing so serves American interests. Israel is an ally in a conflict against a common enemy. The Israeli-Palestinian conflict is nested within a larger clash between freedom and tyranny. On one side are Israel, the United States, and every other nation that upholds the ideal of freedom; and on the other, the Islamic totalitarian movement—a profoundly anti-Western movement that kills and enslaves in the name of Allah.

Freedom vs. "Democracy"

Often Israel is described—and celebrated—as the Middle East's only democracy. To understand what it means to be pro-Israel on principle, however, we need to differentiate between "democracy" and freedom. Many people conflate these two ideas, and George W. Bush greatly helped to amplify that confusion. The Bush administration waged a campaign to bring democracy—essentially, majority rule—to the Middle East and called that policy a

"Forward Strategy for Freedom." It's crucial that we untangle this conceptual mess.

The ideal we should uphold is not democracy, but individual freedom. Notice that while free societies have representative governments and popular elections, you can also find tyrannical regimes that hold elections. For example, France, Germany, and the United Kingdom all of course have elections. But then so did Saddam Hussein's dictatorship in Iraq; so does theocratic Iran; so does the military regime of Abdel Fattah al-Sisi in Egypt. Even the Saudi regime has dabbled with municipal elections. And, while fighting a civil war, Bashar al-Assad of Syria won re-election. Et cetera.

Elections are a means of choosing political representatives, but freedom depends on the structure of those elections (e.g., are all candidates free to run?) and, most crucially, on what political powers those representatives do and do not possess. To the extent "democracy" has a good name, it is because of the regimes with representative government, such as the United States, in which elected political representatives are subordinate to a written or unwritten constitution that restricts them, at least in significant part, to the task of protecting individual freedom. While the ideal of freedom is widely embraced, hardly anyone really understands it. To appreciate fully what it means—and how it differs fundamentally from "democracy"—let's take a brief look at its origin.

The political ideal of freedom is a comparatively recent innovation in political thought. For eons, the default setting in society was some kind of tyranny. Your life belonged to whoever held political power. When you look back at the history of Europe, the cradle of freedom, you can see that for centuries upon centuries, government was a tool of domination over individuals; politics was a brutal scramble for power to lord it over others.

For instance, the English monarchy justified itself by the doctrine of the divine right of kings. The king asserted a God-given entitlement to dispose of your property and life at his whim. And when His Highness did so, it was your duty to bow and thank Him for giving you the honor of serving Him. Europe's kings, popes, emperors, tsars, princes, counts, dukes, and sundry lords ruled in the shadow of the sword. The Church, which dominated the continent, extirpated vice, heresy, blasphemy, unbelief. By force. The Inquisition, relying on the instruments of torture, exposed the unbelieving. Heretics were burned at the stake. Church and Crown both demanded obedience—in action, in thought.

On and on it went, for centuries. The ground began to shift, however, in the late seventeenth century with the dawn of the Age of Enlightenment. The Enlightenment's leading thinkers and philosophers, such as John Locke, advanced a radically different view of the individual and his relationship to the state. They believed that individuals are capable of observing facts and, using reason to understand the world, can guide their own lives. From that conception of the individual as sovereign, what follows is a fundamentally different vision of society. After the Age of Enlightenment, the traditional individual/state relationship was flipped: the state's function became, not to enslave you, but to protect your individual sovereignty.

The Founders of America were deeply shaped by the Enlightenment. Influenced by Locke's political thought, the Founders developed that vision and brought it into reality. The Declaration of Independence signaled a revolt not just against the tyranny of King George III. More broadly, it bucked the entrenched political model commanding human beings to kneel in obedience to authority—whether embodied in the crown, the church, or some other ruler. The Founders re-conceptualized the traditional relationship between the individual and the state: The individual is sovereign, in his own mind and life, whereas government is properly instituted among men *for the sake of* safeguarding the freedom of its citizens to think and act and pursue their own lives.

This kind of government renders the individual's freedom untouchable, by putting it off-limits to the mob or would-be power-lusters. An individual's life remains his own, and he or she is left free to pursue it (while reciprocally respecting the freedom of others to do the same). That was the premise of the original system that the Founding Fathers created in America. They called it a republic, and it was strictly delimited by the Constitution of the United States and the Bill of Rights. It was not a democracy.

The Founders recognized that a democracy—a system that confers unlimited power on the majority—is antithetical to freedom. Democracy rests on the primacy of the group. The system's supreme principle is that the will—the desires—of the collective is the proper standard regarding political matters; thus, the majority can arrogate to itself the power to exploit and tyrannize others. If your gang is large enough, you can get away with whatever you want. James Madison understood a profound lesson of political history. He observed that in a system of unlimited majority rule:

> ...there is nothing to check the inducements to sacrifice the weaker party or an obnoxious individual. Hence it is that such democracies have ever been spectacles of turbulence and contention; have ever been found incompatible with personal security or the rights of property; and have in general been as short in their lives as they have been violent in their deaths.[2]

Contrast that with the proper function of government: to protect your moral entitlement to pursue your own earthly happiness, according to your judgment, and consistent with the freedom of other individuals. Put another way, a proper government's only purpose is to protect the individual rights of its citizens.

Government is *a necessary good* that places the thought, actions, property, and life of the individual beyond the reach of criminals, mobs, clerics, tyrants, majorities. The individual, on this conception, must be left free to advocate and to practice peacefully any ideology, including religion, without fear of being forced to submit to the ideas of another.

The individual/state relationship, on this conception, means that the government answers to the people whose liberty it is responsible for protecting. The Founders, following in Locke's footsteps, held that if the government breached the defined limits of the powers delegated to it, citizens recognized their right to replace their representatives—or in extreme cases, even to dissolve the government and establish one that better serves their lives.

The principle of freedom applies to *all* individuals regardless of sex, race, creed, economic standing. It took many years for its implications to play out, and there were major contradictions in the rollout of America's original system of government. For example, the institution of slavery—an obvious negation of the principle of individual rights—lasted until the 1860s, ending only after the bloody Civil War; state-enforced racism, in the form of Jim Crow, ended a hundred years later; and the 19th Amendment to the U.S. Constitution, enabling women to vote, was ratified in 1920. We all wish that these and other milestones of human progress had been reached much sooner. And to be sure, there's still more work to be done to fully implement the ideal of freedom. Nonetheless, these were considerable advances. We should regard these developments as advances because they more consistently implement the ideal that government must safeguard, not violate, your freedom of thought and action.

What would violate your freedom? Basically, only the use of physical force: think of theft, fraud, assault, rape, murder—and a government run amok. You cannot live, let alone thrive, if you cannot reap and eat the harvest you sow. Take this farming example, and trace out the increasingly complex web of relationships that arise when trade enters the picture. Multiply that complexity further to a modern economy of industrial manufacturing, home mortgages, decades-long medical research, biotech patents, financial contracts for billion-dollar transactions, and you begin to see the need for a government of laws, not men; a government that adjudicates disputes objectively; that protects the liberty and property of its citizens.

Properly understood, individual rights ensure your freedom of action in society, so that you can learn, trade, prosper. The defining feature of a free society is its recognition and protection of individual rights. It is that political ideal, rather than "democracy," that we should live up to and that should inform our foreign policy, and specifically our support for Israel.

Why "Privilege" Freedom? Who Are We to Judge Other Cultures and Political Systems?

When I give talks and write about the crucial importance of freedom—particularly its centrality to Israel and its absence elsewhere in the Middle East—I sometimes get this kind of comment: "OK, the Western way of life and political system are built on the ideal of freedom. But who's to say that it's best for everyone? Why privilege your political values? We may not like how the Saudi regime treats women, say, but they, like us, are just following their own values and ideals. We may dislike what Palestinian self-determination leads to, but that reflects their will. Who are we to apply our values to judge other cultures?"

My answer is that the ideal of freedom is an *objective moral standard*. It is true for all people, in all places, at all times. Because of that, we *should* apply it as our standard for judging any political cause and any government, anywhere. Yes, these are strong claims.

Let me spell out the crucial point that freedom is an objective, universal moral ideal.

An Objective Standard

The underpinning of the ideal of freedom is the observable nature of human beings in all times, in all places. The philosopher Ayn Rand, building on the achievement of Locke and the Founders, observed that individual rights are not some gift from a deity or a permission slip from society. Rather, rights define the necessary freedom of action that you and I and all individuals must have, when we live in society. Factually, in order to thrive we each need to work, produce, trade, think, make decisions. In order to do that, politically we need to be left free to act according to our rational judgment.

Because it is morally right for each of us to have control over our own lives; because it is morally right for each of us to be free to speak our mind, shape the politics of our country; because it is morally right for each of us to pursue our own goals, earn our individual happiness and flourish; because it is morally right for each of us to be free—the proper kind of government is one that leaves us free to think and act. It protects us from criminals and foreign threats, so that we can build a business, raise a family, pursue a career, flourish.

Whereas under freedom you can pursue your own life and goals, that's precisely what every form of tyranny—authoritarianism, dictatorship, monarchy, theocracy—puts beyond your reach, on purpose and methodically.

Essentially, what the facts show us is that in order to thrive, you need to live free. Glance at history, and you can observe a causal relationship between liberty and human flourishing.[3]

Nowadays we Americans take for granted a standard of living that is unprecedented. Since the close of the nineteenth century, life expectancy has roughly *doubled*. When your great grandparents were children, terrible diseases such as diphtheria, rubella, smallpox, scarlet fever, and polio ravaged whole populations, crippling, blinding, and killing thousands. Polio, for instance, crippled millions, poor and rich alike (President Franklin D. Roosevelt was paralyzed by it), but vaccination has made that awful disease practically unheard of. Medical science has tamed, cured, and in certain cases eradicated an astonishing number of lethal diseases. Today, a serious public-health worry is not famine, but ailments stemming from the consumption of abundant, inexpensive calorie-dense food.

Freer than any society in history, we are pampered by innumerable workaday riches—so much so that we take them for granted. Even Americans technically defined as living in poverty own such technological marvels as refrigerators, air conditioning, microwaves, televisions, cell phones. Memes on social media ridicule people for bemoaning "First World problems." Here are some of those tribulations: When the Wi-Fi onboard the San Francisco-New York flight stutters; when the lines for rides at Disneyland are too long; when we must put limits on our children's "screen time," an aggregate of iPhones, iPads, TV, and computer screens.

These are problems that, one hundred years ago, not even America's first handful of billionaires could have imagined. These are problems that today billions of people around the world—disease-ravaged, penniless, underfed, uneducated, subjugated people—would love to have. Our first-world problems underscore just how advanced and wealthy the free world has become.

You can also observe the crucial importance of liberty to human life in the record of an (unplanned) natural experiment. Take one country, cut it in two. Each starts off with the same language, same levels of education, same technology, but they differ in their political system. This is basically what happened to Germany following World War II. West Germany veered toward freedom. East Germany went Communist. Consider the results.

East Germany (officially, the German Democratic Republic) was a satellite of the Soviet Union, and became a police state *par excellence*. The size of the secret police (known as the Stasi) was vast. In addition to its:

> 85,000 full-time employees, the Stasi had approximately 60,000 "unofficial collaborators," 110,000 regular informers, and upwards of half a million 'part time' informers, many of whom had no means of knowing that they even fell into such a category. Husbands spied on wives, professors reported on students, priests informed on their parishioners. There were files on 6 million residents of former East Germany, *one in three of the population*. [Emphasis added.][4]

East Germans were poor, they lived under acute censorship, they were indoctrinated with propaganda. The East German government built the infamous Berlin Wall to stop people fleeing. Anyone attempting to scale the wall was gunned down.

Just on the other side of the Wall, however, West Berlin was like another world. It thrummed with trade, innovation, progress, affluence. By the late 1980s—a generation after the country's division—West Germany was famous for its manufacturing prowess and was a global exporter of goods (the brand names are familiar: Volkswagen, Audi, Mercedes; Braun; Krupp; Bosch). The country became the leading industrial power in post-war Europe, and by one measure the fourth largest economy in the world.[5] West Germany was a country many people dreamed of moving to.

What explains the contrast between two sides of the same country? The West enjoyed actual freedom. The East was in chains.

The point here extends far beyond the Berlin Wall. Consider some of the dictatorships that ravaged the world in the last hundred years. The Soviet Union. Germany under the Nazi (National Socialist) party. Italy under the rule of Fascism. The Khmer Rouge in Cambodia. Communist China. North Korea. These regimes enslaved their subjects. They committed mass murdered. They dehumanized their populations. The common denominator among such regimes is that they dispose of the irreplaceable lives of human beings as cheap. Not in error or by accident, but on purpose and methodically.

The wider point: Freedom enables human flourishing. Every form of tyranny negates it.

Precisely because freedom is a necessary condition for individual flourishing in society, it serves as an objective moral standard. Therefore, our entire approach to political thought, to public policy, to the Middle East, to the Israeli-Palestinian conflict must embrace the fundamental moral distinction between freedom and tyranny.

Israel is a free society facing jihadist and dictatorial enemies. Justice demands that we stand in support of Israel. Morally, we *should* stand alongside everyone in the region and among the Palestinian population who seeks peace, progress, and genuine freedom. And we *should* stand against the Palestinian movement and its cause. On principle.

How consistent with justice is America's foreign policy? What has been our *actual* approach to the Israeli-Palestinian conflict?

CHAPTER 6

HOW OUR APPROACH MUST CHANGE

It's true that in countless ways America is supportive of Israel. It's also true that our leaders and diplomats are occasionally vocal about upholding freedom. But look at the record of American policy, and it's impossible to miss a startling conclusion. Our approach has failed fully to serve U.S. interests, not only in the Israeli-Palestinian conflict, but also in the Middle East broadly.

Indeed, it's actually made matters worse. To be blunt, the approach we've followed sells out good people—in Israel, among the Palestinians, throughout the region—who genuinely seek freedom, and it enables and encourages monsters, notably the Islamists.

What explains that failure? In a word, our approach has been unprincipled and amoral. Instead of looking at the facts and judging the adversaries objectively, our approach evades crucial facts, plays down the impact of the region's prevalent ideas, and flouts the requirements of moral judgment. This is a longstanding, bipartisan problem, and it has manifested in various ways across time. The through line, however, is that America's approach to the conflict (and the region) negated the demands of justice.

By understanding that pattern of failure, we can bring into sharper focus how America's approach must change. This chapter recounts three pivotal episodes in American policy toward the Israeli-Palestinian conflict. For each episode, we look at what it means to take a principled stand in support of Israel, and contrast that with what American policy *actually* did—much to our detriment. These comparisons underscore the necessity of identifying and acting on the demands of justice.

The encouraging takeaway is that there is a path forward. We *can* attain our interests in the Middle East, and the Israeli-Palestinian conflict *is* solvable—if we take justice seriously.

Episode One. The Post-Cold War Era

The Berlin Wall embodied the political-moral conflict of the Cold War. On one side was a free society; on the other, a totalitarian, Soviet-aligned regime. Then, one night in November 1989, the Wall came down. By the early 1990s, the Soviet Union, with its various satellite regimes, had disintegrated. The end of the Soviet bloc, and with it the end of the Cold War, was a world-historical moment. Left standing as the only super-power on the world stage was the United States. It was a grand scale, even poetic, re-affirmation of the moral superiority of a free society.

For Washington, the post-Cold War era was ripe with opportunities for advancing our ideals. Throughout Europe, millions of people were emerging from the dark night of totalitarianism. We were well placed to advocate proudly for our founding ideal of liberty, to stand alongside all who seek freedom, to model that principle in our actions and policy. During the Cold War, Israel was a strong regional ally, persistently assaulted by the neighboring dictatorships and would-be dictators of the Palestinian movement (backed by Soviet Russia). For a number of reasons, the post-Cold War years were a prime opportunity to help our ally end that threat.

The Palestinian cause, by this time, was struggling. It had yet to come even close to fulfilling its purpose of wiping out Israel. The movement, as we have seen, had trailed one bloody failure after another—chased out of Jordan, bloodied in Lebanon. The geographical distance between the PLO's base in Tunisia and Israel served as a further reminder of the movement's failure to achieve its goal of conquest. Meanwhile, the emerging Islamist groups, chiefly Hamas, vied fiercely with the PLO for influence over the Palestinian community.

The PLO also faced serious financial problems. The Soviet Union, now unraveling, was no longer available as a patron. Even more damaging, however, was the PLO's embrace of Saddam Hussein during the 1990–91 Gulf War. By siding with the Iraqi dictator, the PLO alienated its other Arab patrons. In 1990 Saddam Hussein sent his tanks to invade oil-rich Kuwait, seeking to loot and conquer the neighboring country. What followed was a standoff between Iraq and the U.S.-led coalition. When Hussein refused to budge, the American military drove Iraqi forces out of Kuwait. During the war, however, Iraq managed to fire Scud missiles at Israeli cities. Even as these rockets were raining down upon Israel—*rockets that initially were feared to contain chemical weapons*—Yasser Arafat praised Saddam Hussein and celebrated him as a hero (so did some Palestinians, who marched in the streets carrying Iraqi flags chanting "Saddam, you hero, attack Israel with chemical weapons!" and "we are with you till victory.")[1]

Though the Arab states that funded the PLO shed no tears for Israel, they were aghast at Arafat's rallying behind Iraq and its invasion of Kuwait. They were well aware that Kuwait had not only provided Arafat with a refuge for many years, it had also bankrolled the Palestinian cause. For the PLO's Arab patrons, the Palestinian cheerleading of Saddam Hussein was a reminder that just as Arafat and his followers had turned on Kuwait, they might well turn on their other state-sponsors. The river of cash from Arab regimes that kept the Palestinian movement afloat began to dry up.

At that moment in history, here was yet another, eloquent reminder of the Palestinian movement's essential character. It had close ties to the Soviet bloc, one of history's worst dictatorships; it had a longtime alliance with a brutal dictator (Saddam Hussein), openly celebrating his flagrant invasion and looting of Kuwait and bombing of Israel; it was a movement of murderers and would-be dictators, fighting to liquidate Israel's free society. Even as people across the globe were throwing off the yoke of communist tyranny, hungrily drawing their first lungful of air as unshackled individuals, the Palestinian movement persisted in seeking to enslave and butcher human beings.

Observing all of this in real time and considering the history of the Palestinian movement, no one could any longer honestly doubt its malignant nature and goal. If we took seriously the demands of justice, what approach should we have adopted toward the Israeli-Palestinian conflict?

More than any military edge, what Israel needed then, and still, is Washington's moral endorsement and backing. At minimum, we should have denounced, vocally and without reservation, the Palestinian movement as hostile to freedom, and, indeed, to human flourishing. That would have entailed rejecting not merely the movement's vile (usually terrorist) means, but also its animating goal. Moreover, recognizing the Palestinian movement's material weakness as an opportunity, we should have encouraged our ally Israel to dismantle the movement in order to eliminate, for good, the threat that it posed. For a start, that would have entailed capturing, or if necessary killing, the leaders, lieutenants, and officers of the Palestinian cause, putting them on trial publicly and fully discrediting their movement, exposing the scale of their crimes against Israelis and Palestinians, and punishing them.

What did we actually do?

Embracing the PLO

In the wake of the Gulf War, the George H.W. Bush administration (1989–1993) felt that the moment was ripe to bring an end to the Israeli-Palestinian conflict. The goal was not to wind down the Palestinian movement, but to organize an international conference in Madrid, Spain, to foster peace between Israel and its adversaries. One premise animating George H.W. Bush's administration was that the moral character of the adversaries was really beside the point; you could bargain with anyone. The conference created an opening for the PLO to regain a foothold of diplomatic legitimacy; it managed to get some of its people into the delegations which supposedly spoke for the Palestinian community.[2]

The whitewashing of the PLO, however, moved along at warp speed during the so-called Oslo Peace Process (1993 onward). These talks began in secret, under the auspices of the Norwegian government, and (initially) without the official endorsement of Israel's government. PLO representatives sat on one side of the table; on the other, a couple of Israeli academics, winging it, and technically breaking the law (it was illegal under Israeli law to have direct contact with the PLO). The result was a broad-strokes, vague agreement on "principles" that could frame an eventual peace deal. For ill-considered reasons, Israel's government decided to pursue the talks officially, and President Bill Clinton (1993–2001) leaned in to endorse this diplomatic venture.

The Oslo peace process reflected a fuller expression of the premise that animated the George H.W. Bush administration. The peace process was based on the idea (widely accepted in diplomacy) that you need to put aside the nature and goals of the adversaries in a conflict, bring them to the table, and then negotiate a settlement that both sides agree to. The formula at the heart of the peace process was "land for peace." To attain peace, Israel would cede land to the Palestinian movement, for the creation of a future state, and in exchange, the Palestinians would stop their violent attacks.

To regard that formula as something other than extortion of a free society (Israel) by a dictatorial movement (the PLO) seeking to destroy it, you have to hold a number of assumptions that defy the facts and the demands of justice. Among them: That the Palestinian movement is not *really* animated by an ideological commitment to destroying Israel. That the movement's leaders actually give a damn about the Palestinian community that they claim to fight for. That the promises and commitments of would-be dictators and murderers can be taken seriously.

Informed by such assumptions, the peace process worked to whitewash the Palestinian movement and enable its vicious cause. On September 13, 1993, Clinton hosted a ceremony on the White House lawn to mark the signing of the Oslo peace accord. Standing alongside the president of the United States, on an equal footing— literally and morally—were Israel's prime minister, Yitzhak Rabin, and the chairman of the PLO, Yasser Arafat. Clinton, who later went all in to broker the follow-on negotiations, proclaimed the agreement a "victory for peace." Let us go from this place, he said, "to celebrate the dawn of a new era, not only for the Middle East but for the entire world."[3] The Israeli foreign minister, Shimon Peres, gave voice to the supposed spirit of that day. "Let all of us

turn from bullets to ballots, from guns to shovels." And, addressing the Palestinian delegation, he said: "We shall offer you our help
in making Gaza prosper and Jericho blossom again."[4]

The entire peace process made a mockery of justice. The
Palestinians were asked to fulfill certain preconditions: they had
to renounce terrorism, recognize Israel's sovereignty as a state, and
cancel the clauses in the PLO's charter that call for the destruction
of Israel. Presto: The Palestinian leadership, having put out a statement vaguely on that theme, were duly invited to pull up a seat at
the table and begin laying out their demands.

Thus Arafat—a man with the blood of thousands on his hands,
the leader of an officially designated terrorist organization—had
his sins washed away. Instantly, he was anointed a partner for peace,
a statesman.[5] With the pomp of a state visit, he arrived in Washington aboard a plane donated by one of his remaining patrons,
Saddam Hussein.[6] In 1994 Arafat (along with Israel's prime minister and foreign minister) jointly won the Nobel Prize for Peace.[7]
Throughout the remainder of the Clinton administration, Yasser
Arafat was the most frequent foreign visitor to the White House.[8]

The whitewash was slathered on thick. No matter the history
of the movement; no matter its deceit; no matter its essential
character and animating cause; the leader of the Palestinian movement went from being *persona non grata* to being acclaimed a
peace-maker.

The price of this grotesque fiction, to which Israel and the
United States were active parties, would be the lives of numerous individuals. The same day that Arafat stood on the White
House lawn, he had a pre-recorded speech, in Arabic, broadcast
on Jordanian radio. In that speech he explained how the peace
deal fit within the Palestinian movement's "phased strategy." That
strategy, adopted in 1974, called for adding a diplomatic track to

the Palestinian war against Israel. Along with shootings, bomb-ings, and other forms of violent attack, the Palestinians were open to advancing their war of conquest in installments (or, phases) by accepting diplomatic concessions of land, little by little, rather than all at once. Once they gained some land, it would serve as a kind of Trojan Horse for destroying Israel. Nor was that speech the only time Arafat, or his lieutenants, articulated the movement's true agenda.[9]

Creating Another Mideast Dictatorship

The peace process was thus a major opportunity, handed to the Palestinians, for advancing their basic goal. At perhaps the nadir of the movement's existence, the Oslo peace process served to ennoble a vicious cause, whitewash its leadership, and endorse its means and ends. It granted the Palestinians the gloss of legitimacy while rewarding past aggression and further enabling it. That encouragement was given palpable, material reality, in two forms.

The first, and most consequential, was the creation of a new quasi-state, the Palestinian Authority. The PA, as we saw in chapter four, was an interim step toward full sovereignty, and it was granted broad powers over "education and culture, health, social welfare, direct taxation, and tourism" within its jurisdiction in areas of the West Bank and Gaza Strip.[10]

The second, which enabled and armed that dictatorial quasi-state, was the torrent of international aid. In the five years after the signing of the Oslo accord, the total came to about 2.4 billion dollars.[11] During that same period, the World Bank reports, the Palestinians were among the highest per-capita recipients of aid in the world ("averaging over $200 per capita per year, many times the level of official assistance to lower middle income countries or other countries" in the region.).[12] For its part, the United States has been a major donor. From the mid-1990s through 2016, for example, Washington alone committed more than five billion dollars in aid to the Palestinians (averaging about 400 million dollars a year between 2008–16).[13]

The peace process, involving numerous rounds of talks, unfolded across nearly a decade. By the dusk of Clinton's second term, the foreseeable materialized. Israel's ceding of land brought no peace, only continued Palestinian violence. Hoping to salvage the peace process, Clinton hosted a summit intended to hash out all of the remaining issues, once and for all. He rolled up his shirtsleeves and became personally involved in the negotiations. Two things stand out in the story of that 2000 summit.

First, it is highly unusual for an American president to take so hands-on a role, devoting nearly two weeks out of his schedule, and risking his reputation on the outcome. There could be no mistaking the seriousness of Clinton's commitment to the peace talks and thus their fundamental premise: the willful disregard of the moral inequality between Israel and the Palestinian movement.

Second—and a consequence of the first—it is revealing that there was no question of dissolving the Palestinian Authority, despite its moral character. The PA was a dictatorship, and it was complicit in murderous attacks on Israel. Entering its fifth year, the quasi-state was an irreversible gain for the Palestinian cause.

Looking back years later on his peace-making initiatives, Clinton insisted that, "I killed myself to give the Palestinians a state. I had a deal they turned down that would have given them all of Gaza."[14] Evidently, they wanted far more. Flush with foreign aid and controlling a quasi-state from which to fight, they were well positioned to march on. By September of 2000, about two months after Clinton's summit reached a dead end, the PLO launched a ferocious round of war against Israel, the so-called Second Intifada.

More Israelis were injured, maimed, crippled, and killed during a five year span of the Second Intifada than in the *quarter century* prior to the Oslo peace accord.[15]

Put simply, the Oslo peace process afforded the Palestinian movement an urgently needed financial lifeline, an internationally endorsed quasi-state, and, most important of all, moral legitimacy. Essentially and perversely, this was a case of free nations—the United States, Israel, and the freer nations of the United Nations at their forefront—actually *creating* a new militant dictatorship.

Episode Two. The Post-9/11 Era

By late summer 2001, if you looked at the Israeli-Palestinian conflict from the vantage point of Washington, D.C., what would you see? The Palestinian Authority, in keeping with the prevailing norms of the Middle East, was maturing into a full-blown dictatorial regime. Arafat had enthroned himself as absolute ruler, and he oversaw the ongoing terror war on Israel. None of that was fundamentally new, except perhaps the increasing savagery of the attacks. In the more-militant-than-thou dynamic, which (as we've seen) long characterized the Palestinian movement, there was a new development. The Islamist faction Hamas, jockeying to out-martyr its rivals, was on the ascent. Within the Palestinian community it was gaining increasing moral clout; Hamas became notorious for suicide bombings.

But what should have changed everything—about America's approach toward the Middle East, including toward Israel—were the jihadist attacks of September 11, 2001. For American policymakers, the 9/11 suicide attacks should have been a moment of urgent moral reflection and reassessment. The Islamic totalitarian movement had declared war on us years before, though few of us had been willing to take it seriously. The various Islamist factions, despite their strategic, tactical, and sectarian infighting, were united in their common goal; it was what defined them. What this movement stood for—the subjugation all of humanity under a totalitarian Islamic rule—was evil. Clearly, now, it was necessary to confront and eliminate the jihadist menace.

This is precisely what the initial rhetoric of the George W. Bush administration (2001–2009) led many people to expect. Bush's (in)famous slogans—"either you are with us, or you are with the terrorists"; we'll get the terrorists "dead or alive"; the "axis of evil"— were accepted as hallmarks of a new approach, one committed to moral judgment in foreign policy.

In reality, however, Bush's approach negated the demands of justice. The hallmark of objectivity in moral judgment is a commitment to the facts, however unpleasant. Instead, Bush's approach evaded crucial facts about the Palestinian movement, notably the relationship between the leaders and their followers. The Bush administration, moreover, shut its eyes to the link between the Islamist movement goals and its *religious* nature. And it disregarded the evidence that this movement was ascendant within the Palestinian community (and across the region). These evasions— about the Palestinian cause, about the Islamist movement, about the popularity of Islamists—were key to Bush's policy approach. That policy, in its effects, was catastrophically unjust.

Evading the Nature of the Palestinian Cause

In his landmark speeches, Bush denounced "tyranny" and vowed to "rid the world of evil." But even as Palestinian suicide bombers were blowing up buses, nightclubs, cafes, pizzerias, shopping malls across Israel, Bush refrained from condemning Arafat's tyrannical regime and the evil it was inflicting. And just sixty days after the 9/11 attacks, from which Americans were still reeling, Bush made history by pledging his administration's commitment to the two-state solution. The United States had for years given de facto backing to the idea of a sovereign Palestinian state, but Bush was the first formally to go on the record in support of that goal.[16]

To make sense of that commitment to Palestinian statehood, you need to grasp how Bush came to view the Palestinian cause: The problem lay not with its basic goal, but rather with leaders of the movement. And eventually, Bush was embarrassed into criticizing Arafat. The trigger for that was an incident in January 2002, a couple of months after Bush's historic endorsement of a Palestinian state.

Israel's navy intercepted a cargo ship, the *Karine A*, heading for a rendezvous off the shore of Gaza. On board were eighty large submersible canisters tightly packed with "enough weapons and explosives to supply a small army."

> The fifty-ton arsenal included dozens of 122mm and 107mm Katyusha rockets with ranges of twenty and eight kilometers respectively; hundreds of shorter-range 81mm rockets; numerous mortars, SAGGER and RPG 18 anti-tank missiles, sniper rifles, AK-47 assault rifles and mines. The rockets and mortars were of Russian, Chinese, North Korean and Iranian origin. Some were advanced munitions, such as the VR7 anti-tank warhead, capable of penetrating the armor of main-battle tanks. Perhaps most ominously, the boat held about 3,000 pounds of C4 explosive, enough for about 300 suicide bombs.[17]

This arsenal—enclosed in Iranian-made canisters and subsidized by Tehran's Islamist regime—was heading to the Palestinian Authority. The purpose was obvious; the evidence implicating Arafat's regime, conclusive. Nor was this its first war-supply ship; there had been several earlier Palestinian attempts at smuggling weapons by sea.[18] But the sheer quantity of munitions aboard the *Karine A* was staggering.

For the Bush administration, the *Karine A* affair was something of a turning point. It was only *now* that Bush bestirred himself to describe Arafat as a "committed terrorist." In a major speech, the president laid out his administration's view of what had subverted the peace process. Bush called on Palestinians to embrace "new leaders, leaders not compromised by terror," a spectacularly wishy-washy reproach of the killer Arafat. Bush urged the building of a "practicing democracy."[19]

To regard the *Karine A* affair as somehow revelatory of Arafat's character and the nature of his regime is preposterous. The *Karine A* affair "did not actually show anything new about whether he [Arafat] was a committed terrorist" observes the diplomat and scholar Daniel Kurtzer, adding, with academic deadpan: "For that conclusion, the evidence was much older."[20] What the episode did throw into sharp relief was Bush's view that there was a fundamental divide between leaders of the Palestinian movement and their subjects, the Palestinian people.

The Palestinian people, Bush asserted, just wanted peace, a better life, and if given the chance, they'd seize it. Some small number of them? Quite possibly; but *all*? No. Bush's claim evaded a mountain of facts. For decades, many Palestinians revered Arafat as a hero, and under his rule of the Palestinian Authority, they endorsed and took part in the terror war he orchestrated. Many who opposed and criticized Arafat did so because they supported the Islamist faction Hamas; they viewed Arafat and his PLO cronies as impious sellouts who were not militant enough. Indeed, when it came to the Islamists within the Palestinian community, the Bush administration exhibited a mile-wide blind spot.

Empowering the Jihadists

Despite the role of Iran's Islamist regime in the *Karine A* affair, the Bush administration disregarded evidence that within the Palestinian community the Islamists were ascendant. To look even casually at the Palestinian cause at that time was to see the abundant, indisputable evidence of the movement's Islamization. The facts were there. But unwilling to entertain the idea that there can be a connection between religious faith and the desire to dominate and destroy, the Bush administration chose to ignore the facts, and it called for Palestinians to elect new leaders. The result was to pave the way for a new jihadist quasi-state in Gaza.

The prelude to that jihadist triumph came in the summer of 2005; the climax followed a few months later.

For dubious reasons, the Israeli government decided to pull out of the Gaza strip, remove the Israeli settlers living there, and cede the territory to the Palestinian Authority. No strings attached, no conditions, no land-for-something deal. In the summer of 2005, the Israeli government just handed it over. With some plausibility, the Islamists would predictably claim Israel's surrender of Gaza as a victory for the path of jihad. But the Bush administration endorsed the Israeli plan heartily. The Secretary of State, Condoleezza Rice, underscored the point, telling reporters "It cannot be Gaza only." [21]

For many in Gaza, the withdrawal strengthened their resolve to destroy Israel. At a press conference, one Hamas gunman extolled "the choice of jihad, which caused Israel's security theory to fail." "We're going to keep our weapons," he added, "because the battle with the enemy is a long one." The imam at the Caliph Mosque in Gaza explained that Israel's withdrawal was "an achievement of resistance." He went on to praise notable "martyrs of Hamas" and stated that "Allah knows that when we offer up our children, it is much better than choosing the road of humiliation and negoti-ation." The spillover audience, sitting at nearby sidewalks and in alleyways, listened "with expressions alert and thoughtful."[22] By one reckoning, eight out of ten Palestinians (eighty-two percent) viewed the Israeli withdrawal from Gaza as a victory for the "armed struggle."[23]

Then, in January 2006, came Bush's so-called "forward strat-egy for freedom." Essentially, this was a modern-day crusade for democracy, that is, for unlimited majority rule. By its consistent application of this policy, the Bush administration held open the door and ushered the jihadists toward greater power.

The Bush team claimed that bringing democracy to the region was necessary for advancing U.S. security. The theory was that the establishment of Iraqi democracy in the "heart of the Middle East will be a watershed event in the global democratic revolu-tion." Building up a swell in the region, that revolutionary wave was supposed to sweep from Baghdad to Cairo, from Damascus to Tehran, from Beirut to the Palestinian territories.[24] This would happen, it was claimed, because everyone innately wants liberty ("I believe," Bush insisted, "that God has planted in every human heart the desire to live in freedom").[25] This notion was based on faith. To find counter-evidence for it, look at the endless sectarian wars of domination across the globe and, just in the Middle East, the recent ascent and wide popular support of Islamists. Essential to the democracy crusade was an evasion of the prevailing ideas in the Middle East, chiefly the embrace of Islamic totalitarian ideas.

When practiced faithfully, Bush's democracy crusade sowed chaos across the Middle East by empowering Islamists.

That's what happened in Lebanon. Through democratic elec-tions, Hezbollah joined the country's cabinet for the first time and gained control of two ministries.[26]

That's what happened in Egypt. Through democratic elections, the Muslim Brotherhood won eighty-eight seats (almost twenty percent of the total) in the country's assembly, and likely it could have even won more, had it fielded more candidates.[27]

That's what happened in Iraq. Through democratic elections, Iraqis brought to power a government intimately tied to the Islamist regime in Iran, which now exerts enormous power over the country.[28]

That's what happened in the Palestinian territories, too.

The warning signs were abundant. Many voices, across the U.S. political spectrum, raised objections about allowing Hamas to take part. Israel's prime minister warned against allowing Hamas to take part.[29] Prominent organizations such as the National Democratic Institute sounded a warning about Hamas's participation in elections.[30] On this issue, according to former Bush staffers, there was some dissent within the administration.[31] The Bush team, however, dismissed whatever misgivings were voiced.

On the premise that faith is always the solution, never the problem, Bush maintained, contrary to the evidence, that the yearning for liberty was universal; that all Palestinians wanted freedom; that they all wanted peace. Never mind the Palestinian movement's enduring goal. Never mind the movement's indoctrination of its subjects, across many years. For Bush it was unthinkable that some would admire, let alone embrace, the Islamist vision of Hamas—though clearly many did. It was unthinkable that some would turn their backs on the chance for freedom, peace, and prosperity—though many did. Bush exhorted Palestinians to choose new "leaders not compromised by terror."

They chose Hamas.

International monitors blessed the 2006 Palestinian legislative election as "free" and "fair." Turnout was high. But more: the margin was unambiguous. Running candidates under the banner of "Change and Justice," Hamas captured seventy-six seats out of one hundred and thirty-two.[32] It was a landslide.

By summer, the Islamists of Hamas, now galvanized as never before, teamed up with their Lebanese brothers-in-arms, Hezbollah, to initiate a rocket war against Israel. Behind Hamas and Hezbollah, stood their patron: the Iranian regime. The Hezbollah-Hamas-Iran axis managed to fight Israel for thirty-four days. Despite Israel's far greater military strength, the war ended in a stalemate. For members of this jihadist axis, getting to a stalemate was itself a kind of victory.

Within a year of Hamas's electoral landslide, as we saw in chapter four, Hamas had fought its rival Palestinian faction for control of the Gaza Strip, and it won. Then, from its stronghold in Gaza, Hamas and its allied Islamist factions launched rocket and mortar attacks on Israeli towns and cities. (All this, despite Washington's post-election "isolation" of Hamas and the supposedly air-tight Israeli naval blockade on Gaza.) To quell this rocket war, Israel deployed air and ground forces in Operation Cast Lead, or what became known simply as the Gaza War.

Welcome to Hamas-stan, a new Islamic totalitarian quasi-state on the Mediterranean, made possible by the Bush administration's evasion of what justice demands.

Episode Three. How We Got to Today

The rise of Hamas was part of a wider trend. It was unmistakable during George W. Bush's term in office; under Barack Obama, the ascendancy of Islamists became glaring. Leading that decades-spanning trend was the Islamist regime in Iran. Even as it raced to develop a nuclear program, Iran exerted massive influence not only in Iraq, but also in Lebanon, in Gaza, in Syria, in

Yemen, and in Afghanistan. By 2014, the Islamic State (or ISIS) erupted on the world stage. It conquered territory straddling Iraq and Syria, where it established a totalitarian regime under sharia. ISIS became synonymous with videos glorifying human slaughter (think crucifixions; beheadings; burning people to death). Exhibiting its global ambitions, the group was behind a string of deadly attacks in Paris, Brussels, Copenhagen, San Bernardino, Istanbul, Orlando, Nice, Manchester, Beirut.

It's a marker of the Islamic State's appeal—and the robust appeal of the Islamist cause generally—that it attracted tens of thousands of followers from across the Middle East. Even more remarkable, it attracted hundreds from Western nations. They freely chose to turn their backs on their friends, their families, their schooling, their jobs, their future in the world's freest, most prosperous countries. They flocked to live under, and fight for, the Islamic State.[33]

Thus by the mid 2010s, a movement led, inspired, and funded by Iran, Saudi Arabia, and the Gulf states; a movement hostile to reason, hostile to progress, hostile to individual freedom rampaged across the Middle East and far beyond.

If you were to take stock of the Middle East, and the Israeli-Palestinian conflict, at that time, two conclusions were unavoidable.

First, *the* headline story here was the rise of Islamists. To understand the wars, the slaughter, the human devastation convulsing the Middle East, and spilling out globally, you would have to look at the Islamist movement's malignant quest for religious conquest and domination. Thus, the Israeli-Palestinian conflict was now tightly enmeshed in a wider clash between free societies and Islamic totalitarianism.

And, second, with the growing need to confront Islamic totalitarianism, the interests of the United States and of Israel were now even more closely aligned. For American policy makers, then, a commitment to human life, freedom, and justice demanded that Washington stand firmly, vocally alongside Israel and against our common foe, the Islamists.

What, then, has been America's approach to the Israeli-Palestinian conflict (and the region) in the last decade?

Fundamental Misconceptions

On the campaign trail, Barack Obama had promised to depart from Bush's foreign policy, and the Obama administration (2009–2017) worked to live up to that pledge. Inheriting two ongoing wars, in Iraq and Afghanistan, Obama looked to undo what he regarded as errors and wrongs in America's Mideast policy. In the approach that he adopted, two premises were salient.

Like Bush, Obama held the premise that the Islamist movement was fundamentally driven by something other than its religious ideology. Of course the Islamists talked about religion, but that was a veneer for underlying, political and/or economic, motivations. This idea is reflected, for example, in the Obama administration's favored term to describe jihadists: "violent extremists"—a hopelessly broad term that bleached out the distinctive substance, the specific *ideas*, that animate the Islamist movement.

The other salient premise related to the nature of the Israeli-Palestinian conflict, and America's stake in it. For Obama, departing from Bush's policy, what was missing from the conflict was a balanced approach, and to restore that balance entailed greater American pressure on its ally, Israel.

We can see these premises play out in Obama's efforts to resolve the Israeli-Palestinian conflict, and in his approach to the Islamist movement, particularly in the diplomatic engagement with Iran. Combined, the effect of these premises was to shape a policy flagrantly in defiance of the requirements of justice.

Seeking "Balance" in the Israeli-Palestinian Conflict

Resolving the Israeli-Palestinian conflict was one of Obama's top priorities. In a major 2009 speech delivered in Cairo, Egypt, Obama explained: If "we see this conflict only from one side or the other, then we will be blind to the truth: the only resolution is for the aspirations of both sides to be met through two states, where Israelis and Palestinians each live in peace and security."[34] Sure, the Palestinians "must abandon violence," but we must recognize the devastation that Israel's occupation inflicts upon them. Thus "[p]rogress in the daily lives of the Palestinian people must be a critical part of a road to peace, and Israel must take concrete steps to enable such progress."[35]

"Balance," then, translates into evading the militant nature of the Palestinian cause and of Israel's character as a free society. The two sides, in other words, must be viewed as essentially morally equal. This pursuit of "balance" called for rebooting the peace process. The inbuilt logic of that policy, as we've seen, asks both sides to make concessions, but by the nature of the adversaries and their goals, any deal between them really amounts to Israeli appeasement of a hostile movement.

The need to pressure Israel to make concessions was inherent in the logic of the peace process, and it was underscored in Obama's diagnosis of a major obstacle to peace: Israel's building of "settlements." Thus, he stressed that the U.S. "does not accept the legitimacy of continued Israeli settlements," which undermine "efforts to achieve peace. It is time for these settlements to stop."[36] To restore "balance," therefore, America would have to pressure Israel to make (further) concessions to the Palestinian movement.

We've seen, in chapter three, that the term "settlements" packages together phenomena that are essentially dissimilar. Even if you came to the view that some, or even most, "settlements" are wrong, there's something deeply warped about giving such prominence to this aspect of the conflict. It implies that the chief problem is the building of apartment buildings, houses, factories, schools—and not the unrelenting, decades-long campaign led by Arab states and then by the Palestinian movement to liquidate a free society through conventional war, subversion, shootings, bombings, suicide attacks, rockets.

The Obama team's fixation on the settlements revealed a profound misconception about the nature of the conflict. And it led to a major, increasingly acrimonious rift between the United States and Israel—at a time when the two nation's interests were even more closely aligned.

"Linkage" and Another Blind Spot for Islamists

By 2014, the Obama administration's reboot of the peace process collapsed. That summer, the Islamists of Hamas launched yet another a rocket war against Israel (see chapter four). The war belied an assumption in Obama's approach: that Israel was a crucial source of strife, the obstacle to peace. Indeed, there's reason to think that this assumption stemmed from a wider perspective on the region, which illustrates the confluence of Obama's unfounded premise about what animates the Islamist movement and his warped view of the Israeli-Palestinian conflict.

Obama apparently subscribed to the view that the Israeli-Palestinian conflict is causally linked to the region's endless turmoil.[37] Solve this festering conflict, so the logic goes, and the Middle East's upheavals and strife will wind down, along with hostility toward the United States. This view, sometimes called "linkage," has been put forward in various forms by prominent figures in the diplomatic, military, and political communities.[38] In 2014 John

Kerry, the secretary of state, expressed a version of this notion of "linkage," extending it to the Islamist movement. Kerry had been dispatched to the Middle East to recruit an international coalition to help combat the growing menace of the Islamic State in Iraq and Syria. When he returned from that trip, Kerry told journalists that leaders across the Middle East assured him personally that the lack of Israeli-Palestinian peace was a cause of "recruitment and of street anger."[39]

By "recruitment," Kerry meant to the jihadist forces of the Islamic State, a salient faction within the wider jihadist movement. And by "street anger," he meant public hostility in the region about the unresolved Israeli-Palestinian conflict. Let's unpack these claims. For many in the region, the lack of a resolution to the conflict is bound up with hostility toward Israel, which is viewed as the problem, and toward the United States, because of its major role over many years in failed efforts to broker Israeli-Palestinian peace. This perspective integrated with the Obama administration's misconceptions about the conflict and the region's endless turmoil. Because of that, and because this kind of view about the causes of strife in the region commands wider endorsement, let's take a closer look at the two elements Kerry spotlighted, "street anger" and recruitment.

"Street Anger" and Anti-American Hostility?

What of the claim, which Kerry was hardly the first to voice, that the Israeli-Palestinian conflict fuels "street anger" at Israel and anti-American hostility?

If ever there were an opportunity to hear the so-called Arab street express itself—unfiltered, unmanipulated, and uncensored—we got it in the shape of the Arab Spring (which began in

2010/11). The popular upheavals in Tunisia, Egypt, Libya, Syria and elsewhere differed in each case, but they had at least one thing in common. It is what the crowds didn't say. "For anyone who spent time in [Cairo's] Tahrir Square these last three weeks," noted Thomas Friedman, "one thing was very obvious: Israel was not part of this story at all." The story, he noted, is about Egyptians seeking freedom, dignity, and justice.[40] To take another example: The rebels in Libya sought to eliminate the dictator Gen. Muammar el-Qaddafi, and many among them wanted an Islamist regime instead. When ordinary citizens from across the region, by the hundreds of thousands if not millions, vented their outrage, they demanded many different things. But—contrary to what Kerry's linkage viewpoint would lead us to expect—Israel was not part of the story.

Yet hostility toward Israel (and America) is a reality in the Middle East, and it's crucial to recognize what drives so much of it. You can see why theocrats, dictators and authoritarian leaders in the Mideast would seek to exploit the Israeli-Palestinian conflict for their own ends. Some distract their own victimized citizens by redirecting anger at Israel (a convenient scapegoat for the rest of the region's backwardness and poverty), and also its ally, the United States.

For decades, neighboring regimes harped on the Palestinian refugee issue, which they themselves exacerbated, to incite animosity toward Israel. More broadly, state-incited anti-Semitism and hostility toward Israel are commonplaces in the Middle East. For example, "The Protocols of the Elders of Zion" is a fictitious tract, originating in Russia in the early 1900s, that peddles a blatant conspiracy theory. It purports to outline the nefarious secret plans of a Jewish cabal to undermine the health, family life, and morality of non-Jews—on the path to world domination. And yet the "Protocols" have been included in the Jordanian school curriculum; the Saudi government has distributed free copies of the book to visitors and at embassies; Arab-language commentators invoke the tract (treating it as authentic) to explain cultural developments; television stations (both state-run stations and private ones with the blessing of state censors) have aired a big budget drama based on the "Protocols" (incidentally, the tract is cited not only in Hitler's *Mein Kampf* and in statements by various Nazi ideologues, but also in Hamas's founding document).[41] Egyptian news media often echo those themes. The Al Jazeera satellite TV network, owned by Qatar and exerting influence throughout the Middle East, is notorious for its pro-Islamist, anti-Israel news reporting.

The point, however, is that such enmity is commonly manufactured and sustained for ulterior purposes, irrespective of the truth and justice of the matter. Certainly such animosity matters, but what matters more are the dishonest, dictatorial regimes that peddle it. They also incite hatred of neighboring regimes on sectarian and political grounds (for example, Iran and Saudi Arabia constantly denounce each other as heretical).

If you want to isolate a core issue in the region, one that engenders hatred and enemies, look to the region's pre-Enlightenment political culture, with its inexorable power-lust, scapegoating, and vilification of outsiders, especially infidels. It is a feature of tyrannical regimes to foment hostility toward outsiders, not only toward Israel but also America. To the extent we regard the animosity they manufacture as a problem, the starting point for dealing with it is not by pandering to these regimes (by, say, coercing Israel to appease the Palestinian movement), but by recognizing their ploys and calling them on it.

Islamist Recruitment?

What about the claim that Islamic totalitarians leverage the Israeli-Palestinian conflict to recruit for jihad? Many do. It's easy for jihadists to frame the conflict as an egregious case of powerful infidels vs. the (underdog) followers of Allah. In an analysis of Al Qaeda texts spanning 1990 to 2002, the scholar Thomas Hegghammer found no less than one hundred and fifty-eight mentions of the word "Palestine." "Most al-Qaida recruitment videos, including the first such production from early 2001, include images from Palestine." The issue of "Palestine" is "all over al-Qaida's propaganda and has been so for over a decade." Assorted jihadists groups avidly exploit the Palestine issue.[42]

While the Palestine issue does actuate some, though certainly not all, jihadists, to understand the significance of that, you have to see it within the wider Islamist narrative. In that story there is a cosmic struggle for a "just" world, one subservient to religious dogma. The crux of that is the striving of the faithful (Islamists) against the unbelievers (impious Muslims, apostates, infidels, atheists; particularly in the West). Within that narrative framework, a great many issues and conflicts, apart from the Palestine issue, can actuate new recruits, who see themselves as part of a global Muslim community (or, "umma").

Here are a few emotional-ideological "buttons" that the Islamists push in order to galvanize, recruit, and draw them into the movement. The fight against the Soviet Union in Afghanistan, during the 1980s, attracted a significant influx of foreign holy warriors (Osama Bin Laden among them). The Bosnia conflict, during the 1990s, was another trigger, because Muslims were targeted. In his memoir Maajid Nawaz, a British former Islamist, recounts how seeing videos of Muslims being slaughtered in the

Bosnia conflict inflamed him. The victims were all strangers to him, but they belonged to a global Muslim community, and Nawaz felt impelled to fight for the redemption of his co-religionists.[43] The bond of collective religious solidarity was *that* strong. During the 2010s, the rise of Islamic State in Iraq and Syria proved an even more powerful magnet for international jihadists. And one perennial trigger is sectarianism among jihadist groups.

The common factor here is the specifically Islamist narrative that frames the worldview of recruits, manipulating their emotions. They are primed to feel a powerful solidarity with co-religionists throughout the world and to regard anything short of an all-encompassing Islamist regime as a metaphysical injustice that they must fight to rectify.

In the case of the "Palestine" issue, the basic concern of Islamists is not any political grievance about Israeli borders, land-use policy, or alleged oppression of particular individuals. They demand not freedom and prosperity for Palestinians (or anyone else), but submission: Islamists seek to enslave the world under Allah's laws. Their doctrine is specifically hostile to individual rights. There's no policy that Israel can change that would make the "Palestine" issue unattractive to jihadist recruits. Only conquering Israel and raising the flag of Islamic totalitarianism over Palestine and Jerusalem could satisfy them, temporarily.

The fundamental problem here is not that the Israeli-Palestinian conflict is unresolved; the problem is a movement fueled by the boundless ambition to realize the vision of Islamic totalitarianism.

When we step back from examining Kerry's claims about "street anger" and recruitment, it's clear that this perspective negates the available evidence. The upshot is twofold. It downplays—indeed, it trivializes—the actual, ideological-political drivers of the region's turmoil in general and of the Israeli-Palestinian conflict in particular.

At the same time, it denigrates Israel: it implies that, because Israel stubbornly denies the Palestinians their political aspirations, there's continued fighting, which spills beyond their borders.

This helps to make sense of the Obama administration's messianic push to reboot the Israeli-Palestinian peace talks, its fixation on settlements, and its fierce pressure on Israel to make concessions. (The Obama administration underscored that view in December 2016 by taking the historic step of abstaining from a U.N. Security Council resolution condemning Israeli settlements. Unopposed by the U.S., with its decisive influence, the resolution was adopted.[44])

Enabling the Standard Bearer of the Jihad

The Obama administration's other major priority was to achieve a *rapprochement* with Iran. For six years, this diplomatic goal was a centerpiece of Obama's Mideast policy. The Islamist regime, remember, was not only a patron and ammunition supplier of Hamas in its several wars on Israel; Iran was, and remains, a standard bearer of the Islamist cause. And in the dogged pursuit of a diplomatic engagement with the Iranian regime, we can see a manifestation of the Obama administration's (fallacious) premise that Islamists are animated fundamentally by something other than their religious doctrine.

That's what informed the logic of the Iran nuclear deal. Sure, the Iranian regime calls us the "Great Satan" and works to export its Islamic revolution globally, but ultimately they don't really mean it. If offered the right package of "carrots," they'll drop their long-term agenda and abide by the terms of the agreement. To make this diplomatic venture seem plausible, you have to adopt a fractured view of Iran, one that dissolves Iran's defining ideological character.

That means adopting a myopic perspective that treats the actions of Iran in isolation, as if carried out by distinct, firewalled personalities that happen to coexist in the same regime. Iran's drive for nuclear capability (officially: for civilian purposes!) reflects one personality. Iran's pervasive violation of individual rights domestically? That's another. How about its ongoing backing of jihadist groups? Still another. What about Iran's quest for regional domination? Yet another, dissociated personality. The logic of this fractured perspective means that we must handle each personality separately, divorced from any wider context. From this myopic perspective, there's no wider ideological agenda uniting Iran's actions.

Even though the Obama approach was predicated on negating Iran's essentially ideological nature, the Tehran regime continued to provide constant, unmistakable illustrations of its theocratic character.

Take one incident, just six months into Obama's first term. Recall, back in chapter two, that we looked at the massive street demonstrations that took place after Iran's 2009 elections. The clerics in Iran have led crowds in chants of "death to America" for 30-plus years, but here we saw spontaneous protests against the regime itself, with crowds reportedly shouting "death to the dictator" and "death to Khamenei."[45] In a regime predicated on the supremacy of clerical rule, these protesters were, in effect, challenging the legitimacy of Iran's theocracy. The protestors risked death at the hands of regime-backed militia sent to crush them.

In the U.S. reaction to these protests, we can observe yet another way in which the Obama approach flouted the demands of justice. The United States had ample reason to encourage the implosion of the Islamist regime in Tehran. For more than thirty years, that regime has conducted a proxy war against us, it has the blood of hundreds of Americans on its hands, and it is actively pursuing nuclear capability. (In my book *Winning the Unwinnable*

War, I describe the nature of Iran's militant campaign against us and the regime's centrality to the jihadist cause.[46]) When Iranians themselves marched in protest, seeking to remove from power their theocratic oppressors, we faced a prime opportunity to provide (at least) moral support to those brave protestors. If successful, their efforts could have brought to power a non-hostile regime, and drastically reduced the threat to American lives.

What did Obama do? Muttered a few words, belatedly, about being "appalled and outraged." Then we flouted even that perfunctory rhetoric. By reaffirming that "the United States respects the sovereignty" of Iran, we endorsed the regime.[47] We then continued our diplomatic outreach to coax Tehran, stained with fresh blood, to enter into talks over its nuclear program. What about the tens of thousands of Iranians who stuck their necks out? What about those who hoped for a future under a government that protects even a modicum of freedom?

The Obama administration went on to certify Iran's (undeserved) legitimacy in the nuclear deal of 2015. Whatever you might think of that controversial accord, it has resulted in a flow of money into Iran. Ennobled on the international stage and enriched financially, the ayatollahs are now better able to tyrannize their own population and to arm Hamas, Hezbollah, and a host of other jihadists.[48]

Evading the demands of justice, the Obama administration's approach literally enabled a brutal theocracy, with American blood on its hands, at the center of the Islamist movement.

A Wider Pattern: Selling Out Good People, Encouraging Monsters

There's a larger point here. The brave souls in Iran who risked so much to protest against their own oppression; the individuals living under Hamas and the Palestinian Authority who reject the militant cause that purports to fight in their name (however few now remain); the Egyptians genuinely seeking freedom in Tahrir Square; the subjects of Saudi Arabia, and neighboring tyrannies, who yearn to live in a free society; the many Israelis who seek to live unmolested in the region's only free society: all of them are innocent victims, deserving of our concern and support. How does U.S. policy treat them?

It sells them out.

On this point Barack Obama conformed to a wider pattern in America's approach to the Israeli-Palestinian conflict in particular and the Middle East in general. Our leaders, for all their differences, have long negated the demands of justice. They do not merely disregard the principle of freedom, but sell it short. They fail properly to recognize Israel's virtue, its singular character as a free society amid a hellscape of dictatorships, theocracies and rampaging jihadists. Clinton, Bush, Obama, and now Trump all treat Egypt, Lebanon, Jordan, the Gulf Monarchies, and Saudi Arabia as genuine allies. Even though Trump took the sensible, overdue step of recognizing Jerusalem as Israel's capital, he has also welcomed Egypt's president Abdel Fattah al-Sisi at the White House. He even praised Sisi for doing a "fantastic job" and reassured the military dictator that he has a "great friend and ally in the United States and in me."[49] And Trump's first foreign trip began with a visit to Saudi Arabia, where he (like Obama, like Bush) bowed in deference to the king, accepting from him a gilded necklace and medal. Not once did Trump utter a peep about the absence of individual freedom in the religious monarchy or its connection to the Islamist movement.[50]

Iran has been something of an outlier in this U.S. embrace of Mideast tyrannies, but only temporarily. In the 1990s, President Bill Clinton worked hard to woo the ayatollahs, even brushing aside Iranian attacks on American soldiers in Saudi Arabia, and brushing aside the regime's massacre of student protesters, just to win the ayatollahs over.[51] George W. Bush—without deliberate irony—invited Iran to join a post-9/11 coalition against "terrorism"; then he temporarily tagged Tehran as part of an "axis of evil" before rapidly dropping that phrase, and spending the waning years of his administration coaxing the Iranians to the negotiating table. It was Obama who managed that feat, which served to strengthen and enrich Iran's theocratic regime.

If you live in Egypt, Saudi Arabia, Iran, or some other Mideast tyranny, if you value your life and freedom, if you want the chance to define your own path in life, set and reach your own goals, take the steps necessary to realize your personal vision of a thriving life—what would you think of American Mideast policy?

Washington often undercuts and bashes the only free country in your midst. When a minority of people across the Middle East rise up demanding greater freedom—demanding, in effect, that their countries emulate Israel—Washington holds them in contempt. Meanwhile, it whitewashes such monsters as Arafat, awards him the laurels of a peacemaker, and gives him the throne of a new kingdom. When Washington launches a democracy crusade—misleadingly touted as a "forward strategy for freedom"— predictably it is the jihadists who win big, and everybody else loses; the few who actually understand and yearn for freedom lose the most. And for decades, Washington grovels to buy the love of the leading Islamist regime, Iran, which publicly denounces us as its chief enemy, wages holy war against us and our allies, and lusts to subjugate the Middle East under its totalitarian rule.

All of that has a considerable, vastly under-appreciated impact. Even more than any material advantages that we've given the jihadists, it is the ugly spectacle of our moral weakness that galvanizes them. That dynamic is crucial to understanding the region's chaos and the boldness of our enemies. America's conduct in the region works like a flare. From all directions and across vast distances, our conduct signals to our adversaries the seriousness of our commitment to our values and our allies. Leaders in the region, especially Islamists, are acutely sensitive to those signals. The merest whiff that America turns away from its friends and its own interests, and our enemies (rightly) interpret that as weakness.

We've given them much more than a whiff. America's unjust policy has sold out our ally Israel—along with genuinely free-dom-seeking individuals across the region—while enabling, strengthening, and empowering our enemies. Our flagrant moral weakness encourages them in the belief that their faith-based doctrine is somehow viable, that Allah has their back against the materially stronger but spiritually corrupt infidels. Osama Bin Laden, Ayatollah Khomeini of Iran, and sundry other Isla-mist leaders have rallied their followers and recruited new ones by pointing to American cowardice and inconstancy. America's amoral, unprincipled approach to the region and the Israeli-Pales-tinian conflict has played directly into their hands.

The disastrous mess that passes for American policy in the Middle East is an object lesson. It illustrates what comes from disregarding the moral difference between freedom and tyranny. Our policy across decades has demoralized, subverted, and weak-ened the good while enabling, strengthening, and empowering monsters. Because it is unjust, our policy hurts us.

What's Needed to Resolve the Israeli-Palestinian Conflict?

Some people no longer ask "*What* is the solution?" but rather "Is this conflict solvable?"

If you start with the premises currently shaping American foreign policy, then, yes, the Israeli-Palestinian conflict must appear unsolvable. The conventional solutions must all seem futile, because they are. What's more, they have exacerbated the conflict. But the widely held premises shaping our approach are false. If we repudiate those premises, and if we instead embrace the principle of justice, then the Israeli-Palestinian conflict becomes *solvable*.

Let me describe four necessary first steps on the path to a truly just resolution.

1. Recognize the conflict's ideological nature.

Contrary to the views and premises shaping America's approach, the drivers of the Israeli-Palestinian conflict are deep-seated. Fundamentally, the conflict has persisted not because Palestinians lack a sovereign state, nor because of "settlements," nor because of various other political grievances. Instead, the conflict has been fueled by—and reflects—the region's ideological currents and pathologies. We've seen Arab states wage war on Israel at its founding in 1948 for their own self-aggrandizement. Later, Gamal Abdel Nasser and his Arab nationalist allies led the charge, with another unsuccessful war in 1967. Then emerged the Palestinian Liberation Organization. Now jihadists are at the vanguard. The common theme here is a clash between a free society and regimes and ideological movements that are hostile to freedom and contemptuous of human life.

What would it take for Palestinians, now subject to the Palestinian Authority or Hamas rule, to reach a bright future, freedom, prosperity? Lots of time and a willingness to be self-critical, because they first need to undertake some fundamental cultural-ideological changes.

Palestinians need to uproot the perverse values and ideas that, like virulent weeds, strangle their culture. They ought to adopt and nurture the universal values that enable human flourishing. Indeed, the entire region needs precisely that kind of cultural change. Imagine if, for the sake of lifting themselves out of their poverty and backwardness, the people of the region embraced the political ideal of freedom; if they turned their minds wholeheartedly toward embracing secular learning and science; if they recognized the fundamental equality of men and women; if they oriented their thought and culture toward an acceptance of the irreplaceable value of an individual human life.

We can imagine a day when the Middle East, and Palestinian society in particular, has reoriented itself in precisely these ways. That's a future to be hoped for. To get there, however, these communities must first reject their destructive ideas and values and leaders.

2. Step away from the two-state solution and the diplomatic initiative designed to reach that outcome.

Because the conflict is fundamentally ideological, and because the region's political-institutional climate is geared toward domination and conquest, it is a fatal mistake to expect that the remedy lies simply in establishing a Palestinian state (nor can such a polity's failures be fixed through further elections). So it's correct, if overly charitable, to say that the Oslo peace process was premature. It was, and remains, premature—by several generations. Contrary to the assumptions underpinning that diplomatic venture, you can evade the moral difference between the adversaries, you can launder the guilty, you can blacken the name of the good; but nothing can alter the facts. The plain truth is the Palestinian movement never renounced its goal of overthrowing Israel. The peace process had to aid killers and harm Israel.

The conventional view holds, albeit with plummeting enthusiasm, that the only sensible outcome for the conflict is a two-state solution. But we must reject that article of faith, because (as we've seen) it negates the fundamental moral inequality between the adversaries. This approach assumes that Palestinian demands for statehood are on their face legitimate. What's left open to debate is only how to resuscitate the peace negotiations, who's to blame for the obstacles on the road, and what America's role should be.

Those assumptions make no sense. No one who understands the nature and aims of the Palestinian movement can take seriously the idea of rebooting the peace talks. No individual, no group of individuals, no self-identified national community has the moral right to create a tyrannical regime, whether dictatorial or theocratic. Yet that is the kind of state that the leaders of the Palestinian movement would create. And, fundamentally, there are no genuine Palestinian grievances—those involving the infringement of individual rights—that are even partly remedied by the wholesale violation of rights under a Palestinian tyranny.

While in many of its statements and aims American policy has been supportive of Israel, the effects of our unprincipled approach have been destructive. By our support of the Palestinian Authority (through foreign aid) and, indirectly the Gaza regime of Hamas (through "humanitarian" relief), we enabled two vicious, militant regimes that trample on the individual rights of their subjects and that imperil the lives and freedom of Israelis.

We should, therefore, withdraw not only our financial support, but more crucially, our moral backing of the Palestinian movement's goal of a fully sovereign state.

3. Judge according to the objective moral standard of freedom.

It is not only America's approach toward the Israeli-Palestinian conflict that is unprincipled. Washington has a sordid tradition of condoning, abetting, and bolstering the region's authoritarians, dictators, theocrats. There's a lot that we need to change in our approach to the region, far more than we can cover here. But one necessary step forward, in the region and specifically in the Israeli-Palestinian conflict, is to judge all regimes, all ideological movements, all political groups. We need to judge them by the objective moral standard of freedom—and act accordingly. Without exception, across time.

Which means continually evaluating allies and enemies (and everyone in between). Our judgments must be grounded in empirical evidence, and subject to revision when new facts warrant a different conclusion.

No relationship or alliance can be exempt from such moral scrutiny. Let me indicate just three examples. We must end the pretense that Egypt is anything but a military dictatorship that exploits and brutalizes its people. We must end the pretense that Saudi Arabia is an ally; we must recognize that it is a vicious regime predicated on a strain of Islamic totalitarianism. We must end the pretense that Iran is a normal regime with which we can enter into diplomatic agreements. In reality, it is a committed enemy of the United States and a standard-bearer of the Islamist cause, seeking to exert its dominion far and wide.

4. Stand alongside Israel and against our common enemies.

We should endorse the side that upholds freedom. We ought to stand with Israel and everyone else in the region genuinely seeking freedom—uncompromisingly, resolutely, vocally. Such moral support is far more consequential than most people imagine. It also entails supporting Israel's defeat of our common enemy, not only the dictatorial elements of the Palestinian movement, but also, and especially, the jihadists. Inflicting a morale-crushing blow to the jihadist cause would have wider impact.

The essential goal is to render the Palestinian movement non-threatening. For years Israel has pursued an appeasing policy, and it has done so with Washington's stern, at times shrill, urging and endorsement. The result was to encourage the worst, most militant elements within the Palestinian movement in their war-making. This pattern must end. How can the Palestinian movement be made non-threatening? That's largely a policy question, and you could come up with various means of achieving that goal. The scholar Daniel Pipes has outlined a compelling case that can be summed up as: "Israeli victory, then peace."

At the root of the Pipes plan is a historical lesson: wars end decisively when one side is compelled to accept defeat.[52]

Twentieth-century conflicts that ended decisively include World War II, China-India, Algeria-France, North Vietnam-United States, Great Britain-Argentina, Afghanistan-U.S.S.R., and the Cold War. Defeat can result either from a military thrashing or from an accretion of economic and political pressures; it does not require total military loss or economic destruction, much less the annihilation of a population. For example, the only defeat in U.S. history, in South Vietnam in 1975, occurred not because of economic collapse or running out of ammunition or battlefield failure (the American side was winning the ground war) but because Americans lost the will to soldier on.[53]

To accept defeat does not mean to take a pause in fighting, while nursing the hope of winning the next round. It means undergoing a profound mind-shift. It means giving up on one's militant goals. For good. More than merely deploying tough tactics, Pipes's approach would entail long-term, "systemic policies that encourage Palestinians to accept Israel and discourage" their rejection of it. To defeat the Palestinian movement entails inducing a profound, lasting change of heart among the followers and supporters of that movement. The Pipes plan, which I've sketched only briefly, has a lot to recommend it; you can read about it in the articles I cite in the endnotes. The wider point is that the goal is to reach the day when followers of the Palestinian movement give up on their desire to liquidate Israel, when they feel defeated, when they put down their knives and suicide belts and rocket launchers, when they accommodate themselves to Israel's continued existence. History teaches us, as Pipes observes, that you make peace with *"enemies that have been defeated."*[54]

Once the Palestinian movement no longer blights the region, there will be a great many detailed issues and questions to sort out (such as the legal status of the population formerly under the Palestinian Authority and Hamas; what to do with the remnants of their quasi states; when or if to incorporate territories formerly under their control). Many of those questions and challenges intersect Israeli domestic policy, and in that post-conflict future, the people best placed to deal with those issues are the people closest to them, not the United States.

Israel is morally entitled to defeat our common enemy, and we ought to encourage and enable it to succeed in pursuit of victory. The goal of victory, however, does not require that Israel's defeated enemies become its admirers or friends. They just need to feel deterred, permanently, from taking up arms against it.

For Palestinians, however, the experience of defeat could open the door to a better future. For the more militant, it could foster in some of them a willingness to rethink the values and cultural ideas that have caused them so much misery, and adopt the rational values and ideas that enable individual freedom and thriving. And for those who have truly desired freedom, it would give them a chance to rise without fear of being attacked and silenced.

It is only in that kind of future—after the Palestinian movement is defeated, after a new generation or two have arisen in opposition to that movement's animating goal—that it would make sense to ask whether there should exist a new state alongside Israel, for a population that defines itself as Palestinian. They would have to demonstrate that their freedom would be best protected under such a new sovereign state—certainly, a difficult standard to meet—and they would be responsible for building, funding, and maintaining it. That's conceivable, in a thought-experiment sort of way, and it would be reasonable only in a future where the Palestinian community has re-oriented itself toward rational ideals.

Conclusion

The theme of this book is that, if we understand justice properly, we should be supportive of Israel—on principle. To act on that conclusion, however, entails a fundamental re-orientation. It requires questioning assumptions and moral premises that are widespread in our culture—and instead embracing a rational alternative.

That is the choice we face. Either we stay on the path that leads to more of the same, if not worse; the path that continues to empower vicious regimes and movements, the path that sells out the region's freedom-seeking individuals. Or, we take a different path. This new path entails upholding our own moral-political ideals. It entails strengthening our ally and encouraging all those seeking to advance freedom, while combatting our common foes.

It's either/or. The attempt to avoid taking a moral stand, the recourse to some middle ground of moral neutrality, is itself a stand. The belief that you can skirt moral judgment is illusory. Worse, the practice of disregarding moral judgment is itself corrupting of our thinking and action. It can only undermine us, our interests, and our allies. On this point, the philosopher Ayn Rand offers a timeless insight.

> [M]oral neutrality necessitates a progressive sympathy for vice and a progressive antagonism to virtue. A man who struggles not to acknowledge that evil is evil, finds it increasingly dangerous to acknowledge that the good is the good. To him, a person of virtue is a threat that can topple all of his evasions—particularly when an issue of justice is involved, which demands that he take sides. It is then that such formulas as "Nobody is ever fully right or fully wrong" and "Who am I to judge?" take their lethal effect. The man who begins by saying: "There is some good in the worst of us," goes on to say: "There is some bad in the best of us"—then: "There's *got to* be some bad in the best of us"—and then: "It's the best of us who make life difficult—why don't they keep silent?"—who are *they* to judge."[55]

The path we've traveled is leading us toward precisely that kind of moral bankruptcy. The longer we stay on that path, the more it distances us from objective judgment, the more it hampers our ability to define and achieve our interests.

We need to change direction, now.

We know what's at stake in the Israeli-Palestinian conflict. We know the moral character of the adversaries. We know the price of negating moral judgment: our persistently unjust policy has undercut Israel's moral standing and our own regional interests, while empowering our enemies.

Let us, finally, take seriously what justice demands.

ADDITIONAL RESOURCES

For additional resources, such as maps, videos, interviews, articles, and a timeline of events mentioned in the book, please see: elanjourno.com/resources/

ACKNOWLEDGMENTS

I wish to express my profound thanks to Onkar Ghate, senior fellow and chief content officer at the Ayn Rand Institute. For nearly two decades, I've benefited from working alongside Onkar, who is a brilliant scholar of Ayn Rand's philosophy. Partly through Onkar's courses, partly through the example of his own writing, partly through his editing of my work, Onkar has influenced my thinking and writing in more ways than I can enumerate. Onkar has provided extensive, in-depth, and enlightening feedback on my work, thus pushing me to grow intellectually.

Onkar was my editor on this book. Onkar and I discussed the book's outline and basic argument on several occasions, and he commented on numerous drafts at various stages of development. His editorial comments and guidance on how to approach crucial philosophic points were invaluable. His feedback on successive drafts led me to think more deeply about the intended audience, reframe key issues, delimit the book's theme, and bring out the over-arching logic. Without his far-reaching role in the project, this book would have been far less effective in articulating its message.

The idea for a book on this subject originated some years ago, in a conversation I had with Yaron Brook, chairman of ARI's board of directors. Across many years, Yaron and I worked together on several projects related to the topic of this book, a collaboration that I look back on fondly and with gratitude. During that time I learned a great deal from Yaron, and this book reflects his indelible influence on me.

When I began the early research for the book, Debi Ghate, who was then at ARI, recognized the project's value. She encouraged me to pursue it and enabled me to devote time to it.

I'm especially grateful to several friends and colleagues who provided feedback on drafts of the book at different stages of its development: Keith Lockitch, Steve Simpson, Greg Salmieri, Asaf Romirowsky, Amit Ghate, Amesh Adalja, Samantha Goodman, and Maryah Haidery. Their thoughtful observations, criticism, counter-arguments, and questions helped me improve the finished product. (Needless to say, the book reflects my viewpoint, and they may or may not agree with the finished product.)

For helping me locate and compile some research materials, I want to thank Carl Svanberg, Kevin Douglas, Jordan McGillis, Alexander Hutton, Logan Holden, Rebecca Girn, Isabella Morales, Dakin Sloss, and Cristian Reyes.

In many ways, small and large, I benefited from the advice, experience, and assistance of a number of friends and colleagues: Boaz Arad, Julie Ferguson, Rachel Knapp, Duane Knight, Rikki Nedelkow, Jason Bateman, Lew Hendrickson, Richard Ralston, Aaron Smith, Benjamin Weingarten, Sara Leopold Spinnell, Christine Locke, Jim Brown, Peter Schwartz, Jeri Eagan, and Tara Smith.

Thomas Bowden brought a keen eye and deft touch to copy-editing parts of the manuscript. Amanda Maxham was a great help when I was checking the accuracy of certain data points in the manuscript. Donna Montrezza helped with the proofreading of some of the early chapters. Thanks to Stephen Reich for his design work on the maps that appear in this book. I'm grateful to Michael Wilson, Maddie Sturgeon, and the rest of the team at Post Hill Press for their help getting the book into print.

Finally, I'm thankful for the support of my family. My late mother was perennially encouraging. To my brother Ronen, who was a pillar of strength at a dark time for our family, I owe a debt of thanks I can never repay. And I am grateful to my extended family of nieces, nephews, brothers-, sisters-, and parents-in-law, for their help and encouragement. I wish to thank my children, Calista and Tristan, for enriching my life every day, and above all, my wife Lindsay, for her insightful comments on the book, for her buoyant spirit, and for her loving support.

• • •

Special thanks are due to the many individuals whose financial contributions fund the work of the Ayn Rand Institute. Speaking for all of us at ARI, I'm grateful for their continuous support of our mission, and for sharing our vision for the future. In the case of this book, I wish to especially recognize the support of Carl Barney and Alberto Peisach, without whom this project would not have been possible.

ENDNOTES

INTRODUCTION

1   It is also known by other names, notably the Islamic State in Iraq and the Levant (ISIL) and Daesh. To avoid confusion, we'll refer to the group as the Islamic State and ISIS for short.

2   In January 2015, Peter Neumann of the International Centre for the Study of Radicalisation put the total number of foreign fighters at 20,730, which surpasses the total who are believed to have entered Afghanistan to wage holy war during the 1980s. Peter R. Neumann, "Foreign Fighter Total in Syria/Iraq Now Exceeds 20,000; Surpasses Afghanistan Conflict in the 1980s," ICSR (2015), icsr.info/2015/01/foreign-fighter-total-syriairaq-now-exceeds-20000-surpasses-afghanistan-conflict-1980s. (Among the fighters who went to Afghanistan was Osama bin Laden.) By December 2015, The Soufan Group estimated the worldwide total to be between 27,000 and 31,000. The Soufan Group, *Foreign Fighters: An Updated Assessment of the Flow of Foreign Fighters Into Syria and Iraq*, soufangroup.com/wp-content/uploads/2015/12/TSG_ForeignFightersUpdate1.pdf.

3   Rick Noack, "Here's How the Islamic State Compares with Real States," *Washington Post*, Sept. 12, 2014, washingtonpost.com/news/worldviews/wp/2014/09/12/heres-how-the-islamic-state-compares-to-real-states/.

4   John Kerry, "Remarks at a Reception in Honor of Eid al-Adha," Oct. 16, 2014, 2009-2017.state.gov/secretary/remarks/2014/10/233058.htm.

5   See for example the discussion in Thomas Hegghammer and Joas Wagemakers, "The Palestine Effect: The Role of Palestinians in the Transnational Jihad Movement," *Die Welt des Islams* 53, no. 3-4 (2013). We'll return to this issue in chapter six.

6   We return to this issue in chapter six. Regarding Ban Ki Moon, see for example: Herb Keinon, "'Israel-Palestinian Conflict Is Key,'" *Jerusalem Post*, Jan. 01, 2007, jpost.com/International/Israel-Palestinian-conflict-is-key. See also The Iraq Study Group Report, 2007. Regarding Jimmy Carter, see for example: Nathan Gardels, "Jimmy Carter Takes on Israel's Apartheid Policies and the Pro-Israeli Lobby in the U.S." *Huffington Post*, Dec. 12, 2006, huffingtonpost.com/nathan-gardels/

jimmy-carter-takes-on-isr_b_36134.html?view=print. Regarding Petraeus and Mattis, see *Pathways to Peace: America and the Arab-Israeli Conflict*, ed. Daniel C Kurtzer (New York: Palgrave Macmillan, 2012), 4.

7   Barack Obama, "Remarks in Cairo," Jun. 4, 2009, online by Gerhard Peters and John T. Woolley, *The American Presidency Project*, presidency.ucsb.edu/ ws/?pid=86221.

8   Pew Research Center, "Public Divided over Whether Israel, Independent Palestinian State Can Coexist" (Washington, D.C., 2014), 4, people-press.org/files/ legacy-pdf/4-29-14%20Israel-Palestinians%20Release.pdf.

9   78 percent of white evangelicals voted for Bush; 81 percent for Trump. See "Election 2016: Exit Polls," *New York Times*, Nov. 8, 2016, nytimes.com/interactive/2016/11/08/ us/politics/election-exit-polls.html; see also Sarah Pulliam Bailey, "White Evangelicals Voted Overwhelmingly for Donald Trump, Exit Polls Show," *Washington Post*, Nov. 9, 2016, washingtonpost.com/news/acts-of-faith/wp/2016/11/09/ exit-polls-show-white-evangelicals-voted-overwhelmingly-for-donald-trump/.

10 John Hagee, *In Defense of Israel: The Bible's Mandate for Supporting the Jewish State* (Lake Mary, FL: FrontLine, 2007), 84.

11 Hagee, *Defense of Israel*, 111.

12 Hagee, *Defense of Israel*, 58.

CHAPTER 1

1   Isabel Kershner, "Scarlett Johansson and Oxfam, Torn Apart by Israeli Company Deal," *New York Times*, Jan. 30, 2014, nytimes.com/2014/01/31/ world/middleeast/scarlett-johansson-and-oxfam-torn-apart-by-israeli -company-deal.html; see also Scarlett Johansson, "Clearing the Air," *Huffington Post*, Jan. 24, 2014, huffingtonpost.com/scarlett-johansson/sodastream _b_4661895.html.

2   For example: One commission within the vast United Nations bureaucracy (a commission composed of Arab states, most of which do not recognize Israel's legitimacy) published a report in 2017 portraying Israel as an "apartheid" regime. The U.N.'s secretary general, however, disavowed the report, which was later withdrawn. See Rick Gladstone and Somini Sengupta, "U.N. Diplomat Behind Report Accusing Israel of Apartheid Quits," *New York Times*, Mar. 17, 2017, nytimes. com/2017/03/17/world/middleeast/un-rima-khalaf-quits-israel-apartheid.html.

3   See, for example, the attempts to endorse the BDS agenda within the Modern Language Association, one of the largest academic societies in the humanities. Ultimately, MLA members ended up rejecting that agenda in a 2017 vote. Scholars for Peace in the Middle East, a nonprofit organization of academics, reports on and analyzes the campaign for boycotts, sanctions and divestment. See: spme. org.

4   Orin Kerr, "Free Speech on Campus: Michael Oren at UC Irvine," *Volokh Conspiracy* (blog), Feb. 12, 2010, volokh.com/2010/02/12/free-speech-on-campus-michael -oren-at-uc-irvine/.

5   In the first 10 years since its establishment, June 2006 to June 2016, the UN Human Rights Council adopted 134 resolutions criticizing countries, 68 of those

targeted Israel. "The UN and Israel: Key Statistics from UN Watch," Aug. 23, 2016, unwatch.org/un-israel-key-statistics/. The tally in 2017: unwatch.org/2017-unga-resolutions-singling-israel/. See also, May Bulman, "Ban Ki-moon Says UN Has 'Disproportionate' Focus on Israel," *Independent*, Dec. 17, 2016. independent. co.uk/news/world/middle-east/ban-ki-moon-united-nations-disproportionate-israel-focus-resolutions-palestinians-human-rights-danny-a7481961.html

6   Richard Goldstone, *Report of the United Nations Fact-Finding Mission on the Gaza-Conflict* (New York: United Nations, 2009), 13.

7   The Goldstone Report was replete with factual errors, politicized distortions, and an uncritical willingness to take Hamas claims at face value. Nearly a year and a half later, Richard Goldstone publicly retracted some of the report's most egregious claims; tellingly, however, the other U.N. team members unapologetically rejected the need to revise, let alone retract, the report. See Peter Berkowitz, *Israel and the Struggle over the International Laws of War* (Stanford, CA: Hoover Institution Press, 2012), and also my review of that book in *Journal of International Security Affairs* (Fall/Winter 2012), reprinted in *Failing to Confront Islamic Totalitarianism* (ARI Press, 2016).

8   Rashid Khalidi is much more than a sympathizer or surrogate for the Palestinian cause. There's strong evidence that he held a significant role in the movement, serving for a time as a spokesman for the Palestinian Liberation Organization in Lebanon. See Asaf Romirowsky, "Arafat Minion as Professor," *Washington Times*, Jul. 8, 2004, washingtontimes.com/news/2004/jul/8/20040708-083635-4366r/; and Martin Kramer, "Khalidi of the PLO," *Sandbox*, Oct. 30, 2008, martinkramer.org/sandbox/2008/10/khalidi-of-the-plo/.

9   Rashid Khalidi, "Collective Punishment in Gaza." *New Yorker*, Jul. 29, 2014, newyorker.com/news/news-desk/collective-punishment-gaza.

10 The diplomat was Daniel Bernard. "'Anti-Semitic' French Envoy Under Fire," *BBC News*, Dec. 20, 2001, news.bbc.co.uk/1/hi/1721172.stm.

11 In chapter four, we will apply the same framework in evaluating the Palestinian Authority, an interim political body that was meant to develop into a state.

12 Ian Black, "A Look at the Writings of Saudi Blogger Raif Badawi—Sentenced to 1,000 Lashes," *Guardian*, Jan. 14, 2015, theguardian.com/world/2015/jan/14/-sp-saudi-blogger-extracts-raif-badawi.

13 Robin Wright, "A Saudi Whipping," *New Yorker*, Jan. 9, 2015, newyorker.com/news/news-desk/saudi-whipping. This punishment, it's worth noting, also reflected three months for the crime of parental disobedience, stemming from the fact that for some years Badawi argued publicly with his father. Keep in mind that Badawi, well into his thirties, is a married man with three children of his own.

14 Wright, "A Saudi Whipping."

15 Ben Hubbard, "Artist's Death Sentence Follows a String of Harsh Punishments in Saudi Arabia," *New York Times*, Nov. 22, 2015, nytimes.com/2015/11/23/world/middleeast/saudi-artists-death-sentence-follows-a-string-of-harsh-punishments.html; David Batty and Mona Mahmoud, "Palestinian Poet Ashraf Fayadh's Death Sentence Quashed by Saudi Court," *Guardian*, Feb. 2, 2016,

theguardian.com/world/2016/feb/02/palestinian-poet-ashraf-fayadhs-death
-sentence-overturned-by-saudi-court.

16   Hubbard, "Artist's Death Sentence." According to data compiled by The Cornell
     Center on the Death Penalty Worldwide, in Saudi Arabia there were at least 100
     executions in 2017; 153 in 2016; and 158 in 2015; deathpenaltyworldwide.org.

17   Cf. Ahmed Vahdat, "Prominent Iranian Cartoonist Arrested," *Telegraph*, Nov.
     17, 2015, telegraph.co.uk/news/worldnews/middleeast/iran/12001783/Promi-
     nent-Iranian-cartoonist-arrested.html.

18   Rose Troup Buchanan, "Iranian Blogger Found Guilty of Insulting Prophet
     Mohammad on Facebook Sentenced to Death," *Independent*, Sep. 18, 2014,
     independent.co.uk/news/world/middle-east/iranian-blogger-found-guilty-of
     -insulting-prophet-mohammad-on-facebook-sentenced-to-death-9741572.
     html. "Facebook Activist Sentenced to Seven Years in Prison for 'Insulting the
     Prophet,'" Center for Human Rights in Iran, Oct. 1, 2015, iranhumanrights.
     org/2015/10/soheil-arabi-4/.

19   Michael Cavna, "Iranian Artist, Farghadani, Who Drew Parliament as
     Animals, Sentenced to 12-Plus Years," *Washington Post*, Jun. 1, 2015, wash-
     ingtonpost.com/news/comic-riffs/wp/2015/06/01/iranian-artist-farghadani
     -who-drew-parliament-as-animals-sentenced-to-12-plus-years/.

20   David Keyes, "The Poet Iran Executed," *Daily Beast*, Feb. 11, 2014, thedaily-
     beast.com/articles/2014/02/11/the-poet-iran-executed.html. According to
     Reprieve, an NGO that tracks the death penalty worldwide, Iran outstrips
     Saudi Arabia in the number of executions; in 2016 alone, there were more
     than 560. See: reprieve.org.uk/death-penalty-around-world/the-facts/which
     -countries-execute-most/.

21   The schoolteacher's name is Ali al-Malkawi. See: U.S. Department of State,
     Country Reports on Human Rights Practices for 2015, Jordan, state.gov/j/drl/rls/
     hrrpt/humanrightsreport/index.htm?year=2015&dlid=252931.

22   Examples and poll data noted in U.S. Department of State, *Country Reports 2015,
     Jordan*.

23   U.S. Department of State, *Country Reports on Human Rights Practices for 2015,
     Kuwait*, state.gov/j/drl/rls/hrrpt/humanrightsreport/index.htm?year=2015&dlid
     =252933.

24   *Amnesty International Report 2015/16: The State of the World's Human Rights*
     (London, UK: Amnesty International, 2016), 222.

25   Salam Al Amir, "Man Denies Insulting Prophet Mohammad on Facebook,"
     National, Mar. 6, 2017, thenational.ae/uae/courts/man-denies-insulting-prophet
     -mohammed-on-facebook.

26   Abdulla Rasheed, "Emirati Gets 10 Years for Insulting UAE Leadership," May
     25, 2015, gulfnews.com/news/uae/courts/emirati-gets-10-years-for-insulting-
     uae-leadership-1.1521363; U.S. Department of State, *Country Reports on Human
     Rights Practices for 2015, United Arab Emirates*, state.gov/j/drl/rls/hrrpt/human-
     rightsreport/index.htm?year=2015&dlid=252951.

27   *Amnesty International Report 2015/16*, 382.

28 Agence France-Presse, "Egypt Bans 'Zionist' Film *Exodus* and Cites 'Historical Inaccuracies,'" *Guardian*, Dec. 26, 2014, theguardian.com/film/2014/dec/26/egypt-bans-hollywood-exodus-christian-bale.

29 H. A. Hellyer, "The Silencing of Egypt's Jon Stewart," *Foreign Policy*, Jun. 3, 2014, foreignpolicy.com/2014/06/03/the-silencing-of-egypts-jon-stewart/.

30 Josie Ensor, "Egypt Expels Former BBC Journalist in Crackdown on Dissenting Media," *Telegraph*, Jun. 28, 2016, telegraph.co.uk/news/2016/06/28/egypt-expels-former-bbc-journalist-liliane-daoud.

31 Ruth Michaelson, "Egypt Jails Author Ahmed Naji for Sexually Explicit Book," *Guardian*, Feb. 20, 2016, theguardian.com/world/2016/feb/20/egypt-author-ahmed-naji-book-sex-drugs; Alison Flood, "Egyptian Writer Ahmed Naji's Jail Term Upheld Over Sexually Explicit Book," *Guardian*, Aug. 30, 2016, theguardian.com/books/2016/aug/30/egypt-upholds-ahmed-naji-jail-term-over-sexually-explicit-book-the-use-of-life.

32 Akiva Eldar, "Are Israel and Apartheid South Africa Really Different?" *Haaretz*, Jan. 4, 2010, haaretz.com/are-israel-and-apartheid-south-africa-really-different-1.265580.

33 Joshua Muravchik, "Trashing Israel Daily," *Commentary*, Jun. 1, 2013, commentarymagazine.com/articles/trashing-israel-daily.

34 For an in-depth historical analysis of Shavit's major allegation of an Israeli massacre during the 1947–48 war, see Martin Kramer, *The War on Error: Israel, Islam, and the Middle East* (New Brunswick: Transaction Publishers, 2016), 169–218; we'll touch on this issue in chapter three.

35 Note that in 2016 Shavit resigned his newspaper and television posts, not because of the content of his book, but because of accusations of sexual misconduct. See: Ruth Eglash, "'My Promised Land' author Ari Shavit resigns journalism posts in wake of sexual-harassment accusations," *Washington Post*, Oct. 30, 2016, washingtonpost.com/news/worldviews/wp/2016/10/30/my-promised-land-author-ari-shavit-resigns-journalism-posts-in-wake-of-sexual-harassment-accusations/.

36 Cf. Pnina Lahav, "American Influence on Israeli Law," in *Israel and the United States: Six Decades of U.S.-Israeli Relations*, ed. Robert Freedman (Philadelphia, PA: Westview Press, 2012), 205.

37 Daphne Barak-Erez, "The Law of Historical Films: In the Aftermath of *Jenin, Jenin*," *Southern California Interdisciplinary Law Journal* 16, no. 3 (2007): 513. lawweb.usc.edu/why/students/orgs/ilj/assets/docs/16-3%20Barak-Erez.pdf.

38 Lahav, "American Influence," 200.

39 Barak-Erez, "Law of Historical Films," 498

40 Barak-Erez, "Law of Historical Films," 512.

41 Barak-Erez, "Law of Historical Films," 513.

42 Barak-Erez, "Law of Historical Films," 515 [footnotes omitted].

43 The Censorship Board itself, whose purview has shrunk and whose bans have been overturned, ought to be abolished completely. A more complicated question is the validity of Israel's military censor, whose authority has been hemmed in. There's a case to be made for preventing the media from disseminating information about troop movements and other military operations in an embattled

country, surrounded by hostile neighbors and continually on a war footing. The presumption, though, should be that such authority is illegitimate, except in time-limited periods of war.

44 Phyllis Chesler, the feminist scholar and psychologist, has done a great deal to raise awareness of the phenomenon of Islamic "gender apartheid" and give wider currency to that term. See, for example, her 2005 speech before a Senate hearing on that topic, reprinted as chapter seven in Phyllis Chesler, *Islamic Gender Apartheid: Exposing a Veiled War Against Women* (Nashville, TN: New English Review Press, 2017).

45 The decree was announced in September 2017, with the changes in the law scheduled to take effect in 2018. Ben Hubbard, "Saudi Arabia Agrees to Let Women Drive," *New York Times*, Sep. 26, 2017, nytimes.com/2017/09/26/world/middleeast/saudi-arabia-women-drive.html.

46 The Saudi king reportedly decided in 2017 to adjust the guardianship system, only slightly loosening the chains that still bind Saudi women. The monarchy has also made noises about somewhat curtailing the power of the "morality police" and enacting other superficial reforms, but sadly none come close to real liberalization.

47 Mona El-Naggar, "'I Live in a Lie': Saudi Women Speak Up," *New York Times*, Oct. 28, 2016, nytimes.com/2016/10/29/world/middleeast/saudi-arabia-women. html. The *Times* invited these testimonials using Twitter, and where possible, it used email to verify the identity of the respondents. It gave the women the option of anonymity. The quoted passages above omit the names and locations that the newspaper attributed to some of the women.

48 El-Naggar, "Saudi Women Speak."

49 Ben Hubbard, "Saudi Arabia Releases Woman Arrested for Wearing Skirt in Public," *New York Times*, Jul. 19, 2017, nytimes.com/2017/07/19/world/middleeast/saudi-woman-khulood-released-skirt-video.html.

50 "Saudi Court Ups Punishment for Gang-Rape Victim," CNN, Nov. 17, 2007, cnn. com/2007/WORLD/meast/11/17/saudi.rape.victim.

51 Lizzie Dearden, "Iranian Women Arrested for Posting 'Vulgar' Photos on Instagram Without Wearing Headscarves," *Independent*, May 17, 2016, independent. co.uk/news/world/middle-east/iranian-women-arrested-for-posting-vulgar -photos-on-instagram-without-wearing-headscarves-a7033236.html.

52 Data from the Egypt Health Issues Survey 2015, published by the Egyptian Ministry of Health and Population, and referenced in U.S. Department of State, *Country Reports on Human Rights Practices for 2016, Egypt*, state.gov/documents/organization/265706.pdf.

53 Bob Drogin, "Egypt's Women Face Growing Sexual Harassment," *Los Angeles Times*, Feb. 23, 2011, articles.latimes.com/print/2011/feb/23/world/la-fg-egypt -women-abuse-20110223.

54 Poll data cited in Magdi Abdelhadi, "Egypt's Sexual Harassment 'Cancer,'" Jul. 18, 2008, BBC News, newsvote.bbc.co.uk/mpapps/pagetools/print/news.bbc. co.uk/2/hi/middle_east/7514567.stm. For comparison, the U.S. Department of Justice estimates that in 2010, the total rate of "rape and sexual assault victimization" of U.S. females aged 12 and older was 2.1 per 1,000. This figure encompasses

what the Department of Justice calls "attempted," "threatened," and "completed" victimizations. (Michael Planty et al., "Female Victims of Sexual Violence, 1994–2010," U.S. Department of Justice, Office of Justice Programs, March 2013.) It is commonly noted that rape and sexual assault are underreported crimes.

55 Abdelhadi, "Egypt's Sexual Harassment 'Cancer.'"

56 On how the Jordanian penal code has dealt with such crimes, see Fadia Faqir, "Intrafamily Femicide in Defence of Honour: The Case of Jordan," *Third World Quarterly* 22, no. 1 (2001); and Yotam Feldner, "'Honor' Murders—Why the Perps Get Off Easy," *Middle East Quarterly* 7, no. 4 (2000), meforum.org/50/honor-murders-why-the-perps-get-off-easy. Note that Jordan abolished its law providing leniency to rapists in 2017; Lebanon revoked the article applying to adult victims of rape, but left unchanged the article exempting from punishment the rapist of a minor if he marries the victim. See: "Jordan Abolishes Article 308 Protecting Rapists From Punishment If They Marry Their Victims," Inquiry & Analysis Series No.1328, *Middle East Media Research Institute*, Aug. 23, 2017, memri.org/reports/jordan-abolishes-article-308-protecting-rapists-punishment-if-they-marry-their-victims. See also, "Campaign in Lebanon Against Law Exempting Rapists from Punishment if They Marry Their Victim: 'A White [Dress] Does Not Cover Up Rape,'" Special Dispatch No. 6720, *Middle East Media Research Institute*, Dec. 22, 2016, memri.org/reports/campaign-lebanon-against-law-exempting-rapists-punishment-if-they-marry-their-victim-white.

57 In a survey of trends in "honor killings," Phyllis Chesler found that worldwide "more than half of victims were tortured; i.e., they did not die instantly but in agony," and in the Muslim world, half were tortured. Further, Chesler notes that "Torturous deaths include: being raped or gang-raped before being killed; being strangled or bludgeoned to death; being stabbed many times (10 to 40 times); being stoned or burned to death; being beheaded, or having one's throat slashed." Phyllis Chesler, "Worldwide Trends in Honor Killings," *Middle East Quarterly* 17, no. 2 (2010), meforum.org/2646/worldwide-trends-in-honor-killings.

58 Fadia Faqir notes that "honor killings" occur in a cultural context wherein the "individual has less importance than the community of the extended families," and that collective honor depends centrally on the virginity of unmarried daughters and the chastity of married ones. Faqir, "Intrafamily Femicide," 71. To glimpse the arbitrariness of the accusations leveled against the victims of "honor killings," see the various examples noted in Faqir, Chesler ("Worldwide Trends"), and Feldner ("'Honor' Murders"). Two anecdotes, noted in a 2000 report by the United Nations Population Fund, illustrate the mindset behind "honor killings": "Kifaya, a Jordanian girl of 12, was intelligent and full of curiosity. But when she returned home one evening from a walk in the neighbourhood with some friends, she was confronted by her enraged father. Shouting that she had dishonoured the entire family, her father proceeded to beat Kifaya with sticks and iron chains until she was dead. He told police he killed his only daughter because she went for walks without his permission. About the same time, Hanan, 34, was shot dead by her brother for the 'crime' of marrying a Christian. Her brother left her body in the street and smoked a cigarette while he waited for the police to arrive."

United Nations Population Fund, *The State of World Population 2000* (New York: UNFP), 29.

59 For many years, under Jordan's legal code—notably Articles 98 and 340—the perpetrators of "honor" murders could receive trivially light sentences. Proposals to amend or abolish Article 340, notes Feldner, were met with fierce public opposition (some 62 percent of Jordanians opposed such changes to the law, according to one poll). See Feldner, "'Honor' Murders."

60 U.S. Department of State, *Country Reports 2015, Kuwait.*

61 Data cited in Michael Curtis, "The International Assault against Israel," *Israel Affairs* 18, no. 3 (2012): 347.

62 They are Miriam Naor; Esther Hayut; Daphne Barak-Erez; and Anat Baron. Naor's role is known as the "president" of the court; elyon1.court.gov.il/eng/judges/judges.html.

63 IDF website, idf.il/1589-en/dover.aspx.

64 Hassan M. Fattah, "Saudi Arabia Begins to Face Hidden AIDS Problem," *New York Times*, Aug. 8, 2006, nytimes.com/2006/08/08/world/middleeast/08saudi.html.

65 "Saudi Religious Police Target 'Gay Rainbows,'" *France24*, Jul. 24, 2015, observers.france24.com/en/20150724-saudi-police-rainbows-gay-school; Brian Whitaker, "Everything You Need to Know About Being Gay in Muslim Countries," *Guardian*, Jun. 21, 2016, theguardian.com/world/2016/jun/21/gay-lgbt-muslim-countries-middle-east.

66 See: U.S. Department of State, *Country Reports on Human Rights Practices for 2015, Qatar,* state.gov/j/drl/rls/hrrpt/humanrightsreport/index.htm?year=2015&dlid=252943; U.S. Department of State, *Country Reports 2015, Kuwait*; U.S. Department of State, *Country Reports 2015, United Arab Emirates.*

67 "Ahmadinejad Speaks; Outrage and Controversy Follow," *CNN*, Sep. 24, 2007, cnn.com/2007/US/09/24/us.iran; videos of his statement can be found on YouTube.

68 Liam Stack, "Gay and Transgender Egyptians, Harassed and Entrapped, Are Driven Underground," *New York Times*, Aug. 10, 2016, nytimes.com/2016/08/11/world/africa/gay-egyptians-surveilled-and-entrapped-are-driven-underground.html.

69 Stack, "Gay and Transgender Egyptians." See also Mona Eltahawy, "Why Is the Egyptian Government So Afraid of a Rainbow Flag?" *New York Times*, Oct. 26, 2017, nytimes.com/2017/10/26/opinion/egypt-gay-lgbt-rights.html; Declan Walsh, "Egyptian Concertgoers Wave a Flag, and Land in Jail," *New York Times*, Sep. 26, 2017, nytimes.com/2017/09/26/world/middleeast/egypt-mashrou-leila-gays-concert.html.

70 Farah Wael, "Gay Rights in Lebanon: The Good, the Bad, and the Ugly," *Index on Censorship*, Apr. 24, 2014, indexoncensorship.org/2014/04/gay-rights-lebanon-good-bad-ugly/.

71 Dan Littauer, "Lebanon Medical Chiefs Ban Gay Anal Probe Tests," *GayStarNews.com*, Aug. 8, 2012, gaystarnews.com/article/lebanon-medical-chiefs-ban-gay-anal-probe-tests080812/. Reports indicate that the Lebanese police continued to use such probes; see Nick Duffy, "Lebanon: Anal Exams Still Being Conducted

on 'Suspected Homosexuals' Despite Ban," *PinkNews*, Jul. 16, 2014, pinknews. co.uk/2014/07/16/lebanon-anal-exams-still-being-conducted-on-suspected-homosexuals-despite-ban/.

72 It is notable that a Pride Parade was held in Beirut, Lebanon, for the first time in 2017, despite threats from Islamists.

73 Associated Press, "Tel Aviv Gay Pride Parade Is Mideast's Biggest," *Washington Times*, Jun. 3, 2016, washingtontimes.com/news/2016/jun/3/200000-party -in-tel-aviv-gay-pride-parade-regions-/.

74 Isabel Kershner, "Blacklisted in Iran, Gay Poet Seeks Asylum in Israel," *New York Times*, Mar. 2, 2016, nytimes.com/2016/03/03/world/middleeast/blacklisted-in-iran-gay-poet-seeks-asylum-in-israel.html.

75 According to NASDAQ.com as of Jan. 4, 2018, the number of U.S. companies listed was 2,829; Chinese, 99; Israeli, 82; Canadian, 52; U.K., 35; Korean, 2; French, 9; German 4; Indian, 4.

76 Data summarized on IVC-online.com, Jan. 17, 2018, ivc-online.com/Portals/0/ RC/Survey/IVC_Q4-17%20Capital%20Raising_Survey-Final.pdf

77 Data reported by PriceWaterhouseCoopers, cited in Nati Yefet, "Exits in Israel Totaled $7.44 Billion in 2017, and The Average Exit Was $106 Million," *Globes*, Dec. 27, 2017, globes.co.il/en/article-pwc-israeli-exits-up-110-in-2017 -1001217180.

78 It's worth noting a fascinating paradox: although Israel's high concentration of start-ups suggests a strong capitalist streak, many Israelis in fact view themselves as loyal to socialist ideals. Steven Plaut offers some illuminating observations on this paradox in "Israel's Socialist Dreams vs. Capitalist Realities," *Middle East Quarterly*, Summer 2016, meforum.org/6046/israel-socialist-dreams-capitalist-realities. Indeed, once upon a time, the Israeli economy looked a lot like the "social democrat" model of France and Germany. Within a marketplace of private companies and businesses, the government and labor unions ran major industrial companies (for example, electric and water utilities; the phone company) and state-enforced monopolies (for example, in dairy production). The inefficient public sector fell far short of delivering reliable prosperity. By 1985, a massive budget deficit "triggered inflation of more than 400 percent annually." (Ofira Seliktar, "The Israeli Economy," in *Contemporary Israel*, ed. Robert Freedman [Philadelphia, PA: Westview Press, 2009], 160.) That was a turning point. What followed in Israel has been likened to the so-called Thatcher Revolution in Britain. During Margaret Thatcher's time as prime minister, the U.K. government began privatizing government-run utilities (telephone, gas), corporations (British Petroleum, British Airways) and lightened the regulatory burden. Similarly, the Israeli government "undertook measures to deregulate the economy and sold off many of its biggest businesses, including Israel Chemicals (1995), telephone operator Bezeq (2005), and Oil Refineries (2007)." (Barry Rubin, *Israel: An Introduction* [New Haven: Yale University Press, 2012], 263.) The government also worked to unravel state-enforced monopolies and cartels, notably in the financial sector, and reform the tax code. (Seliktar, "The Israeli Economy," 165.) So far, Israel's economic makeover has been remarkable. Another change in society: In Israel's early years, the countryside was dotted with socialist

agricultural collectives, called kibbutzim. Members of a kibbutz typically abjured private property, often had their jobs assigned to them, received an equal wage and dined in communal halls. I spent about a year of my childhood on a kibbutz called Mishmar David. When we moved there, it was a condition of joining that we cede ownership of our family's VW Beetle, for all kibbutz members to use. Years later, Mishmar David was one the first to dissolve itself into an ordinary (non-communal) village. Kfar Menachem, the kibbutz where my mother grew up, has converted into a privately held operation. Others have collapsed into bankruptcy; some kibbutzim linger on, barely.

79   Guy Rolnik, "World's Biggest Investor Buys Iscar from Wertheimers for $4 Billion," *Haaretz*, Jun. 7, 2006, haaretz.com/world-s-biggest-investor-buys -iscar-from-wertheimers-for-4-billion-1.186996.

80   Dan Senor and Saul Singer, in *Start-up Nation* (2009), among other observers contend that the Israeli government was instrumental in enabling the mushrooming of Israeli start-ups. The point is highly debatable. The strongest claim, in my view, is that a high concentration of engineering talent emerged because of time spent in military units that focus on high tech. Considering the amount of outside venture funding that has flowed into Israel, however, it is an overstatement to claim that government initiatives had a decisive role in the start-up scene. Under-appreciated here are two factors: political freedom and the drive of individual business leaders.

81   World Bank Indicators, 2013, the year for which the most recent data were available, data.worldbank.org/indicator/IP.JRN.ARTC.SC. For the per-capita figures, I used the World Bank's population data (indicator "SP.POP.TOTL") for the year 2013.

82   Three Israelis—Menachem Begin; Yitzhak Rabin; Shimon Peres—have won or co-won Nobel Prizes for Peace, and another—S. Y. Agnon—has won the prize for Literature. Two Egyptians—Anwar Sadat; Mohammad ElBaredai—have won or co-won the Peace Prize; and one—Naguib Mahfouz—garnered the prize for Literature. Iran's sole Nobel laureate is Shirin Ebadi, a dissident and activists for human rights. See, nobelprize.org.

83   *Arab Human Development Report: Building a Knowledge Society*, United Nations Development Programme Arab Fund for Economic and Social Development (United Nations, New York 2003), 67. See also: "Innovation in the Arab World: From Zero to Not Much More," *Economist*, Jun. 4, 2016, economist.com/news/ middle-east-and-africa/21699955-how-be-creative-stifling-region-zero-not-much-more.

84   World Bank, "World Development Indicators," mortality rate, infant (per 1,000 live births). Data for 2016, the most recent year available, data.worldbank.org/ indicator/SP.DYN.IMRT.IN. For the U.S. data, the period is 1966-2016. For the comparison with Iran and Egypt: the rate in Israel was 12.8 in 1984, and 18.6 in 1977.

85   World Bank, "World Development Indicators," life expectancy at birth, total (years). Data for 2015, the most recent year available, data.worldbank.org/indicator/SP.DYN.LE00.IN.

CHAPTER 2

1 In the UAE, the monarchs (emirs) of these seven emirates form a council, and select from among themselves who will serve as president and vice-president of the federation. Political allegiances are bound up with patriarchal and tribal loyalties.

2 Sean L. Yom and Mohammad H. Al-Momani, "The International Dimensions of Authoritarian Regime Stability: Jordan in the Post-cold War Era," *Arab Studies Quarterly* 30, no. 1 (2008): 46-50.

3 The examples and the quotation appear in Rod Norland, "Holding Hands, Drinking Wine and Other Ways to Go to Jail in Dubai," *New York Times*, Feb. 11, 2017, nytimes.com/2017/11/11/world/middleeast/dubai-crimes-united-arab-emirates-jail.html.

4 William Booth, "Prominent Jordanian Writer Fatally Shot After He Shared Cartoon Said to Offend Islam," *Washington Post*, Sep. 25, 2016, washingtonpost.com/world/middle_east/prominent-jordanian-writer-fatally-shot-after-he-posted-cartoon-said-to-offend-islam/2016/09/25/68557a34-e3ce-46a9-a14b-b9ceec005288_story.html.

5 Booth, "Jordanian Writer."

6 Rana F. Sweis and Peter Baker, "Writer Charged With Insulting Islam Is Killed as Extremism Boils Over in Jordan," *New York Times*, Sep. 25, 2016, nytimes.com/2016/09/26/world/middleeast/nahed-hattar-jordanian-writer-killed.html.

7 Booth, "Jordanian Writer"; Sweis and Baker, "Writer Charged."

8 U.S. Department of State, *Country Reports 2015, Jordan*. See also, for example, Neil MacFarquhar, "Heavy Hand of the Secret Police Impeding Reform in Arab World," *New York Times*, Nov. 14, 2005, nytimes.com/2005/11/14/world/middleeast/heavy-hand-of-the-secret-police-impeding-reform-in-arab-world.html.

9 U.S. Department of State, *Country Reports on Human Rights Practices for 2015, Bahrain*, state.gov/j/drl/rls/hrrpt/humanrightsreport/index.htm?year=2015&dlid=252919.

10 U.S. Department of State, *Country Reports 2015, United Arab Emirates*.

11 On political influence and nepotism, see for example: U.S. Department of State, *Country Reports 2015, United Arab Emirates*.

12 On the impunity of government officials and police officers, see for example: U.S. Department of State's country reports on Kuwait, Jordan, and Lebanon: *Country Reports on Human Rights Practices for 2015*, state.gov/j/drl/rls/hrrpt/humanrightsreport

13 This incident is reported in Cynthia Farahat's speech for *Accuracy in Academia*, Jun. 7, 2013, youtube.com/watch?v=ahB8doC8TKI

14 For an illuminating account of how Morsi pushed his Islamist agenda, see Eric Trager, *Arab Fall: How the Muslim Brotherhood Won and Lost Egypt in 881 Days* (Georgetown University Press, 2016), Chapter 10.

15 Steven A Cook, "Egypt's Nightmare: Sisi's Dangerous War on Terror", *Foreign Affairs*, Nov./Dec. 2016, foreignaffairs.com/articles/middle-east/egypt-s-nightmare.

16 Hazel Haddon, "In Sisi's Egypt, Blasphemy Is Still a Crime," *Foreign Policy*, Apr. 21, 2015, foreignpolicy.com/2015/04/21/in-sisis-egypt-blasphemy-is-still-a-crime.

17 David A. Kirkpatrick, "Vow of Freedom of Religion Goes Unkept in Egypt," *New York Times*, Apr. 25, 2014, nytimes.com/2014/04/26/world/middleeast/egypt-religious-minorities.html.

18 Dahlia Kholaif and Tamer El-Ghobashy, "Bomb at Egypt's Main Coptic Cathedral Compound Kills Dozens," *Wall Street Journal*, Dec. 11, 2016, wsj.com/articles/bomb-at-egypts-main-coptic-christian-cathedral-compound-kills-dozens-1481461752.

19 Nina Shea, "Do Copts Have a Future in Egypt?" *Foreign Affairs*, Jun. 20, 2017, foreignaffairs.com/articles/egypt/2017-06-20/do-copts-have-future-egypt.

20 Apparently because of an international outcry, the court reconsidered the sentences of the 529 people it condemned to death. It commuted the sentences of all but 37 to life in prison. Karl Vick, "Egypt's Courts Mock Justice With More Mass Death Sentences," *Time.com*, Apr. 28, 2014, time.com/79530/egypt-mass-death-sentence-courts-muslim-brotherhood.

21 Declan Walsh, "Egypt Roared as Mubarak Fell. It's Mute as He's Freed." *New York Times*, Mar. 24, 2017, nytimes.com/2017/03/24/world/africa/hosni-mubarak-egypt.html.

22 Thanassis Cambanis, "Michel Aoun Rises to Lebanese Presidency, Ending Power Vacuum," *New York Times*, Oct. 31, 2016, nytimes.com/2016/11/01/world/middleeast/michel-aoun-lebanon-president.html.

23 U.S. Department of State, *Country Reports on Human Rights Practices for 2015, Lebanon*, state.gov/j/drl/rls/hrrpt/humanrightsreport/index.htm?year=2015&dlid=252935.

24 Joe Parkinson, Sam Schechner, and Emre Peker, "Turkey's Erdogan: One of the World's Most Determined Internet Censors," *Wall Street Journal*, May 2, 2014, online.wsj.com/news/articles/SB10001424052702304626304579505912518706936

25 Parkinson, et al., "Turkey's Erdogan,"

26 See for example, Andrew C. McCarthy, *Spring Fever: The Illusion of Islamic Democracy* (New York: Encounter Books, 2013).

27 Safak Timur and Tim Arango, "Turkey Seizes Newspaper, Zaman, as Press Crackdown Continues," *New York Times*, Mar. 4, 2016, nytimes.com/2016/03/05/world/middleeast/recep-tayyip-erdogan-government-seizes-zaman-newspaper.html

28 Constanze Letsch, "Seized Turkish Opposition Newspaper Toes Government Line," *Guardian*, Mar. 6, 2016, theguardian.com/world/2016/mar/06/seized-turkish-opposition-newspaper-zaman-erdogan-government.

29 Dexter Filkins, "The End of Democracy in Turkey," *New Yorker*, Jan. 3, 2017, newyorker.com/news/news-desk/the-end-of-democracy-in-turkey; Committee to Protect Journalists, cpj.org/imprisoned/2016.php

30 Patrick Kingsley, "Erdogan Claims Vast Powers in Turkey After Narrow Victory in Referendum," *New York Times*, Apr. 16, 2017, nytimes.com/2017/04/16/world/europe/turkey-referendum-polls-erdogan.html.

31 Patrick Clawson and Michael Rubin, *Eternal Iran: Continuity and Chaos* (New York: Palgrave Macmillan, 2005), 101.

32 Nassrin Farzaneh, "Children at High-Risk: A Comparative Analysis of the Case of Child Soldiers in Iran and in El Salvador," (Ph.D. thesis, Columbia University, 2007), 42.

33 Sara Terry, "For Iran's Child Soldiers, Capture By the Iraqis Is a Mixed Blessing," *Christian Science Monitor*, Jul. 7, 1987, csmonitor.com/1987/0707/zbtot4.html.

34 Matthias Küntzel, "Ahmadinejad's Demons," *New Republic*, Apr. 2006. Archived at matthiaskuentzel.de/contents/ahmadinejads-demons.

35 Quoted in A. Savyo, Yossi Mansharof, and M. Nissimov, "Iranian Women's Magazine Shut Down for Publishing Investigative Article on Martyrdom Movement," Middle East Media Research Institute, Inquiry and Analysis Series No. 439, Mar. 31, 2009, memri.org/reports/iranian-womens-magazine-shut-down-publishing-investigative-article-martyrdom-movement

36 Cf. "Community Under Siege: The Ordeal of the Bahá'ís of Shiraz," Iran Human Rights Documentation Center, Sep. 2007, iranhrdc.org/files.php?force&file=reports_en/Community_Under_Siege_Sep07_775623222.pdf.

37 On Saudi Arabia, see for example: Carlotta Gall, "Saudis Bankroll Taliban, Even as King Officially Supports Afghan Government," *New York Times*, Dec. 6, 2016, nytimes.com/2016/12/06/world/asia/saudi-arabia-afghanistan.html; regarding Qatar, see for example, Jonathan Schanzer, "Assessing the U.S.-Qatar Relationship," Testimony Before the House Foreign Affairs Committee, Subcommittee on Middle East and North Africa, Jul. 26, 2017, docs.house.gov/meetings/FA/FA13/20170726/106329/HHRG-115-FA13-Wstate-SchanzerJ-20170726.pdf.

38 Quoted in Efraim Karsh, *Islamic Imperialism: A History* (New Haven, CT: Yale University Press, 2005), 217.

39 See Rouhollah K. Ramazani, "Constitution of the Islamic Republic of Iran," *Middle East Journal* vol. 34, no. 2 (1980): 186. This translation reputedly hews closely to the original Persian. Cf. another translation reads: "...expanding the sovereignty of the law of God in the world." See "Constitution of the Islamic Republic of Iran 1979 (as last amended on July 28, 1989)," wipo.int/wipolex/en/text.jsp?file_id=332330.

40 Ilan Berman, *Iran's Deadly Ambition: The Islamic Republic's Quest for Global Power* (New York: Encounter Books, 2015), 13.

41 For an excellent analysis of Hezbollah and its relationship with Iran, see Matthew Levitt, *Hezbollah: The Global Footprint of Lebanon's Party of God* (Georgetown University Press, 2013). This patron/subcontractor relationship is ongoing; see, for example, Ben Hubbard, "Iran Out to Remake Mideast With Arab Enforcer: Hezbollah," *New York Times*, Aug. 27, 2017, nytimes.com/2017/08/27/world/middleeast/hezbollah-iran-syria-israel-lebanon.html.

42 For more about that video clip, see Brian Stelter, "Honoring Citizen Journalists", *The New York Times*, Feb 21, 2010, nytimes.com/2010/02/22/business/media/22polk.html?mcubz=0

43 Basic Law: Human Dignity and Liberty, knesset.gov.il

44 For the party lists in the 2015 election, see knesset.gov.il/description/eng/eng_mimshal_res20.htm

45 Lahav, "American Influence," 188-89.

46 Pnina Lahav, "Israel's Supreme Court," in *Contemporary Israel*, ed. Robert Freedman (Philadelphia, PA: Westview Press, 2009), 143-144. The case is HCJ 2056/04 Beit Sourik Village Council v. The Government of Israel; June 30, 2004; elyon1. court.gov.il/Files_ENG/04/560/020/A28/04020560.A28.pdf

47 Rami Amichai, "Former Israeli PM Olmert Sentenced to Six Years for Corruption," *Reuters*, May 13, 2014, uk.reuters.com/article/2014/05/13/uk-israel-olmert-idUKKBN0DT0F020140513.

48 The op-ed was by Daniel Doron, "Olmert Isn't Alone," *Israel Hayom*, May 15, 2014, israelhayom.com/opinions/olmert-isnt-alone.

49 Nicolo Nourafchan "Judging Torture: Lessons From Israel," *Georgetown Journal of International Law* 43 (2012): 1294.

50 HCJ 5100/94, *Public Committee Against Torture v. Government of Israel* (1998-1999), 28, 36-37, elyon1.court.gov.il/files_eng/94/000/051/a09/94051000.a09.pdf.

51 Lee Gancman, "Israel Police to Appoint First Muslim Deputy Commissioner," *Times of Israel*, Feb. 11, 2016, timesofisrael.com/israel-police-to-appoint-first-muslim-deputy-commissioner/.

52 Dov Lieber, "Israel Appoints Its First Female Muslim Diplomat," Apr. 5, 2017, timesofisrael.com/israel-appoints-its-first-female-muslim-diplomat/.

53 Joshua Muravchik, *Liberal Oasis: The Truth About Israel* (New York: Encounter Books, 2014), Kindle Edition, Location 247.

54 Muravchik, *Liberal Oasis*, Location 705.

55 Theodor Herzl, *The Jewish State* (New York: Dover Publications, 1988), 145. It must be noted that the political vision Herzl articulates here is rather mixed; in a number of ways, it reflects an inconsistent application of the principle that underlies political freedom, the principle of individual rights.

56 Herzl, *The Jewish State*, 116.

57 Herzl, *The Jewish State*, 146.

58 Herzl, *The Jewish State*, 146, 133.

59 Walter Laqueur, *A History of Zionism: From the French Revolution to the Establishment of the State of Israel* (New York: MJF Books, 1972), 132-133.

60 See, for example, Howard Sachar, *A History of Israel: From the Rise of Zionism to Our Time* (New York: Alfred A. Knopf, 2007), 67-70. Also, Laqueur, *History of Zionism*.

61 Yuval Elizur and Lawrence Malkin, *The War Within: Israel's Ultra-Orthodox Threat to Democracy and the Nation* (New York; London: Overlook Duckworth, 2013), 52-3.

62 Ami Pedahzur, *The Triumph of Israel's Radical Right* (New York: Oxford University Press, 2012), 31.

63 Bernard Avishai, *The Hebrew Republic: How Secular Democracy and Global Enterprise Will Bring Israel Peace at Last* (New York: Harcourt, 2008), 94.; See also the discussion Elizur and Malkin, *War Within*, Chapter. 7.

64 Avishai, *Hebrew Republic*, 94.

65 Elizur and Malkin, *War Within*, 128.

66 Both polls can be found in Rafi Smith and Olga Paniel, "2015 Israel Religion and State Index Report #7," Sep. 2015, Hiddush, Freedom of Religion For Israel, hiddush.org.

67 U.S. Department of State, *France 2014 International Religious Freedom Report*, state.gov/documents/organization/238592.pdf.

68 Agnès Leclair, "Le Rapporteur Public Du Conseil d'État Pour L'autorisation Des Crèches Dans Les Mairies," *Le Figaro*, Oct. 21, 2016, lefigaro.fr/actualite-france/2016/10/20/01016-20161020ARTFIG00344-l-epineuse-question-des-creches-devant-le-conseil-d-etat.php.

69 See, for example: "How Members Are Appointed," parliament.uk/business/lords/whos-in-the-house-of-lords/members-and-their-roles/how-members-are-appointed/

70 Large shops (defined as having more than 280 square meters) can only open on Sundays for six consecutive hours, between 10 a.m. and 6 p.m., and must close on Easter Sunday and Christmas Day.

71 Cf. U.S. Department of State, *United Kingdom 2014 International Religious Freedom Report*, state.gov/documents/organization/238658.pdf.

CHAPTER 3

1 Mahmoud Abbas, "The Long Overdue Palestinian State" May 17, 2011, *New York Times*, nytimes.com/2011/05/17/opinion/17abbas.html.

2 Yasser Arafat, "Palestine at the United Nations," *Journal of Palestine Studies* 4, no. 2 (1975): 189.

3 Edward Said, *The Question of Palestine* (New York: Vintage Books, 1992), 171-2. Said claims that he regards "many acts of individual adventure (hijacking, kidnapping, and the like)" as in some sense "immoral," but he quickly hedges by noting circumstances that he seems to suggest actually warrant such acts (172; see also, xx-xxi).

4 Said, *Question of Palestine*, xx-xxi. Said articulates a commonly held theme. In later years, he soured on the leadership of the Palestinian Liberation Organization (PLO) and elements of its strategy.

5 George W. Bush, "Remarks on the Middle East," Jun. 24, 2002. Online by Gerhard Peters and John T. Woolley, *The American Presidency Project*. presidency.ucsb.edu/ws/?pid=73320.

6 Barack Obama, "Remarks in Cairo," Jun. 4, 2009. Online by Gerhard Peters and John T. Woolley, *The American Presidency Project*. presidency.ucsb.edu/ws/?pid=86221.

7 In a summary formulation, Said names three broad issues which he puts in terms of "the irreducible and functional meaning of being a Palestinian": these are the Zionist acquisition of Palestine; the dispossession and exiling of Palestinians; and a denial of their rights (*Question of Palestine*, 180-181). Our discussion in this chapter will deal with these issues, but subdivide them into four broad grievances. Furthermore, note that in his book Said uses the term dispossession mainly in connection with the effects of the 1948 war (such as the refugee crisis and related issues), but the term "dispossession" is also used by other scholars, for example by Rashid Khalidi (who shares common ground with Said), in connection with

the acquisition of land in Palestine by Jews prior to 1948 (see, Rashid Khalidi, *Palestinian Identity: The Construction of Modern National Consciousness* [New York: Columbia University Press, 1997], ch. 5). In this chapter when we look at the claim of "dispossession," it is during the period prior to that war. We will look at the effects of the 1948 war, including refugees and their property, in a later section of this chapter.

8   See for example, "What is BDS?" bdsmovement.net/what-is-bds.

9   Here, for example, are several other grievances of varying degrees of complexity: control over the city of Jerusalem, particularly including its holy sites; disputes over access to water; the supply of electricity; curfews; check points; travel restrictions; crowd control during riots; home demolitions; administrative detention. While these and others are beyond the scope of the book, they do merit exploration, and in certain cases the grievances may point to actual wrongs; in others, not at all. The present chapter argues that to analyze such grievances, it's crucial to question the conventional moral assumptions and instead adopt a framework grounded in the principle of individual rights.

10 I say "dormant," because there's some evidence that can be interpreted as manifestations of a Palestinian national identity prior to the 1960s. For the purposes of this book, we need to set aside many questions related to the general phenomenon of national identity, and specifically the Palestinian identity, and how to define it. Rashid Khalidi, the Columbia professor and PLO-linked activist, has offered an account to explain what he calls the "lost years," the decades when the Palestinian identity was essentially absent from the cultural-political scene. Khalidi notes some factors that shed light on the issue. See Khalidi, *Palestinian Identity*, chapter 8.

11 *The Palestinian National Charter: Resolutions of the Palestine National Council July 1-17, 1968*, avalon.law.yale.edu/20th_century/plocov.asp.

12 Kenneth W. Stein, *The Land Question in Palestine, 1917-1939* (Chapel Hill: University of North Carolina Press, 1984), 10-11.

13 Stein, *Land Question*, 10-15. Stein notes that the Land Law of 1858 "enumerated six classes of land: *mulk, miri, waqf, mawat, mahlul,* and *matruka*" and he describes each of these in turn.

14 Stein, *Land Question*, 52.

15 Stein, *Land Question*, 37.

16 Stein, *Land Question*, 69.

17 Stein, *Land Question*, 69.

18 Stein, *Land Question*, 228-239, 67.

19 Stein, *Land Question*, 52-54.

20 Stein, *Land Question*, 36.

21 Stein, *Land Question*, 4-5, 11.

22 Stein, *Land Question*, 20-22.

23 Stein discusses the ways that some Zionist purchasers and Arab landlords worked to circumvent various land-transfer regulations during the British Mandate. See, *Land Question*, Chapter 3.

24 Stein notes that "Trespass was a perennial problem in agriculturally predominant Palestine, and boundaries between land areas were not properly defined." Stein, *Land Question*, 13; for examples of vague boundary descriptions, see 22.

25 Cf. Khalidi, *Palestinian Identity*, 102.

26 We're concerned here with contrasting acquisition of land through voluntary trade from the legal (and thus presumably legitimate) owner, from wrongful (i.e. rights-violating) acquisition of land. With the purchase of land through voluntary trade, though, there were still disputes and friction, for example over compensation and resettlement (how much is a fair monetary compensation? is the alternate tract of land for resettlement of comparable size and quality?) The wider point is not that land purchases took place without friction, but rather that there's a fundamental difference between trade and theft. (It's a difficult question to assess the standing of buyers and sellers who circumvented the various land-transfer restrictions imposed by the British authorities, because it's debatable if these regulations, on their own terms, were proper or fair.)

27 The Palestine Mandate, Jul. 24, 1922, Article 2, avalon.law.yale.edu/20th_century/palmanda.asp.

28 Over time, however, the British authorities severely limited Jewish immigration, particularly in the run-up and during World War II, when many in Europe sought to flee the Nazis.

29 Sachar, *History of Israel*, 154-162. .

30 Sachar, *History of Israel*, 162,168.

31 The span of time indicated is 1920-37. *Palestine Royal Commission Report (Cmd. 5479)*, Presented by the Secretary of State for the Colonies to Parliament by Command of His Majesty (London: H.M. Stationery Office, 1937), 125, https://unispal.un.org/pdfs/Cmd5479.pdf. The report speaks of the "Arab" population, but for reasons discussed later in this chapter (in the section on minority rights), I refer to that community as composed of Muslims and Christians, because these terms are clearer.

32 According to the British government's report, the number of these industrial undertakings increased from about 1200 to 2200. *Palestine Royal Commission Report*, 126.

33 "Outsiders" at this point meant not only the Zionists but also the British. Baruch Kimmerling and Joel S. Migdal, *Palestinians: The Making of a People* (New York: Free Press, 1993), 56.

34 Quoted in Sachar, *History of Israel*, 199.

35 Matthias Küntzel, *Jihad and Jew-Hatred: Islamism, Nazism and the Roots of 9/11* (New York: Telos Press Pub., 2007), 32-3.

36 Küntzel, *Jihad and Jew-Hatred*, 33.

37 Küntzel, *Jihad and Jew-Hatred*, 33.

38 Efraim Karsh, *Palestine Betrayed* (New Haven, CT: Yale University Press, 2010), 35.

39 Sachar, *History of Israel*, 213. Sachar notes that the Mufti was bent on eliminating political rivals; indeed, one of the Mufti's henchmen issued a "death warrant" against a particular rival. Kenneth Stein observes that there's evidence the Mufti carried out "personal vendettas indirectly through intermediaries in hopes of

settling scores against those who opposed his leadership and against those who supported the suggested partition of Palestine in 1937." Kenneth Stein, "The Intifada and the Uprising of 1936-1939: A Comparison of the Palestinian Arab Communities," in *The Intifada: Its Impact on Israel, the Arab World, and the Superpowers,* ed. Robert O. Freedman (Florida International University Press, 1991).

40　The Mufti's pursuit of domination persisted well after the 1936-39 riots; cf. Sachar, *History of Israel,* 315.

41　Cf. Barry Rubin, *The Arab States and the Palestine Conflict* (Syracuse University Press, 1981), iv.

42　Note that the fledgling Muslim Brotherhood, an Islamist organization that would spawn a host of factions including Al Qaeda and Hamas, was energized by the 1948 war over Palestine. It stood in solidarity with the uprisings in the 1930s, and during the 1948 war, Brotherhood operatives trained fighters in Palestine and also volunteered to join the war against the Zionists. See: Richard P. Mitchell, *The Society of the Muslim Brothers* (New York: Oxford University Press, 1993), 55-58.

43　This conversation occurred on Nov. 28, 1941. A written record of it can be found in Walter Laqueur and Barry Rubin, *The Israel-Arab Reader: A Documentary History of the Middle East Conflict,* 6th revised edition (New York: Penguin, 2001), 51-55.

44　Küntzel, *Jihad and Jew-Hatred,* 44.

45　After World War II, the Mufti went to Cairo. The Muslim Brotherhood's newspaper was among the voices calling on the Egyptian government to grant him asylum, which he eventually received. Mitchell, *Muslim Brothers,* 56.

46　Quoted in David Barnett and Efraim Karsh, "Azzam's Genocidal Threat," *Middle East Quarterly,* Fall (2011): 87, meforum.org/meq/pdfs/3082.pdf.

47　This definition of the aim was formulated by the Arab League's political committee at a meeting in Cairo, quoted in Karsh, *Palestine Betrayed,* 105. In a May 15, 1948 cablegram to the Secretary General of the United Nations, the head of the Arab League articulated these basic goals as the rationale for the war. Notably, the statement also asserts that the Arab League had "declared that Palestine had become an independent country since its separation from the Ottoman Empire, but that all the appertaining external rights and privileges attendant upon formal independence had to be subdued temporarily for reasons beyond the will of its people" (i.e., during the British Mandate). Thus the Arab League's war was supposed to ensure that preexisting independence. See "Cablegram Dated 15 May 1948 Addressed to The Secretary-General By The Secretary-General Of The League Of Arab States," S/745, May 15, 1948, unispal.un.org/DPA/DPR/unispal. nsf/0/A717E30BD2F6E5EC8525761E0072E9B3.

48　Adeed Dawisha, *Arab Nationalism in the Twentieth Century: From Triumph to Despair* (Princeton University Press, 2009), 129.

49　Barnett and Karsh, "Azzam's Genocidal Threat," 87.

50　Dawisha, *Arab Nationalism,* 129 [footnotes omitted].

51　Dawisha, *Arab Nationalism,* 130.

52　The total number of refugees has been the subject of a long debate between Benny Morris and Efraim Karsh. Karsh estimates the number to be no higher than

609,071 (Karsh, *Palestine Betrayed*, 272.); Benny Morris estimates the number at closer to 700,000 (Benny Morris, *The Birth of the Palestinian Refugee Problem Revisited* [Cambridge; New York: Cambridge University Press, 2004], 604.). Further below I note some of the inherent problems of accounting for the number of refugees, a discussion informed by the scholarship of Asaf Romirowsky and Alexander H. Joffe in *Religion, Politics, and the Origins of Palestine Refugee Relief* (New York: Palgrave Macmillan, 2013).

53   Karsh, *Palestine Betrayed* 183-184.

54   There were about 5.4 million registered Syrian refugees, according to the United Nations refugee agency, UNHCR, as of Jan. 2, 2018. Syria's population in 2010, a year before the war, was 21 million, according to the World Bank.

55   Karsh, *Palestine Betrayed*, 138-142, 237. See also Morris, *Palestinian Refugee Problem*, 589-90.

56   Karsh, *Palestine Betrayed*, 239; Morris, *Palestinian Refugee Problem*, 588.

57   Karsh, *Palestine Betrayed*, 182.

58   See for example the exchange between Martin Kramer and Benny Morris in Kramer's book, *The War on Error: Israel, Islam, and the Middle East*. See also Eliezer Tauber's research, presented in English in "Deir Yassin: The Complete Story," Lecture delivered at the ASMEA Conference (2014); "Deir Yassin: Propaganda and Historiography," Lecture delivered at the ASMEA Conference (2015); "Deir Yassin as a Trigger for the Palestinian Exodus, 1948," *Lecture delivered at the ASMEA (2016).*

59   It was the U.S. view for many years, it was the view of the main nongovernmental organization (the American Friends Service Committee) that cared for the refugees before the United Nations formed its own agency for that purpose (the United Nations Relief Works Agency), and it was UNRWA's view for a time as well. See Romirowsky and Joffe, *Palestine Refugee Relief*, 147-150. See also Alexander H Joffe, "UNRWA Resists Resettlement," *Middle East Quarterly*, Fall (2012).

60   It is worth noting that Palestinian refugees in Israeli camps have faced hardships, too. The fundamental culpability for their plight lies with the instigators of the war, and it is under Israel's political system that they and advocates on their behalf stand the best chance of seeking redress for wrongs suffered in the camps.

61   The above discussion of the challenges inherent in tallying the refugees draws upon the work of Romirowsky and Joffe in *Palestine Refugee Relief*, esp. 8-9, and 90-96.

62   "Palestinian Refugees," UNRWA, unrwa.org/palestine-refugees.

63   Cf. Romirowsky and Joffe, *Palestine Refugee Relief*, 88.

64   Quoted in Barnett and Karsh, "Azzam's Genocidal Threat," 88.

65   In seeking his own dominance in the region, Nasser sought to overthrow neighboring governments, and he pursued various schemes to form a political union between Egypt and other countries in the Arab world, notably with Syria in the form of the United Arab Republic. Note also that inherent in his vision of "Arab nationalism," Egypt arrogated to itself the right to disregard the sovereignty of other nations in order to pursue the "interests" of the Arab "nation." Cf. Dawisha, *Arab Nationalism*, 151-53 and ch. 8.

66 Nasser's statement and the excerpts from Cairo Radio appear in Yehosh-afat Harkabi, *Arab Attitudes to Israel* (Jerusalem: Israel Universities Press, 1974), 2.

67 Laqueur and Rubin, *Israel-Arab Reader,* 99.

68 In 1981, Israel annexed the Golan Heights, putting the area under the state's the law, jurisdiction, and administration. That move came after the surprise 1973 war launched by Egypt and Syria (sometimes called the Yom Kippur War). In that war, Syrian forces attacked Israel via the Golan Heights, which were a point of vulnerability.

69 I list the Golan Heights here as arguably "occupied," because some question the propriety of Israel's annexation.

70 The following omits discussion of the far smaller Golan Heights, which came under Israeli law in 1981.

71 One consequence of Israeli temporizing is an inordinately complicated legal-po-litical situation. "The basic law in the Territories was the Jordanian law in the West Bank and Egyptian law in the Gaza Strip," Gazit notes, but on top of that the Israeli administration added its own decrees and regulations. This confusing arrangement is at odds with a rule of law system; so, Israeli citizens within the territories and the Palestinians living there are subject to differing legal regimes. Shlomo Gazit, *Trapped Fools: Thirty Years of Israeli Policy in the Territories* (London: Frank Cass, 2003), 282.

72 Moshe Shemesh, *The Palestinian Entity 1959-1974: Arab Politics and the PLO* (London: Frank Cass, 1988), 60.

73 For a more detailed comparison of the U.S. in Japan with Israel's experience in the territories, see Menahem Milson, "How Not to Occupy the West Bank," *Commentary,* Apr. 1, 1986, commentarymagazine.com/articles/how-not-to-occupy-the-west-bank/

74 "U.S. Initial Post-Surrender Policy for Japan (SWNCC150/4/A)," State-War-Navy Coordinating Committee, 21 September 1945, ndl.go.jp/constitution/e/shiryo/01/022_2/022_2tx.html.

75 "Basic Initial Post Surrender Directive to Supreme Commander for the Allied Powers for the Occupation and Control of Japan (JCS1380/15)," Joint Chiefs of Staff, 3 November 1945, ndl.go.jp/constitution/e/shiryo/01/036/036tx.html.

76 "Basic Initial Post Surrender Directive (JCS1380/15)," Part I.

77 "U.S. Initial Post-Surrender Policy for Japan (SWNCC150/4/A)," Part I, (c).

78 For an excellent discussion of the impact of the occupation, see John David Lewis, *Nothing Less Than Victory: Decisive Wars and the Lessons of History* (Princeton: Princeton University Press, 2010), Chapter 7. Judged according to its basic goals, the occupation of Japan was largely effective, but not without its shortcomings and errors. Even with its problems, it remains an instructive comparison.

79 Quoted in Gazit, *Trapped Fools,* 48. Gazit also characterizes the intended policy as "invisible" and "unobtrusive."

80 Gazit, *Trapped Fools,*48.

81 Sachar, *History of Israel,* 670-671.

82 The examples of sanitation problems and the economy appear in Gazit's description of this guiding principle. Gazit, *Trapped Fools,* 48.

83 Barry Rubin, *Revolution Until Victory?: The Politics and History of the PLO* (Cambridge, Mass.: Harvard University Press, 1994), 16. On the strong ties between Jordan and the occupied West Bank, see also Milson, "How Not to Occupy."

84 Shachar, *History of Israel*, 672. See also Milson, "How Not to Occupy," which offers a helpful description of Israel's attitude toward the inflow of foreign money into the territories.

85 Sachar, *History of Israel*, 672.

86 Gazit, *Trapped Fools*, 39, 41n15, 41n16. I touched on the issue of Israel's military censor in chapter one, endnote 43.

87 Efraim Karsh, "What Occupation?" *Commentary*, Jul./Aug. 2002, commentary-magazine.com/articles/what-occupation.

88 Quoted in Karsh, "What Occupation?"

89 In the case of Gaza, the initial targets of such attacks were Palestinians, with the goal of deterring them from cooperating with Israel; the focus then shifted to Israeli targets. See Gazit, *Trapped Fools*, 61.

90 Gazit, *Trapped Fools*, 45.

91 Sachar, *History of Israel*, 671-2.

92 Sachar, *History of Israel*, 706-7.

93 Gazit, *Trapped Fools*, 59.

94 Israel's own economy at the time was highly regulated and protectionist. It applied many of these socialist-oriented policies and protectionist ideas toward the occupied territories. By the mid 1980s, Israel's heavily regulated economy was on the brink of collapse. Its regulations and protectionism also had a negative impact on aspects of the economies of the territories.

95 Zeev Schiff and Ehud Yaari, *Intifada: The Palestinian Uprising—Israel's Third Front*, trans. Ina Friedman (New York: Simon and Schuster, 1990), 84.

96 Karsh, "What Occupation?"

97 Rubin, *Revolution Until Victory*, 16-18.; See also Schiff and Yaari, *Intifada*, 49.

98 See, for example, Schiff and Yaari, *Intifada*, 143, 145, 146-148. Israel continued these practices during the so-called second intifada (about 2000–2005), targeting the perpetrators and enablers of terrorist attacks. In 2005, Israel announced that the procedure of home demolitions would no longer be used.

99 See for example, Schiff and Yaari, *Intifada*, Chapter 8. It's worth noting the significant role of Islamist groups, notably Palestinian Islamic Jihad and Hamas, which were salient during the intifada.

100 Barack Obama viewed settlements as an obstacle to peace and demanded a complete halt on settlement construction (see chapter six); Donald Trump has said that settlements are not "good for peace." (Jack Moore, "U-Turning Trump Now Labels Settlements Unhelpful To Peace", *Newsweek*, Feb. 10, 2017, newsweek.com/trump-u-turn-says-settlements-unhelpful-peace-555056.)

101 These broad categories in turn have further, derivative claims nested within them. For example, the claim that Israel made certain agreements, under various peace deals, to limit the "settlements," but did not live up to those promises. These we must bracket, though it is worth noting that such claims about violated

agreements presuppose the legitimacy of the particular peace agreements, which, as we'll see later in the book, is dubious.

102 See Yigal Allon's argument in "Israel: The Case for Defensible Borders," *Foreign Affairs* 55, no. 1 (1976): 38-53.

103 For the view of Israel's government, see for example "Israeli Settlements and International Law," Israel Ministry of Foreign Affairs, Nov. 30 2015, mfa.gov.il, and Gazit, *Trapped Fools*, 18, 35.

104 This point is developed in Dore Gold, "From 'Occupied Territories' To 'Disputed Territories,'" Jerusalem Letter / Viewpoints, No. 470, Jan. 2002, Jerusalem Center for Public Affairs, jcpa.org/jl/vp470.htm.

105 A helpful summary of some of the arguments can be found in Nicholas Rostow, "Are the Settlements Illegal?" *The American Interest*, vol. 5, no. 4, Mar. 1, 2010, the-american-interest.com/2010/03/01/are-the-settlements-illegal.

106 Abraham Bell and Eugene Kontorovich, "Palestine, Uti Possidetis Juris and the Borders of Israel," *Arizona Law Review* 58, no. 633 (2016): 637.

107 HCJ 6698/95, Ka'adan v. Israel Land Administration, 32, elyon1.court.gov.il/files_eng/95/980/066/a14/95066980.a14.pdf

108 Hesketh, *The Inequality Report: The Palestinian Arab Minority in Israel*, 31, 34. But, Adalah reports, the attorney general decided that when a non-Jew "wins a tender for a plot of JNF land, the [state authority] will compensate the JNF with an equal amount of land." This practice is being challenged in court. Another kind of problem arises with committees that select applicants for plots of land and housing units in agricultural and rural towns, because the committees include members from quasi-state organizations.

109 Gazit, *Trapped Fools*, 263-5.

110 Gazit, *Trapped Fools*, 275-78, 79.

111 See, for example, the data compiled by Yesh Din, which also points to evidence that police have been negligent in investigating such crimes and pursuing offenders, "NGO: Law Enforcement On Israeli Civilians In The West Bank", Oct. 2015, files.yesh-din.org/userfiles/Datasheet_English_Oct%202015.pdf. Consider one tiny but ominous faction, reported on in Hillel Gershuni, "A Jewish ISIS Rises in the West Bank," Jan. 11, 2016, tabletmag.com/jewish-news-and-politics/196516/jewish-isis-in-the-west-bank.

112 Allison Kaplan Sommer, "Explained: Israel's New Palestinian Land-grab Law and Why It Matters," *Haaretz*, Feb. 7, 2017, haaretz.com/israel-news/1.770102; See also, John Reed, "Israel Passes Law To Legalise Expropriation of Private Palestinian Land," *Financial Times*, Feb. 6, 2017, ft.com/content/46c69e4d-b5ee-36cf-a100-50ff5f338367.

113 An example is the Amona outpost, which the courts deemed illegal, and the government eventually moved in to dismantle. Rory Jones, "Israeli Police Clear West Bank Settler Outpost," *Wall Street Journal*, Feb. 2, 2017, wsj.com/articles/israeli-police-continue-clearing-west-bank-settler-outpost-1486039074.

114 See, for example, a scathing 2005 report, commissioned by the Israeli government, that was researched and written by an independent lawyer, Talya Sason. Among other findings, Sason notes egregious cases of bureaucratic connivance, at varied levels of authority, with settlers bent on flouting the law. Talya Sason,

"Summary of the Opinion Concerning Unauthorized Outposts," The State of Israel, Prime Minister's Office, Communication Department, Mar. 10, 2005, mfa. gov.il.

115 The "second class citizens" theme goes back at least to 1974, when the PLO's leader Yasser Arafat invoked it in his landmark speech at the United Nations, cf. Arafat, "Palestine at the United Nations"; it reverberates through Edward Said's book *The Question of Palestine* (1992); and it continues to figure in the work of analysts, for instance As'ad Ghanem, "Israel's Second-Class Citizens: Arabs in Israel and the Struggle for Equal Rights", *Foreign Affairs* 95, no. 4 (2016): 37-42; and scholars such as Ilan Peleg and Dov Waxman, *Israel's Palestinians: The Conflict Within* (New York: Cambridge University Press, 2011).

116 Keep in mind that the Palestinians in Gaza are subjects of Hamas's rule; those in the West Bank are subjects of the Palestinian Authority or else the Israeli authorities. Yet another population, in East Jerusalem, have been offered citizenship; some have accepted, others have sought it out, and still others have rejected it.

117 Just as there are difficulties with the term "Arab" (see above), the term "Jew" raises its own challenges. Beyond the state of Israel's official definition of a "Jew," which some people object to, there are wider challenges. "Jew" often means someone who follows the religion of Judaism, but it also means someone—regardless of his or her own beliefs—who was born to parents who are Jewish. So you can find "Jews" who are in fact agnostics, atheists, or Buddhists. Further, for many people being a "Jew" means belonging to a community defined by its traditions, customs, and culture, which largely overlap with the religion of Judaism, but not entirely. There are "cultural Jews" who mark certain religious holidays but are themselves nonbelievers. In being a "Jew," there is a strong component of shared history and experiences. Ancestry is another significant feature of being a "Jew." Under the common definition, to be a Jew you have to be born to a Jewish mother, which puts the matter outside your control. Nonetheless, people can and do convert to Judaism, and in that sense they become Jews. Further complicating this picture is the fact that within the Jewish community, there are distinct subgroups, with differing customs and traditions; for example, after the Passover holiday, Jews from the North African country of Morocco customarily hold a celebration called "mimouna," which features special foods; Jews of Eastern Europe, often called Ashkenazi Jews, do not. Finally, it's important to note a phenomenon evident in Europe at the turn of the twentieth century and through the next four decades. There was a growing tide of racist and anti-Semitic hostility to "Jews": what mattered was not an individual's own choices, beliefs, and practices, but rather his or her unchosen ancestry. If you were born of Jewish ancestry, you were a target. Thus "Jews" who were nonbelievers and fully assimilated to the culture of their European societies found that they were still singled out for enmity. (See for example, Laqueur, *History of Zionism*, 19-39.) It is for these reasons that throughout this book I continually point out that Israel's population of "Jews" encompasses not only religionists and observant Jews, but also secularists, agnostics, atheists, and still others.

118 They settled in Palestine before the end of the British Mandate; some years later (around the middle of the twentieth century) there was a wave of Jews who left,

fled, or were expelled from their homes in Muslim countries (which in some cases expropriated them, too). See the discussion of this point in Sachar, *History of Israel*, 396-403.

119 For an outline of the various groups in Israel, see Peleg and Waxman, *Israel's Palestinians*, 22-23. There are internal conflicts among certain subgroups; the Druze community in Israel, for example, is split because some members believe themselves to be a distinct, non-Arab group, whereas others feel loyal to the wider Arab world. See Jacob M. Landau, *The Arab Minority in Israel, 1967-1991: Political Aspects* (Oxford: Clarendon Press; New York : Oxford University Press, 1993), 124.

120 Bishara's statements are quoted in Avishai, *Hebrew Republic*, 49.

121 Ron Ben Yishai, " Bishara recommended that Hizbullah attack south of Haifa," *Ynet*, May 3, 2007, http://www.ynetnews.com/articles/0,7340,L-3395153,00.html; Jonathan Lis and Shahar Ilan, "Ex-MK Bishara Suspected of Treason, Passing Data to Hezbollah," *Haaretz*, May 2, 2007, https://www.haaretz.com/1.4818672.

122 Alona Ferber, "No Apologies: Lucy Aharish Is Honored to Be Both Arab and Israeli on Independence Day," *Haaretz*, Apr. 22, 2015, haaretz.com/news/features/1.652936.

123 An excerpt of her statement is available here: "WATCH: Arab-Israeli Journalist Lucy Aharish Blasts Palestinian Leadership for Incitement," *Haaretz*, Oct. 15, 2015, haaretz.com/israel-news/watch-lucy-aharish-blasts-palestinian-leadership-for-incitement-1.5409544.

124 Peleg and Waxman, *Israel's Palestinians*, 37.

125 Peleg and Waxman, *Israel's Palestinians*, 33.

126 Peleg and Waxman, *Israel's Palestinians*, 33.

127 Peleg and Waxman, *Israel's Palestinians*, 33.

128 Peleg and Waxman, *Israel's Palestinians*, 33.

129 Peleg and Waxman, *Israel's Palestinians*, 34.

130 Peleg and Waxman, *Israel's Palestinians*, 39.

131 Quoted in Peleg and Waxman, *Israel's Palestinians*, 96.

132 For example, Hesketh, *Inequality Report*.

133 Jacob Landau, *The Arab Minority in Israel, 1967-1991: Political Aspects* (New York: Oxford University Press, 1993), 60.

134 Landau, *Arab Minority*, 67.

135 This reckoning, based on government statistics published in 2004, appears in Hesketh, *Inequality Report*, 40.

136 There's a distinct, but related, issue pertaining to unincorporated villages in the Negev area, which the government regards as illegal. In those villages, it is a matter of policy to prevent the hook-up of utilities, the building of homes, and neighborhoods.

137 Hesketh, *Inequality Report*, 29.

138 One Texas law required all abortion clinics to meet the standards that apply to ambulatory surgical centers, which entailed regulations on buildings, equipment and staffing. Doctors performing abortions were required to have admitting privileges at nearby hospitals, too. In 2016, the U.S. Supreme Court overturned parts of this Texas law. See Steve Simpson and Kevin Douglas, "In SCOTUS Abortion

Case, Both Liberals And Conservatives Undercut Themselves," *Voices for Reason*, Apr. 7, 2016, ari.aynrand.org/blog/2016/04/07/in-scotus-abortion-case-both-liberals-and-conservatives-undercut-themselves; see also Adam Liptak, "Supreme Court Strikes Down Texas Abortion Restrictions", *New York Times*, Jun. 27, 2016, nytimes.com/2016/06/28/us/supreme-court-texas-abortion.html.

139 Peleg and Waxman, *Israel's Palestinians*, 39.
140 Peleg and Waxman, *Israel's Palestinians*, 37.
141 Hesketh, *Inequality Report*, 8.
142 Hesketh, *Inequality Report*, 28, 29.
143 For example, here's one contrarian analysis of the data. Steven Plaut, "The Myth of Ethnic Inequality in Israel," *Middle East Quarterly*, Summer (2014), meforum.org/3839/israel-inequality.
144 Don Watkins and Yaron Brook, "Turning the Tables on the Inequality Alarmists," Ayn Rand Institute, 2015, ari.aynrand.org/-/media/pdf/turning_the_table_on_the_inequality_alarmists.ashx.
145 For a fuller discussion of the difference between political equality and economic equality, and on the crucial role of individual choices in a person's circumstances, see Don Watkins and Yaron Brook, *Equal Is Unfair: America's Misguided Fight Against Income Inequality* (New York: Macmillan, 2016).
146 Peleg and Waxman, *Israel's Palestinians*, 35.
147 Peleg and Waxman, *Israel's Palestinians*, 35-6.
148 Landau, *Arab Minority*, 67.
149 For an illuminating discussion of this issue, see Elizur and Malkin, *War Within*, esp. chapter 6.

CHAPTER FOUR

1 Abd al-Rahman al-Bazzaz, a law professor and later prime minister of Iraq, quoted in Yehoshafat Harkabi, *Arab Attitudes to Israel* (Jerusalem: Israel Universities Press, 1974), 97.
2 Quoted in Shemesh, *Palestinian Entity*, 3; regarding Nasser's pursuit of inter-Arab cooperation against Israel, see Shemesh, *Palestinian Entity*, 38-39.
3 Shemesh, *Palestinian Entity*, 103.
4 Shemesh, *Palestinian Entity*, 107, 112-118.
5 For example, see Shemesh, *Palestinian Entity*, 65-66, and Yezid Sayigh, "Turning Defeat Into Opportunity: The Palestinian Guerrillas After the June 1967 War," *The Middle East Journal* 46, no. 2 (1992), and also Yezid Sayigh, "The Politics of Palestinian Exile," *Third World Quarterly* 9, no. 1 (1987): 42-47. Further examples can be found in Rubin, *Revolution Until Victory*, 128-130. Such patron-mercenary relationships predated the formation of the PLO. For example, at Nasser's direction the Movement of Arab Nationalists, a group originating in Lebanon, worked to foment *coups d'*état in Jordan (late 1950s), in Yemen (1960-62) and in Syria (1963): See Helga Baumgarten, "The Three Faces/phases of Palestinian Nationalism, 1948—2005," *Journal of Palestine Studies* 34, no. 4 (2005): 30.
6 On this tension between Palestinian factions and Arab states, see Shemesh, *Palestinian Entity*, 59; Baumgarten, "Three Faces/Phases," 35; Rubin, *Revolution Until Victory*, 9.

7   Rashid Hamid, "What Is the PLO?" *Journal of Palestine Studies*, 4, no. 4 (1975): 96.

8   Baumgarten, "Three Faces/Phases," 33-35; see also, Shemesh, *Palestinian Entity*, 80-81; and Rubin, *Revolution Until Victory*, 19.

9   The reversal in popular attitudes toward Israel and its adversaries has been noted elsewhere; for example, one illuminating analysis can be found in Joshua Muravchik, *Making David Into Goliath: How the World Turned on Israel* (New York: Encounter Books, 2014).

10 "Middle East: Bullets, Bombs and a Sign of Hope," *Time*, May 27, 1974.

11 Arafat, "Palestine at the United Nations," 192. I have added paragraph breaks to reflect the cadence of Arafat's speech as delivered.

12 Stéphane Courtois, Nicolas Werth, et al., *The Black Book of Communism: Crimes, Terror, Repression* (Cambridge, Mass.: Harvard University Press, 1999), 464.

13 For example, Courtois et al., *Black Book*, Part I, and chapter 25.

14 Sayigh, "Palestinian Exile," 32n9.

15 For examples of infighting and murder among factions, see Rubin, *Revolution Until Victory*, 30-31, 230n11.

16 "The Palestinian National Charter," Articles 9, 10.

17 "The Palestinian National Charter, Article 7.

18 "The Palestinian National Charter, Article 7.

19 "The Palestinian National Charter, Articles 2, 15.

20 John Nagl, *Learning to Eat Soup With a Knife: Counterinsurgency Lessons from Malaya and Vietnam* (Chicago: Chicago University Press, 2005), 15.

21 Rubin, *Revolution Until Victory*, 27.

22 Muravchik, *David Into Goliath*, 40-41.

23 Muravchik, *David Into Goliath*, 46.

24 Bernard Gwertzman, "Hostage's Body Clearly Identified With Signs Of 2 Gunshot Wounds," *New York Times*, Oct. 17, 1985, nytimes.com/1985/10/17/world/hostage-s-body-clearly-identified-with-signs-of-2-gunshot-wounds.html.

25 Rubin, *Revolution Until Victory*, 31-32.

26 Shemesh, *Palestinian Entity*, 161.

27 Shemesh, *Palestinian Entity*,160; see also Sayigh, "Turning Defeat," 250.

28 Tony Walker and Andrew Gowers, *Arafat: The Biography* (London: Virgin Books, 2003), 47.

29 Daniel Byman, *A High Price: The Triumphs and Failures of Israeli Counterterrorism* (New York: Oxford University Press), 45.

30 On the phenomenon of "outbidding," see Andrew H. Kydd and Barbara F. Walter, "The Strategies of Terrorism," *International Security* 31, no. 1 (2006); and Mia M. Bloom, "Palestinian Suicide Bombing: Public Support, Market Share, and Outbidding," *Political Science Quarterly* 119, no. 1 (2004); more on this later in the chapter.

31 Shemesh, *Palestinian Entity*, 132-3.

32 Kimmerling and Migdal, *Palestinians*, 229-230. The extortion of "donations" is reported in Walker and Gowers, *Arafat: The Biography*, 66, 66.

33 Shemesh, *Palestinian Entity*, 135.

34   Kimmerling and Migdal, *Palestinians,* 230.
35   Shemesh, *Palestinian Entity,*140.
36   Shemesh, *Palestinian Entity,* 229-230; Rubin, *Revolution Until Victory,* 37-38.
37   Kimmerling and Migdal, *Palestinians,* 231-234.
38   Zeʼev Schiff and Ehud Yaʼari, *Israel's Lebanon War* (New York: Simon and Schuster, 1984), 79-80
39   Rex Brynen, "PLO Policy in Lebanon: Legacies and Lessons," *Journal of Palestine Studies* 18, no. 2 (1989): 56.
40   Schiff and Yaʼari, *Israel's Lebanon War,* 80.
41   Brynen, "PLO Policy in Lebanon," 62.
42   Sayigh, "The Politics of Palestinian Exile," 55.
43   David Shipler, "Lebanese Tell of Anguish of Living Under the P.L.O.," *New York Times,* Jul. 25, 1982, nytimes.com/1982/07/25/world/lebanese-tell-of-anguish-of-living-under-the-plo.html.
44   Israel's involvement in Lebanon was an altogether tragic affair, and it was deeply unpopular within Israel. The tactical alliances Israel forged with certain Lebanese factions were, at best, morally dubious; one notorious episode, involving an allied Lebanese force, led to horrendous results. The Israeli military allowed the Phalangist (Christian) faction to enter two Palestinian areas, the Sabra and Shatilla camps, to clear out remaining fighters. The Phalangists, however, appear to have been hungry for revenge against the Palestinians and killed hundreds of them, including women and children, sometimes in barbaric ways (estimates of the death toll range between 700 and 2,000). Though the Phalangists carried out the massacre, an Israeli government commission faulted several IDF leaders for the incident, and imputed personal responsibility to the minister of defense, Ariel Sharon, for failing to foresee and prevent such brutality. On this issue, see for example Zeʼev Schiff and Ehud Yaʼari, *Israel's Lebanon War* (New York: Simon and Schuster, 1984).
45   Formally, the "Palestinian Interim Self-Government Authority."
46   Nadav Haetzni, "In Arafat's Kingdom," in *The Mideast Peace Process: An Autopsy,* ed. Neal Kozodoy (San Francisco: Encounter Books, 2002), 60. Note that Issa reports there were as many as twelve security forces, pitted against each other: Issam Abu Issa, "Arafat's Swiss Bank Account", *Middle East Quarterly* 11, no. 4 (2004). See also Cf. Bassem Eid and Eitan Felner, *Neither Law nor Justice: Extra-Judicial Punishment, Abduction, Unlawful Arrest, and Torture of Palestinian Residents of the West Bank by the Palestinian Preventive Security Service* (Jerusalem, Israel: B'Tselem, The Israeli Information Center for Human Rights in the Occupied Territories, 1995).
47   Daniel Polisar, "Yasser Arafat and the Myth of Legitimacy," *Azure,* no. 13 (2002), azure.org.il/article.php?id=469.
48   Douglas Frantz, "Israel Says Arafat Signed Pay Slips to 'Terrorists,'" *New York Times,* Apr. 4, 2002, nytimes.com/2002/04/04/international/israel-says-arafat-signed-pay-slip-to-terrorists.html; David Rohde, "Israelis Release More Documents Accusing Arafat of Terror," *New York Times,* May 6, 2002, nytimes.com/2002/05/06/international/middleeast/06DOCU.html.

49 Rory Jones, "U.S. Pressures Abbas to End Controversial Family Payments," *Wall Street Journal,* May 6, 2017, wsj.com/articles/u-s-pressures-abbas-to-end-controversial-family-payments-1494087597.e

50 Calculations, using data from the official PA budget, by Yossi Kuperwasser, "Palestinian Payments to Incarcerated Terrorists and Martyrs' Families Rise in 2017," Institute for Contemporary Affairs, Vol. 17, No. 19, Jerusalem Center for Public Affairs, Israel, jcpa.org/article/palestinian-payments-incarcerated-terrorists-martyrs-families-rise-2017/. See also, Y. Yehoshua and B. Shanee, "2017 Palestinian Authority Budget Shows: Salaries, Benefits For Prisoners, Released Prisoners Several Times Higher Than Welfare For Needy," Inquiry & Analysis Series No.1327, August 22, 2017, The Middle East Media Research Institute, memri.org/reports/2017-palestinian-authority-budget-shows-salaries-benefits-prisoners-released-prisoners.

51 B'Tselem and The Palestinian Human Rights Monitoring Group, *Human Rights in the Occupied Territories Since the Oslo Accords: Status Report* (Jerusalem, Israel: The Palestinian Human Rights Monitoring Group and B'Tselem: The Israeli Information Center for Human Rights in the Occupied Territories, December 1996), 16-20, 21.

52 Yizhar Be'er and Saleh Abdel-Jawad, *Collaborators in the Occupied Territories: Human Rights Abuses and Violations.* (Jerusalem, Israel: B'Tselem, The Israeli Information Center for Human Rights in the Occupied Territories, 1994), 60, btselem.org/publications/summaries/199401_collaboration_suspects

53 Be'er and Abdel-Jawad, *Collaborators,* 85, 89-90. Kenneth Stein notes that, "By the end of the second year of the Intifada, about *one-fifth* of the Palestinians killed were victims of other Palestinians." [Emphasis added] The persecution of "collaborators" was also a feature of the 1936-39 uprisings (see chapter three). Rebel bands intimidated, assaulted, and at times killed Arabs who had sold land to Jews and/or who were deemed to be disloyal to the uprising. See Kenneth Stein, "The Intifada and the Uprising of 1936-1939: A Comparison," *Journal of Palestine Studies* 19, no. 4 (1990).

54 Some more recent examples, involving both the Palestinian Authority and the Hamas-ruled Gaza Strip, are noted in Jodi Rudoren, "Collaboration in Gaza Leads to Grisly Fate," *New York Times,* Dec. 2, 2012, nytimes.com/2012/12/03/world/middleeast/preyed-on-by-both-sides-gaza-collaborators-have-grim-plight.html. See also: B'tselem has compiled a list of Palestinians killed by Palestinians (between Sep. 29, 2000 and Dec. 26, 2008), identifying those put to death on suspicion of "collaborating" with Israel, btselem.org/statistics/fatalities/before-cast-lead/by-date-of-event/wb-gaza/palestinians-killed-by-palestinians

55 Jonathan Schanzer, *State of Failure: Yasser Arafat, Mahmoud Abbas, and the Unmaking of the Palestinian State* (New York: Palgrave Macmillan, 2013), 60-63, 70.

56 Quoted in Schanzer, *State of Failure,* 57.

57 Bloomberg report cited in Schanzer, *State of Failure,* 60.

58 Issaam Abu Issa, "Arafat's Swiss Bank Account," *Middle East Quarterly,* Fall (2004), meforum.org/645/arafats-swiss-bank-account [footnotes omitted].

59 Issa, "Arafat's Swiss Bank Account" [footnotes omitted].

60 Regarding *Al-Nahar*, see Haetzni, "In Arafat's Kingdom," 65; regarding the closure of papers aligned with rival factions, see for example B'Tselem, *Human Rights*, 21-22.

61 Haetzni, "In Arafat's Kingdom," 65.

62 Noah Browning, "Palestinian Journalist Gets Jail for Abbas Insult," *Reuters*, Mar. 28, 2013, reuters.com/article/us-palestinians-abbas-facebook/palestinian-journalist-gets-jail-term-for-abbas-insult-idUSBRE92R0US20130328. See also, Schanzer, *State of Failure*, 164-165.

63 Itamar Marcus and Nan Jacques Zilberdik, "PA TV glorifies terror Attack that Killed 22 Children," *Palestinian Media Watch*, Feb. 29, 2012, palwatch.org/main. aspx?fi=157&doc_id=6520.

64 Itamar Marcus, "From Terrorists to Role Models: The Palestinian Authority's Institutionalization of Incitement," *Palestinian Media Watch*, May 2010, palwatch.org/STORAGE/special%20reports/PA%20honors%20terrorists%20 Final%20Eng.pdf.

65 "Glorifying Terrorists and Terror," *Palestinian Media Watch*, palwatch.org/main. aspx?fi=448; a public square in El Bireh was dedicated in honor of Mughrabi; see Isabel Kershner, "Palestinians Honor a Figure Reviled in Israel as a Terrorist," *New York Times*, Mar. 11, 2010, nytimes.com/2010/03/12/world/middleeast/12west-bank.html.

66 See, for example, Itamar Marcus and Barbara Crook, "From Nationalist Battle to Religious Conflict: New 12th Grade Palestinian schoolbooks present a world without Israel," *Palestinian Media Watch*, Feb. 2007, palwatch.org/STORAGE/ special%20reports/SchoolBooks_English_Final_for_web.pdf

67 In 2017, for example, Fatah ran summer camps for teenagers in conjunction with the Palestinian Authority; some of the camps took place on the bases of the PA's National Security Forces in the West Bank. At these camps, they glorify "martyrs" to the cause, indoctrinate campers in the movement's ideology, and provide military training (e.g. how to assemble and disassemble weapons). B. Chernitsky and S. Schneidmann, "2017 Summer Camps In The Palestinian Authority – Part I: Military Training, Glorification of 'Martyrs' In Camps Run By Higher Council For Youth And Sports Headed By Jibril Rajoub," Middle East Media Research Institute, Inquiry & Analysis Series No.1334, Aug. 27, 2017, memri.org/reports/2017-summer-camps-pa---part-i-military-training-glorification-martyrs-camps-run-higher; and "2017 Summer Camps In The Palestinian Authority – Part II: Military Training, Glorification Of 'Martyrs' At Camps Held By Fatah And National Security Forces," Middle East Media Research Institute, Inquiry & Analysis Series No.1335, Aug. 29, 2017, memri.org/ reports/2017-summer-camps-palestinian-authority---part-ii-military-train-ing-glorification-martyrs.

68 Ziad Abu-Amr, *Islamic Fundamentalism in the West Bank and Gaza* (Bloomington: Indiana University Press, 1994), 94.

69 Gilles Kepel, *Jihad: The Trail of Political Islam* (London: I.B. Tauris, 2006), 122.

70 Kepel, *Jihad*, 123.

71 Abu-Amr, *Islamic Fundamentalism*, 15-16.

72 This characterization appears in Abu-Amr, *Islamic Fundamentalism*, 102.

73　"The Covenant of the Islamic Resistance Movement (Hamas)," 1988, Article 15, avalon.law.yale.edu/20th_century/hamas.asp.

74　Matthew Levitt, *Hamas: Politics, Charity, and Terrorism in the Service of Jihad* (New Haven, CT: Yale University Press, 2008), 19-23.

75　Quoted in Levitt, *Hamas*, 9.

76　"The Covenant of the Islamic Resistance Movement (Hamas)."

77　Levitt, *Hamas*, 108, 109.

78　Levitt, *Hamas*, 83.

79　"Promoting Violence for Children," *Palestinian Media Watch*, palwatch.org/main. aspx?fi=845&fld_id=845&doc_id=1340&sort=d

80　C. Jacobs, "Hamas Children's Magazine Al-Fateh Encourages Terrorism, Glorifies Martyrdom," Inquiry & Analysis Series No.393, Middle East Media Research Institute, Oct. 16, 2007, memri.org/reports/hamas-childrens-maga-zine-al-fateh-encourages-terrorism-glorifies-martyrdom [footnotes omitted].

81　Abu-Amr, *Islamic Fundamentalism*, 71.

82　Quoted in Abu Amr, *Islamic Fundamentalism*, 29.

83　The emergence of the so-called phased strategy is traced in Shemesh, *Palestinian Entity*, 272-295.

84　Abu-Amr, *Islamic Fundamentalism*, 70.

85　The point is developed in Baumgarten, "The Three Faces/Phases," 40. In reality, Hamas has gained considerable financial backing from state sponsors.

86　"The Covenant of the Islamic Resistance Movement (Hamas)," Article Eight.

87　"The Covenant of the Islamic Resistance Movement (Hamas)," Articles Six, Eleven.

88　Bloom, "Palestinian Suicide Bombing," 73.

89　On this development, see Byman, *High Price*, 121, 131, and 137.

90　Jonathan Schanzer, *Hamas vs. Fatah: The Struggle for Palestine* (New York: Palgrave Macmillan, 2008), 108 [footnotes omitted].

91　Regarding the fate of Palestinian gays and the attempts by some to seek asylum in Israel, see for example the testimonies compiled in Michael Kagan and Anat Ben-Dor, *Nowhere to Run: Gay Palestinian Asylum-Seekers in Israel* (Tel Aviv, Israel: Tel Aviv University, Faculty of Law, Public Interest Law Program, 2008). On the persecution of the Christian minority under the Palestinian Authority, see for example the incidents described in Justus Reid Weiner, "Middle Eastern Christians Battered, Violated, And Abused, Do They Have Any Chance Of Survival?" Jerusalem Center for Public Affairs, May 22, 2014, jcpa.org/article/middle-eastern-christians-battered.

92　Quoted in Schanzer, *Hamas vs. Fatah*, 110.

93　This incident, along with several others targeting Christians, is recounted in Schanzer, *Hamas vs. Fatah*, 110-112.

94　Schanzer, *Hamas vs. Fatah*, 116.

95　Schanzer, *Hamas vs. Fatah*, 114.

96　For an overview, see C. Jacob, "Hamas's Gaza–Four Years Later Chapter 5: Islamization in Gaza" Inquiry and Analysis No. 717, Middle East Media Research Institute, Jul. 26, 2011, memri.org/report/en/0/0/0/0/0/94/5505.htm.

97 Yazid Sayigh, "*We Serve the People*": *Hamas Policing in Gaza* (Waltham, Mass.: Brandeis University, Crown Center for Middle East Studies, 2011), 94.

98 The analyst is Mkhaimar Abusada, quoted in Sayigh, "*We Serve the People*," 95.

99 Jonathan Schanzer, "The Talibanization of Gaza: A Liability for the Muslim Brotherhood," Current Trends in Islamist Ideology, Hudson Institute, Aug. 19, 2009, hudson.org/research/9899-the-talibanization-of-gaza-a-liability-for-the-muslim-brotherhood.

100 Ethan Bronner, "Hamas in Largest Arms Buildup Yet, Israeli Study Says," *New York Times*, Apr. 10, 2008, nytimes.com/2008/04/10/world/middleeast/10mideast.html

101 This tactic long predated Hamas's takeover of Gaza. Matthew Levitt, "Hamas from Cradle to Grave," *Middle East Quarterly*, Winter (2004), meforum.org/582/hamas-from-cradle-to-grave. See also, Terrence McCoy, "Why Hamas Stores Its Weapons Inside Hospitals, Mosques and Schools," *Washington Post*, Jul. 31, 2014, washingtonpost.com/news/morning-mix/wp/2014/07/31/why-hamas-stores-its-weapons-inside-hospitals-mosques-and-schools.

102 Estimate based on data for 2007 and 2008, presented by the IDF, idfblog.com/facts-figures/rocket-attacks-toward-israel.

103 See "Renewal of Rocket Attacks on Israel," IDF Blog, Aug. 21, 2016, idfblog.com/2016/08/21/renewal-of-rocket-attacks-on-israel.

104 For some examples specific to Hamas, see Itamar Marcus, "Hamas: We 'Love Death for Allah,'" *Palestinian Media Watch*, Jul. 31, 2014, palwatch.org/main.aspx?fi=157&doc_id=12235.

105 Steven Erlanger and Fares Akram,"Israel Warns Gaza Targets by Phone and Leaflet," *New York Times*, Jul. 8, 2014, nytimes.com/2014/07/09/world/middleeast/by-phone-and-leaflet-israeli-attackers-warn-gazans.html; William Booth, "Israeli Troops Raid Rocket-Launching Sites In Gaza As Residents Are Urged to Evacuate," Jul. 13, 2014, *Washington Post*, washingtonpost.com/world/israeli-troops-raid-rocket-launching-sites-in-gaza-as-residents-are-urged-to-evacuate/2014/07/13/4c1a0528-0a68-11e4-bbf1-cc51275e7f8f_story.html; Steven Erlanger, "As Israel Hits Mosque and Clinic, Air Campaign's Risks Come Home," *New York Times*, Jul. 12, 2014, nytimes.com/2014/07/13/world/middleeast/israel-gaza-strip.html.

106 "Operation Protective Edge in numbers," *Ynet*, Jul. 28, 2014, ynetnews.com/articles/0,7340,L-4564678,00.html.

107 Lahav Harkov "MKs Read Testimony From Soldiers Defending IDF's Morality," *Jerusalem Post*, Jun. 23, 2015, jpost.com/Arab-Israeli-Conflict/MKs-read-testimony-from-soldiers-defending-IDFs-morality-406894.

108 The spokesman is Sami Abu Zuhri, and the interviewer asks him to react to eyewitness accounts that Gazans are acting as human shields; he endorses it as effective and calls for more to adopt that policy. "Hamas Spokesman Encourages Gazans To Serve As Human Shields: It's Been Proven Effective," Middle East Media Research Institute, Jul. 08, 2014, memri.org/tv/hamas-spokesman-encourages-gazans-serve-human-shields-its-been-proven-effective/transcript. See also, Erlanger and Akram,"Israel Warns Gaza," in which a resident of Gaza

says that "Our neighbors came in to form a human shield." The practice of Palestinians volunteering themselves as human shields appears to date back at least to 2006; for example, Conal Urquhart, "Palestinians use human shield to halt Israeli air strike on militants' homes," *Guardian*, Nov. 20, 2006, theguardian.com/world/2006/nov/20/israel.

109 Clyde Haberman, "At Least 14 Dead As Suicide Bomber Strikes Jerusalem," *New York Times*, Aug. 10, 2001, nytimes.com/2001/08/10/world/at-least-14-dead-as-suicide-bomber-strikes-jerusalem.html.

110 Hamas and Palestinian Islamic Jihad both claimed credit for the attack, but PIJ later withdrew its claim. Haberman, "Suicide Bomber."

111 Haberman, "Suicide Bomber."

112 Masri's mother is quoted, along with several others, in Itamar Marcus and Nan Jacques Zilberdik, "Palestinian Mother Celebrates Her Son's Death: 'This Is The First Time I See Joy In My Heart,'" *Palestinian Media Watch*, Sep. 21, 2014, palwatch.org/main.aspx?fi=157&doc_id=12690.

113 Several examples are quoted in Marcus and Zilberdik, "Palestinian Mother Celebrates Her Son's Death." Note that mothers of such murderers are celebrated as role models; Itamar Marcus and Nan Jacques Zilberdik, "Mother of 4 Terrorists Honored Again By PA As Model For Palestinian Women," *Palestinian Media Watch*, Apr. 9, 2015, palwatch.org/main.aspx?fi=157&doc_id=14438.

114 Ian Fisher, "An Exhibit on Campus Celebrates Grisly Deed," *New York Times*, Sep. 26, 2001, nytimes.com/2001/09/26/world/an-exhibit-on-campus-celebrates-grisly-deed.html.

115 Bloom, "Palestinian Suicide Bombing," 74.

116 Lee Gancman, "Songs In Praise Of Stabbing Are Huge Hits On Palestinian Street, And May Be Motivators Too," *Times of Israel*, Jan. 28, 2016, timesofisrael.com/songs-in-praise-of-stabbing-are-huge-hits-on-palestinian-street-and-may-be-motivators-too.

CHAPTER FIVE

1 Barack Obama, for example, spoke about his commitment to Israel's "qualitative military edge," claiming that he had done "more than any other President to strengthen Israel's security." See Barack Obama, "Remarks by the President on the Iran Nuclear Deal" Aug. 5, 2015, whitehouse.gov/the-press-office/2015/08/05/remarks-president-iran-nuclear-deal.

2 The Federalist No. 10 (James Madison) in Alexander Hamilton, James Madison, John Jay, *The Federalist Papers*, ed. Charles Kessler (New York: Signet Classics, 2003), 76.

3 Economic theory and historical experience attest to the causal relationship between prosperity and the protection of individual rights, notably including intellectual property rights, such as patents. The importance of intellectual property is often under-appreciated. In an eye-opening essay, Stephen Haber examines the relationship between the strength of protection for patents and the consequences for innovation, and thus wealth-creation. Haber spotlights how the strong patent system of the newly independent United States played a role in its rapid industrial development, leading it eventually to outshine Britain. Stephen

Haber, "Patents and the Wealth of Nations," *George Mason Law Review* 23, no. 4 (2016). See also, Adam Mossoff, "How Copyright Drives Innovation: A Case Study of Scholarly Publishing in the Digital World," *Michigan State Law Review* (January 2015), and consider the negative impact on innovation of weakening the protections for IP; Kevin Madigan and Adam Mossoff, "Turning Gold to Lead: How Patent Eligibility Doctrine Is Undermining U.S. Leadership in Innovation," *George Mason Law Review* (forthcoming); *George Mason Law & Economics Research Paper No. 17-16* (2017).

4   Tony Judt, *Postwar: A History of Europe Since 1945* (New York: Penguin, 2006), Kindle edition, location 16122 [footnotes omitted].

5   Cf. "Two Germanys United Would Pose Challenge to Other Economies," *Wall Street Journal*, Nov. 13, 1989, online.wsj.com/public/resources/documents/wsj19891113-united.pdf.

CHAPTER SIX

1   Joel Brinkley, "Confrontation in the Gulf; At Border Kibbutz, Tension and Fear," *New York Times*, Aug. 15, 1990, nytimes.com/1990/08/15/world/confrontation-in-the-gulf-at-border-kibbutz-tension-and-fear.html. Saddam Hussein continues to be lionized in the Palestinian community. Cf. "Palestinians Erect Memorial To Saddam Hussein In Qalqilya, Bearing Slogan 'Arab Palestine From River To Sea,'" Special Dispatch No.7141, Middle East Media Research Institute, Oct. 20, 2017, memri.org/reports/palestinians-erect-memorial-saddam-hussein-qalqilya.

2   Daniel C. Kurtzer, et al. *The Peace Puzzle: America's Quest for Arab-Israeli Peace, 1989-2011* (Ithaca, NY: Cornell University Press; Washington: United States Institute of Peace, 2013), 22-32.

3   William J. Clinton, "Remarks at the Signing Ceremony for the Israeli-Palestinian Declaration of Principles," Sep. 13, 1993. Online by Gerhard Peters and John T. Woolley, The American Presidency Project. presidency.ucsb.edu/ws/?pid=47063.

4   Quoted in "Mideast Accord; Statements by Leaders at the Signing of the Middle East Pact," *New York Times*, Sep. 14, 1993, nytimes.com/1993/09/14/world/mideast-accord-statements-by-leaders-at-the-signing-of-the-middle-east-pact.html?pagewanted=print.

5   After the *Achille Lauro* incident (see chapter four), Congress passed the Anti-Terrorism Act of 1987, which held that the PLO "(1) is a terrorist organization; (2) is a threat to the interests of the United States, its allies, and to international law; and (3) should not benefit from operating in the United States." (S.1203—100th Congress), congress.gov/bill/100th-congress/senate-bill/1203. On December 14, 1988, however, the Regan administration announced that it would enter into diplomatic talks with the PLO. The U.S. rationale for this was that *the day before,* the Palestinian National Council (the PLO's legislative body) had voted to renounce terrorism, recognize Israel's right to exist, and accept U.N. resolutions pertaining to the original partition plan. The rationale some PLO leaders offered for their vote was that diplomacy was a means of advancing their goal of liberating all of Palestine, step by step rather than all at once (which evoked the "phased strategy"). Many supporters and surrogates of the Palestinian cause point to that 1988 vote as an historic and laudable move. But it was, in fact, a hollow gesture.

This mouthing of empty words was thoroughly refuted by the deeds of the PLO. Since 1988, of course, Palestinian attacks on Israel continued. In 1990, because of a terrorist attack, U.S. dialogue with the PLO was again suspended.

6   Reflecting on that historic White House signing ceremony, Dennis Ross, a Middle East envoy and lead U.S. negotiator in the peace process, reports that Arafat had to be prevailed upon not to bring his gun and not to wear a military uniform. Although Arafat left his gun at home, he wore an olive-colored military uniform. Dennis Ross, *The Missing Peace: The Inside Story of the Fight for Middle East Peace* (New York: Farrar, Straus and Giroux, 2004), 119-120.

7   One of the co-winners, Israel's prime minister, Yitzhak Rabin, was assassinated in 1995 by a Jewish religionist who believed himself to be "acting on orders from God." Joel Greenberg, "Assassination In Israel: The Suspect; Suspect Says He Tried to Kill Rabin Before" *New York Times*, Nov. 5, 1995, nytimes.com/1995/11/05/world/assassination-in-israel-the-suspect-suspect-says-he-tried-to-kill-rabin-before.html.

8   Tony Karon, "Clinton Saves the Last Dance for Arafat," *Time*, Jan. 2, 2001, content.time.com/time/world/article/0,8599,93339,00.html.

9   The emergence of the so-called phased strategy is traced in Shemesh, *Palestinian Entity*, 272-295. Arafat's pre-recorded radio speech is quoted and analyzed in Efraim Karsh, "Arafat's Grand Strategy," *Middle East Quarterly* Spring (2004), meforum.org/605/arafats-grand-strategy. Arafat conveyed a similar theme on other occasions. See for example his 1994 speech in Johannesburg, South Africa: "Arafat Compares Oslo Accords To Muhammad's Hudaybiyyah Peace Treaty, Which Led To Defeat Of The Peace Partners" *Palestinian Media Watch*, palwatch.org/main.aspx?fi=711&doc_id=486.

10   "Israel-Palestine Liberation Organization Agreement: 1993," avalon.law.yale.edu/20th_century/isrplo.asp.

11   Data from the PA's Ministry of Planning and International Cooperation, quoted in Scott Lasensky, "Paying for peace: The Oslo process and the limits of American foreign aid," *Middle East Journal* vol. 58, no. 2 (2004): 220.

12   World Bank, "West Bank and Gaza: An Evaluation of Bank Assistance," Report No. 23820, Mar. 7, 2002, 4, documents.worldbank.org/curated/en/751761468779120369/pdf/multi0page.pdf.

13   Jim Zanotti, "US Foreign Aid to the Palestinians" (RS22967), Congressional Research Service, Dec. 16, 2016, fas.org/sgp/crs/mideast/RS22967.pdf.

14   Jessie Hellmann, "Bill Clinton: 'I killed myself to give Palestinians a state.'" *The Hill*, May 14, 2016, thehill.com/blogs/ballot-box/presidential-races/279912-bill-clinton-i-killed-myself-to-give-palestinians-a-state.

15   Calculated using "RAND Database of Worldwide Terrorist Incidents," for the years 1968 through 2009; excluding deaths and injuries known to be caused by Jewish religionist groups (notably, Kach, Kahane Chai, and Shalevet Gilead), rand.org/nsrd/projects/terrorism-incidents/download.html. For the period 1968-1993, the number of injuries is approximately 2,000; fatalities, approximately 500. For the period 2000-2004, the injuries total approximately 4,000 and the fatalities, approximately 1000. For both periods, these approximate totals include some tourists visiting Israel who were injured or killed in various attacks.

16 Kurtzer et al., *Peace Puzzle*, 163. Bush was speaking before the United Nations General Assembly, Nov. 10, 2001.

17 Robert Satloff, "The Peace Process at Sea: The Karine-A Affair and the War on Terrorism," *National Interest*, Spring 2002, washingtoninstitute.org/ policy-analysis/view/the-peace-process-at-sea-the-karine-a-affair-and-the-war-on-terrorism. See also, James Bennet, "Seized Arms Would Have Vastly Extended Arafat Arsenal," *New York Times*, Jan. 12, 2002, nytimes.com/2002/01/12/world/seized-arms-would-have-vastly-extended-arafat-arsenal.html?pagewanted=all.

18 One prior smuggling operation used a vessel called the *Santorini* (May 2001); there have been several attempts since the *Karine A*.

19 George W. Bush, "Remarks on the Middle East," Jun. 24, 2002. Online by Gerhard Peters and John T. Woolley, *The American Presidency Project*, presidency.ucsb. edu/ws/?pid=73320

20 Kurtzer et al., *Peace Puzzle*, 165.

21 Joel Brinkley and Steven R. Weisman, "Rice Urges Israel and Palestinians to Sustain Momentum," *New York Times*, Aug. 18, 2005, nytimes.com/2005/08/18/world/middleeast/rice-urges-israel-and-palestinians-to-sustain-momentum. html. Cf. Elliot Abrams, who served as deputy national security advisor to George W. Bush, reports that the administration advised the Israeli government to "[d]o something in the West Bank as well," which appears to mean: to explore the idea of withdrawing from those territories, as well. Elliott Abrams, *Tested by Zion: The Bush Administration and the Israeli-Palestinian Conflict* (Cambridge University Press, 2013), 100, 102.

22 James Bennet, "Hamas Pushing for Lead Role in a New Gaza," *New York Times*, Aug. 21, 2005, nytimes.com/2005/08/21/world/middleeast/hamas-pushing-for-lead-role-in-a-new-gaza.html.

23 Yaacov Shamir and Khalil Sikaki, "Joint Palestinian-Israeli Poll 18 - December 2005," Palestinian Center for Policy and Survey Research, Dec. 2005, pcpsr.org/en/node/436.

24 George W. Bush: "Remarks on the 20th Anniversary of the National Endowment for Democracy," Nov. 6, 2003. Online by Gerhard Peters and John T. Woolley, *The American Presidency Project*, presidency.ucsb.edu/ws/?pid=844.

25 George W. Bush, "Address Before a Joint Session of the Congress on the State of the Union," Jan. 20, 2004. Online by Gerhard Peters and John T. Woolley, *The American Presidency Project*, presidency.ucsb.edu/ws/?pid=29646.

26 Ramsay Short, "Key Job for 'Terrorist' Hizbollah in Lebanon's New Cabinet," *Telegraph*, Jul. 20, 2005, telegraph.co.uk/news/worldnews/middleeast/lebanon /1494451/Key-job-for-terrorist-Hizbollah-in-Lebanons-new-cabinet.html.

27 Michael Slackman, "Egyptians Rue Election Day Gone Awry," *New York Times*, Dec. 9, 2005, nytimes.com/2005/12/09/international/africa/09egypt.html.

28 Islamic Dawa Party and Supreme Council for the Islamic Revolution in Iraq (SCIRI) were prominent in the bloc that dominated Iraq's government following elections in 2005. Both have longstanding ties to Iran's regime. Iran's influence over Iraq has persisted and arguably increased over time. Cf. Tim Arango, "Iran Dominates in Iraq After U.S. 'Handed the Country Over.'" *New York Times*, Jul.

15, 2017, nytimes.com/2017/07/15/world/middleeast/iran-iraq-iranian-power. html.

29 Abrams, *Tested by Zion*, 140. The willful blindness to the ascendance of Islamists is all the more shocking, when you consider that Israeli authorities were well aware of this phenomenon since the late 1980s. In a classic example of shortsighted policy, early on Israel believed it was advantageous to allow the Islamist factions to grow into a serious rival that could counterbalance the influence of the PLO. Accordingly, Israeli authorities let Islamist groups develop and spread—until, realizing their error, the Israelis began trying to curb them. See, for example, Schiff and Yaari, *Intifada*, chapter 8.

30 Kurtzer et al., *Peace Puzzle*, 197. See "Statement of The National Democratic Institute/Carter Center Pre-Election Assessment of The Palestinian Legislative Council Elections," Jan. 6, 2006, cartercenter.org/documents/2269.pdf.

31 Kurtzer et al., *Peace Puzzle*, 198-203.

32 Jonathan Schanzer notes that there were 74 candidates and two independents; "Ten Years Of Hamas Rule: The Palestinians Must Solve Their Divide Before Peace With Israel," *Newsweek*, Jan 25, 2016, newsweek.com/ ten-years-hamas-palestinians-divide-peace-israel-418497.

33 See, for example, Peter R Neumann, *Radicalized: New Jihadists and the Threat to the West* (London: IB Tauris, 2016).

34 Obama, "Remarks in Cairo."

35 Obama, "Remarks in Cairo."

36 Obama, "Remarks in Cairo."

37 For example, see Obama's statements in "Remarks Following a Meeting With Prime Minister Benjamin Netanyahu of Israel and an Exchange With Reporters," May 18, 2009. Online by Gerhard Peters and John T. Woolley, *The American Presidency Project*, presidency.ucsb.edu/ws/?pid=86174; see also Obama's view before taking office, on NBC's *Meet the Press*. Having met Jordan's King (who has himself voiced a version of the "linkage" view), Obama stated: "King Abdullah is as savvy a analyst of the region and player in the region as, as there is, one of the points that he made and I think a lot of people made, is that we've got to have an overarching strategy recognizing that all these issues are connected. If we can solve the Israeli/Palestinian process, then that will make it easier for Arab states and the Gulf states to support us when it comes to issues like Iraq and Afghanistan." "Meet the Press" transcript for Jul. 27, 2008, nbcnews.com/id/25872804/ns/ meet_the_press/t/meet-press-transcript-july/.

38 Figures who have voiced some version of the "linkage" view include President Jimmy Carter (e.g. Nathan Gardels, "Jimmy Carter takes on Israel's Apartheid Policies and the Pro-Israeli Lobby in the US." *Huffington Post*, Dec. 12, 2006, huffingtonpost.com/nathan-gardels/jimmy-carter-takes-on-isr_b_36134. html?view=print); former U.N. Secretary General Ban Ki Moon (e.g. Herb Keinon, "'Israel-Palestinian Conflict Is Key,'" *Jerusalem Post*, Jan. 1, 2007, jpost. com/International/Israel-Palestinian-conflict-is-key); Gen. David Petraeus, former commander of U.S. Central Command and CIA director; Gen. James Mattis, former commander of U.S. Central Command and U.S. Secretary of Defense in the Trump administration (both Petraeus and Mattis are quoted in

Daniel Kurtzer et al., *Pathways to Peace: America and the Arab-Israeli Conflict* [New York: Palgrave Macmillan, 2012], 4); Sen. Chuck Hagel, later secretary of defense in the Obama administration (e.g. Martin Kramer, *The War on Error: Israel, Islam, and the Middle East* [New Brunswick, NJ: Transaction, 2016], 153-165); and at least some of the prominent individuals who compiled the (bipartisan) Iraq Study Group Report, commissioned by Congress (Dec. 6, 2006; usip.org/sites/default/files/files/USIP-full_iraq_study_group_report.pdf). The discussion in this chapter touches on one form of the "linkage" view; there are variations of this outlook, but exploring them all is beyond the scope of this book. For more on the "linkage" view, see, for example, the analysis by Martin Kramer and the responses to it from several commentators in "The Myth of Linkage," Middle East Strategy at Harvard (MESH), John M. Olin Institute for Strategic Studies, Harvard University, Jun. 12, 2008, blogs.harvard.edu/mesh/2008/06/the_myth_of_linkage/

39 John Kerry, "Remarks at a Reception in Honor of Eid al-Adha," Oct. 16, 2014, 2009-2017.state.gov/secretary/remarks/2014/10/233058.htm.

40 Thomas L. Friedman, "Postcard from Cairo, Part 2" *New York Times*, Feb. 13, 2011, nytimes.com/2011/02/13/opinion/13-friedman-Web-cairo.html.

41 Regarding Jordanian and Saudi use of the tract, see Daniel Pipes, *The Hidden Hand: Middle East Fears of Conspiracy* (New York: St. Martins Griffin, 1996), 311; on the widespread reprinting, excerpting, and citing of the "Protocols," see Menahem Milson, "A European Plot on the Arab Stage," Posen Papers in Contemporary Arab Antisemitism No. 12, The Vidal Sassoon International Center for the Study of Antisemitism, The Hebrew University of Jerusalem (2011), sicsa.huji.ac.il/sites/default/files/sicsa/files/pp12_with_milsons_corrections.pdf. See also, for example, "Jordanian TV Show: The Rothschilds Rule the World, Assassinated 6 U.S. Presidents; Jews Withhold Cure for Cancer and AIDS," Clip No. 6165, Middle East Media Research Institute, Jun. 28, 2017, memri.org/tv/jordanian-analyst-rothschilds-rule-world-assassinated-american-presidents/transcript. Regarding the origin of the "Protocols," see "Protocols of The Elders of Zion: Timeline," U.S. Holocaust Memorial Museum, ushmm.org/wlc/en/article.php?ModuleId=10007244.

42 These statements and data (based on research by Hegghammer) appear in Hegghammer and Wagemakers, "The Palestine Effect," 287, 293.

43 Maajid Nawaz and Tom Bromley, *Radical: My Journey Out of Islamist Extremism* (Lanham, MD: Globe Pequot Press, Lyon Press, 2013), 56-61.

44 See U.N. Resolution 2334, "Israel's Settlements Have No Legal Validity, Constitute Flagrant Violation of International Law, Security Council Reaffirms," Dec. 23, 2016, un.org/press/en/2016/sc12657.doc.htm.

45 Consider this video which apparently aired on CNN, youtube.com/watch?v=iNDTpYlR48g; and Karim Sadjadpour, *Reading Khamenei: The World View of Iran's Most Powerful Leader* (Carnegie Endowment for International Peace: Washington, 2009), v.

46 Elan Journo, ed., *Winning The Unwinnable War: America's Self-Crippled Response to Islamic Totalitarianism* (Lanham, MD: Lexington Books, 2009).

47   What was widely viewed as the administration's firmest response came, eventually, more than a week after the protests began. Barack Obama: "The President's News Conference," Jun. 23, 2009. Online by Gerhard Peters and John T. Woolley, *The American Presidency Project*, presidency.ucsb.edu/ws/?pid=86323.

48   For example, Thomas Erdbrink, "In Iran, State-Backed Companies Win From Lifted Sanctions," *New York Times*, Feb. 5, 2016, nytimes.com/2016/02/06/world/middleeast/in-iran-state-backed-companies-win-from-lifted-sanctions.html; Stanley Reed, "Total Signs Deal With Iran, Exposing It to Big Risks and Rewards," *New York Times*, Jul. 3, 2017. Note that U.S. Department of State routinely flags Iran as the world's leading ("foremost") state-sponsor of terror groups. See for example, U.S. Department of State, *Country Reports on Terrorism 2016*, Jul. 2017, state.gov/documents/organization/272488.pdf

49   "Donald J. Trump: "Remarks Prior to a Meeting With President Trump and President Abdelfattah Said Elsisi of Egypt," Apr. 3, 2017. Online by Gerhard Peters and John T. Woolley, *The American Presidency Project*, presidency.ucsb.edu/ws/?pid=123690. Note that Trump (like Obama) adjusted the flow of aid to Egypt, but that was overshadowed by the ongoing endorsement of Sisi.

50   America's policy toward the smaller Gulf monarchies is also warped. For example: Jonathan Schanzer, "These days, it's the clash of the Arabian Gulf cash in Washington" *The Hill*, Jun. 23, 2017, thehill.com/blogs/pundits-blog/foreign-policy/339150-these-days-its-the-clash-of-the-gulf-cash-in-washington.

51   On the Clinton administration's attempted rapprochement with Iran, see Clawson and Rubin, *Eternal Iran*, 151-152. See also Elaine Sciolino, "Chaotic Protests Reign in Teheran; Vigilantes Active," *New York Times* Jul. 14, 1999, nytimes.com/1999/07/14/world/chaotic-protests-reign-in-teheran-vigilantes-active.html.

52   Daniel Pipes, "A New Strategy for Israeli Victory," *Commentary*, Jan. 2017, 13-18, commentarymagazine.com/articles/a-new-strategy-for-israeli-victory-palestinian/. On the wider historical lesson, see in particular Lewis, *Nothing Less Than Victory*.

53   Pipes, "New Strategy," 15.

54   Pipes, "New Strategy," 15 [Emphasis in original]. See also Daniel Pipes, "Peace Process or War Process?" *Middle East Quarterly* Fall (2009).

55   Ayn Rand, "How Does One Lead a Rational Life in An Irrational Society?" in *The Virtue of Selfishness* (New York: Signet, 1964), 74. Rand's essay can be found online, campus.aynrand.org/works/1962/01/01/how-does-one-lead-a-rational-life-in-an-irrational-society.

INDEX

9/11, *see* September 11, 2001, attacks

Abbas, Mahmoud, 75, 77, 87, 158
Achille Lauro, 146
Afghanistan, ix, 9, 52, 212-213, 219,
    231, 239n2
Agha-Soltan, Neda, 57
Aharish, Lucy, 125-27
Ahmedinijad, Mahmoud, 29
Al Qaeda, ix, 42, 45, 145, 168, 219,
    256n42
Algeria, 139
Apartheid: as policy of South Africa,
    4, 20-21; accusations of in Israel,
    xv, 4, 6; *see also,* Boycott, Divest-
    ment, Sanctions (BDS) movement;
    "Gender Apartheid"
Apostasy: *see* religion/state *for various
    countries*
Apple, 33
"Arab" (identity), 78, 79, 124-27,
    255n31, 262n119; *see also,* "Palestin-
    ian" (identity)
Arab League, 91-95, 101
Arab nationalism, 101-102, 137-143,
    160, 161, 165, 227, 257n65
Arab Spring upheavals, 24, 25, 44, 45,
    216-17, 224
Arabi, Soheil, 12

Arafat, Yasser, 75-76, 140-42, 146-48,
    153-58, 197, 198, 200-202, 204-207,
    225, 261n115
Assad, Bashar al-, 45, 56, 186
Atheism/ists, 46, 57, 64, 71, 127, 128,
    131, 219, 261n117
Azzam, Abdul Rahman, 91, 101

Ba'ath movement, 59, 111, 140
Badawi, Raif, 10-11, 16, 40, 241n13
Badie, Mohamed, 47
Baha'i, 54-55
Bahrain, 27, 40, 43, 58
Bakri, Mohammad, 18-20
Ban, Ki-moon, x
Barak-Erez, Daphne, 19-20
Bedouin, 98, 129
Ben-Gurion, David, 66-67
Berlin Wall, 193-94, 196
Bin Laden, Osama, 219, 226, 239n2
Bishara, Azmi, 125-126
Blasphemy, 16, 46; *see* religion/state *for
    various countries;*
Boko Haram, 7
Bosnia, 219-20
Boycott, Divestment, Sanctions (BDS)
    movement, xv, 4, 38, 76, 78
British Mandate (formally, The Pales-
    tine Mandate), 82, 83, 87-88, 254n23,
    255n27, 256n47, 261n118

Nawaz, Maajid, 219-20
Nazism (National Socialism), 19, 33,
    88, 91, 108, 194, 218, 255n28
Nobel Prize(s), x, 4, 28, 35, 201, 248n82
Noel, Cleo, 145-46
North Korea, 5, 194

Obama, Barack, x, xii, 61, 77, 211,
    213-16, 221-25, 259n100, 270n1
Occupation, see entries under Israel,
    United States, Palestinian movement
Olmert, Ehud, 61-62
Oman, 40
Oren, Michael, 4-5
Ottoman Empire, 79, 81, 83, 87, 181,
    256n47
Oxfam International, 3-4

"Palestinian" (identity), 78-81, 254n10;
    see also, Palestinian movement
Palestinian Authority, 103, 106, 114,
    122, 147-48, 202-204; authoritarian-
    ism of, 152-60, 183; elections (2006),
    167-168, 210-211
Palestinian grievances, xii-xvi, 73-74,
    81, 253n7, 254n9; "right of return,"
    99-101; denial of rights, 77, 123-35,
    147; dispossession, 77, 81-87;
    homeland/statehood, 77, 93, 147-60,
    228-29, 233; occupation, 77, 101-23,
    258n68, 258n69, 258n71; refugees,
    75, 77, 87-101, 217, 256n52, 257n59,
    257n60; settlements, 116-123, 227;
    see also, Palestinian Movement
Palestinian Islamic Jihad (PIJ), 162,
    163, 167, 169, 259n99, 270n110
Palestinian Liberation Organization
    (PLO), 111, 113, 115, 139, 140-61,
    165-67, 170, 198-97, 227, 241n8,
    271-272n5, 274n29; see also, Pales-
    tinian movement
Palestinian Movement: aims, 73-75, 96,
    99, 123, 136, 142, 144-45, 148-160,
    167-72, 165-66, 176-77, 181, 183,
    200-202, 210, 227, 232-33; differen-
    tiated from Palestinian population,

79, 115-16, 127, 182-83, 194, 197,
    205, 210-211, 227-28, 232-33;
    factional dynamics, 142-43, 146-47,
    160-168, 176-77, 204, 227, 263n6;
    270n110; gays and, 168, 268n91;
    glorification of martyrdom, 158-59,
    172-77, 208-209; identity, definition
    of, 79-81; ideology, 142-44, 160-170;
    Islamization of, 160-170, 205-212,
    274n29; occupation, definition of,
    103-104; origins, 137-42; patrons/
    allies, 137-34, 139-40, 143, 165,
    197-98, 263n5; quasi-state in Jordan,
    147-49; quasi-state in Lebanon,
    49-50, 149-52; refugee camps, 49;
    religious persecution, 168; self-de-
    termination, 190, 228-220, 232-33;
    statehood/quasi-states, 147-60,
    167-77, 190, 206, 210-211, 227, 229,
    232-33; strategy, 137-45, 143, 162,
    165-66, 201; tactics, 76, 144-57,
    151, 167, 170-177, 241n7, 269n108;
    terrorism 76, 144-47; thought
    control, 143-44, 153, 157-59, 164,
    168-69, 172-77, 267n67; treatment
    of "collaborators," 155, 266n53,
    266n54; women and, 169; see also,
    Palestinian Liberation Organization
    (PLO); Palestinian Authority; Hamas
    (Islamic Resistance Movement);
    Palestinian Islamic Jihad (PIJ); Fatah,
    Suicide bombings
Palestinian National Charter, 79-80,
    143, 165, 201
Peace Process (aka Oslo agreement),
    xii-xiii, 103, 106, 115, 152, 159-160,
    199-221, 213 224-33; see also
    Palestinian Authority; United States
    Foreign Policy
Peres, Shimon, 200, 248n82
Petraeus, David, x
Pipes, Daniel, 231-32
Protocols of the Elders of Zion, 217-18

Qaddafi, Muammar el-, 45, 217
Qatar, 13, 29, 41, 55, 156-57, 218

Mideast, x, 216-21; Islamist movement and, x, xvii, 204-26, 230-31; Israeli settlements and, 116, 227; "linkage" view, x-xi, 215-217, 274n37, 274n38; occupation of Japan post-World War II, 108-110; Palestinian movement and, 76-77, 179, 195-234, 271-72n5, 272n6; rapprochement with Iran, 221-26; *see also*, Peace Process; Bush, George W.; Bush, George H. W.; Obama, Barack; Trump, Donald J.

Wahdi, Abdullah Al, 14
Wars and armed conflicts: 1936-39 uprising, 90; 1948 war, 75, 91-94, 101, 138, 139, 256n47; 1967 war ("Six Day War"), 102-107, 117; 1973 war ("Yom Kippur War"), 103, 258n68; 2006 Hezbollah-Hamas-Israel war, 211;

2008-09 Hamas-Israel war, 170, 211; 2012 Hamas-Israel war, 170; 2014 Hamas-Israel war, 170-172, 215; World War I, 79, 83, 87, 88; World War II, 88, 91, 96, 98, 99, 108, 193, 231, 255n28, 256n45; *see also*, Intifada, Second Intifada, Gulf War (1991)
Wertheimer, Stef, 33-34
West Bank territories, 3, 102-23, 148, 152-60, 161-67
World Bank, 34-35, 202

Yemen, 9, 91
Yonath, Ada, 28
Youssef, Bassem 15, 16
YouTube, 51, 57

Zionism/Zionist movement, 66-67, 81-83, 85, 88, 91, 93, 144, 164

ABOUT THE AUTHOR

Elan Journo is a fellow and director of policy research at the Ayn Rand Institute. He is co-author of *Failing to Confront Islamic Totalitarianism*, a contributor to *Defending Free Speech,* and editor of *Winning the Unwinnable War.* His articles have appeared in a wide range of publications, from *Foreign Policy* and *Middle East Quarterly* to *The Hill* and the *Los Angeles Times.* He has been interviewed on numerous television and radio programs, and he often speaks at conferences and universities. Born in Israel and raised in the United Kingdom, he earned a BA in philosophy from King's College London and an MA in diplomacy from SOAS, University of London.

elanjourno.com
facebook.com/elan.journo
@elanjourno